Object-Oriented Programming in the BETA Programming Language

ACM PRESS BOOKS

SELECTED TITLES

Object-Oriented Reuse, Concurrency and Distribution *Colin Atkinson*

Advances in Database Programming Languages *Francois Bançilhon and Peter Buneman (Eds)*

Algebraic Specification *J.A. Bergstra, J. Heering and P. Klint (Eds)*

Software Reusability (Volume 1: Concepts and Models) *Ted Biggerstaff and Alan Perlis (Eds)*

Software Reusability (Volume 2: Applications and Experience) *Ted Biggerstaff and Alan Perlis (Eds)*

Object-Oriented Software Engineering: A Use CASE Driven Approach *Ivar Jacobson, Magnus Christerson, Patrik Jonnson and Gunnar Övergaard*

Object-Oriented Concepts, Databases and Applications *Won Kim and Frederick H. Lochovsky (Eds)*

Computing: a Human Activity *Peter Naur*

The Oberon System: User Guide and Programmer's Manual *Martin Reiser*

Programming in Oberon: Steps Beyond Pascal and Modula *Martin Reiser and Niklaus Wirth*

Project Oberon: The Design of an Operating System and Compiler *Niklaus Wirth and Jürg Gutknecht*

The Programmer's Apprentice *Charles Rich and Richard C. Waters*

User Interface Design *Harold Thimbleby*

Advanced Animation and Rendering Techniques *Alan Watt and Mark Watt*

Distributed Systems (2nd edn) *Sape Mullender (Ed)*

Object-Oriented Programming in the BETA Programming Language

OLE LEHRMANN MADSEN
Aarhus University

BIRGER MØLLER-PEDERSEN
Norwegian Computing Center

KRISTEN NYGAARD
University of Oslo

ACM PRESS

ADDISON-WESLEY PUBLISHING COMPANY

Wokingham, England · Reading, Massachussetts · Menlo Park, California · New York
Don Mills, Ontario · Amsterdam · Bonn · Sydney · Singapore
Tokyo · Madrid · San Juan · Milan · Paris · Mexico City · Seoul · Taipei

Cover designed by Hybert Design and Type, Maidenhead
and printed by The Riverside Printing Co. (Reading) Ltd.
Printed in Great Britain by T.J. Press (Padstow) Ltd, Cornwall.

First printed 1993.

British Library Cataloguing in Publication Data
A catalogue record for this book is available from the British Library.

Library of Congress Cataloging in Publication Data
Madsen, O. Lehrmann (Ole Lehrmann), 1950–
Object-oriented programming in the BETA programming language / Ole Lehrmann Madsen, Birger Møller-Pedersen, Kristen Nygaard.
p. cm.
Includes index.
ISBN 0–201–62430–3
1. Object-oriented programming. 2. BETA (Computer program language) I. Møller-Pedersen, Birger. II. Nygaard, Kristen, 1926– . III. Title.
QA76.64.M33 1993
005. 13′3—dc20 93–1150
CIP

Preface

This is a book on object-oriented programming and the BETA programming language. Object-oriented programming originated with the Simula languages developed at the Norwegian Computing Center, Oslo, in the 1960s. The first Simula language, Simula I, was intended for writing simulation programs. Simula I was later used as a basis for defining a general purpose programming language, Simula 67. In addition to being a programming language, Simula[1] was also designed as a language for describing and communicating about systems in general. Simula has been used by a relatively small community for many years, although it has had a major impact on research in computer science. The real breakthrough for object-oriented programming came with the development of Smalltalk. Since then, a large number of programming languages based on Simula concepts have appeared. C++ is the language that has had the greatest influence on the use of object-oriented programming in industry. Object-oriented programming has also been the subject of intensive research, resulting in a large number of important contributions.

The authors of this book, together with Bent Bruun Kristensen, have been involved in the BETA project since 1975, the aim of which is to develop concepts, constructs and tools for programming. The BETA language is one main result of this project, the various stages of which have been described in many different reports and articles (Kristensen *et al.*, 1976; 1983a,b; 1985; 1987a,b; 1988; Madsen, 1987; Madsen and Møller-Pedersen, 1988; 1989a,b; 1992; Madsen *et al.*, 1983). This book contains a description of the BETA language together with the conceptual framework on which BETA has been based.

The Mjølner[2] BETA System is a programming environment supporting object-oriented programming in BETA. The Mjølner BETA System has been developed by the Mjølner project (Dahle *et al.*, 1986; Knudsen *et al.*, 1992), which was a cooperative Nordic project with participants from Sweden, Norway, Finland and Denmark. The Mjølner

[1] Simula 67 was later renamed to just *Simula*, which is used in this book.

[2] The name Mjølner is taken from Nordic mythology, where Mjølner is the name of the god Thor's hammer. According to mythology, this hammer is the perfect tool that cannot fail, grows with the task, and always comes back to Thor's hand.

BETA System includes an implementation of BETA and a large number of libraries and application frameworks. It also includes a Hyper Structure Editor and an object-oriented CASE tool for supporting design using BETA. The system is a commercial product marketed by Mjølner Informatics ApS. Appendix B contains a more detailed description of the Mjølner BETA System. Readers should consult the Mjølner manuals for further details before trying to run the examples in this book. The Mjølner BETA System is currently available for the Macintosh, and for a number of UNIX-based workstations runnning X-Window Systems.

Draft versions of this book and pre-releases of the Mjølner BETA System have been used for teaching object-oriented programming at the Department of Information and Media Sciences (IMV) and the Computer Science Department (DAIMI), both at Aarhus University. At IMV, BETA is used for introductory programming and at DAIMI it is used as a second year course in programming languages. They have also been used for teaching at a number of other places, including the Universities of Copenhagen, Oslo, Bergen and Odense. Draft versions have also been used for BETA tutorials given at the OOPSLA '89, '90 and '91 conferences (Object-Oriented Programming, Languages, System and Applications), at the TOOLS '91 and '92 conferences (Technology of Object-Oriented Languages and Systems), and at EastEurOOPe '91 (East European Conference on Object-Oriented Programming).

The book is organized as follows: Chapters 1 and 2 introduce the basic concepts of object-oriented programming; Chapters 3–12 are a description of subjects such as objects, patterns, sequential execution, the virtual concept, block structure and procedural programming. The multi-sequential aspects of BETA, including coroutines and concurrency, are described in Chapters 13–15. Chapter 16 deals with exception handling, Chapter 17 describes the modularization of large programs, and Chapter 18 presents the conceptual framework underlying BETA. Appendix A includes a grammar for BETA, and Appendix B gives a description of the Mjølner BETA System.

When reading the book, there are three main subject areas that should be covered at the same time:

- The BETA language, Chapters 3–16
- Modularization, Chapter 17
- The conceptual framework, Chapters 2 and 18.

It is recommended that readers start with Chapters 1–6; Chapter 2 introduces part of the conceptual framework, and Chapters 3–6 introduce part of BETA.

Chapter 18, the main chapter on the conceptual framework, may then be read before reading Chapters 7–16. Depending on the reader's previous experience, it may be difficult to grasp Chapter 18 on a first reading, so it is recommended that this is read again after having read the book's remaining chapters. In a teaching situation it is recommended that the concepts detailed in Chapter 18 are discussed while reading the remaining chapters of the book.

Chapter 17, on modularization, may be read after Chapters 3–6. In a teaching situation it is recommended that it is read as soon as the students have to write other than just trivial programs. Experience shows that, from the beginning, students should be trained in splitting a program into convenient modules, including the separation of interface and implementation.

Acknowledgements

The BETA project was initiated in 1976 as part of what was then called *The Joint Language Project.* People from The Regional Computing Center and Computer Science Department at Aarhus University, the Institute for Electronic Systems at Aalborg University Centre, and the Norwegian Computing Center, Oslo participated in that project. The initiative for the project was taken in the autumn of 1975 by Bjarner Svejgaard, Director of The Regional Computing Center.

The BETA language was developed by the authors together with Bent Bruun Kristensen. In addition, a large number of people have been involved in the development of BETA and the Mjølner BETA System, including colleagues and students at Aarhus University, The Norwegian Computing Center, Oslo University, Aalborg University, and Mjølner Informatics. In particular, the contributions of Dag Belsnes and Jørgen Lindskov Knudsen are acknowledged.

Development of the Mjølner BETA System in the Nordic Mjølner project has been supported by The Nordic Fund for Technology and Research. Participants in the Mjølner Project come from Lund University, Telesoft, EB Technology, The Norwegian Computing Center, Telenokia, Sysware ApS, Aalborg University and Aarhus University. The main implementors of the Mjølner BETA System are Peter Andersen, Lars Bak, Jørgen Lindskov Knudsen, Ole Lehrmann Madsen, Kim Jensen Møller, Claus Nørgaard, and Elmer Sandvad. In addition, Karen Borup, Søren Brandt, Jørgen Nørgaard, Claus H. Pedersen, Tommy Thorn, Per Fack Sørensen and Peter Ørbæk have participated in various parts of the implementation.

The development of the Mjølner BETA System has been supported through a contract with Apple Computer Europe, Paris. We are grateful to Larry Taylor for the great support he has provided for BETA. Development of the system has also been supported by a contract with Apollo Computer, Finland, and by the donation of workstations from Hewlett-Packard.

The development of BETA and the Mjølner BETA System has been supported by the Danish Natural Science Research Council, grant. no. 11-3106, FTU 5.17.5.1.25, the Danish Natural Research Council, grant. no. 11-8285, the Danish Research Programme for Informatics, grant nos. 5.26.18.29. (the Devise Project), The Royal Norwegian Council for Scientific and Industrial Research, grant no. ED 0223.16641 (the Scala project), and through the European Commission's Esprit EuroCoOp (5303) and EuroCODE (6155) projects.

We would like to thank colleagues and students for valuable comments, inspiring criticisms, and the discovery of errors in preliminary versions of this book. Kim Halskov Madsen and Randell Trigg deserve special thanks for their use of preliminary versions of the book in teaching at IMV; their experience and comments have had a large influence. Other useful comments have been provided by Birger Andersen, Peter Andersen, Lars Bak, Lone Faber, Carsten Hansen, Dag Helstad, Anette Hviid, Jørgen Lindskov Knudsen, Kim Jensen Møller, Elmer Sandvad, Alexandre Valente Sousa, Kristine Stougaard Thomsen, and the many students who have been exposed to previous versions of the book.

We would like to thank Peter Wegner for his useful comments and encouragement to write this book and Simon Plumtree of Addison-Wesley for his patience. During the preparation of the manuscript we received great help from Susanne Brøndberg, Karen Kjær Møller and the production staff at Addison-Wesley.

The authors would like to thank their families (Ole: Marianne, Christian, Anne Sofie; Birger: Kirsten, Kamilla, Kristine; Kristen: Johanna and to a moderate extent children and grandchildren). The BETA project would not have been the same and this book would not have come into existence without their patience and understanding, and without their participation in many lively gatherings[3] throughout the years.

Ole Lehrmann Madsen
Birger Møller-Pedersen
Kristen Nygaard

May 1993

[3]We also thank the white wine producers in Germany, France, Italy and California.

Contents

Chapter 1

Introduction

This is first and foremost a book on the programming language BETA, but it is also a book on object-oriented programming, and issues such as object-oriented analysis and design are also covered.

Introducing a programming language is not just a matter of introducing language constructs and giving guidelines and hints on how to use them. It is also a matter of introducing a way of thinking that is associated with the underlying conceptual framework. For languages based on well established underlying concepts such as functions, relations or equations, the way of thinking may be obtained from other sources, and will often be part of the background and education of the prospective programmers. For object-oriented programming there is no well established theory or conceptual framework. Furthermore, there is no established consensus on what object-orientation is. Despite this, a large number of programmers practice object-oriented programming. They use a number of different languages such as Simula (Dahl *et al.*, 1968), Smalltalk (Goldberg and Robson, 1989), C++ (Stroustrup, 1991), Eiffel (Meyer, 1988), and CLOS (Keene, 1989). These languages have a common core of language constructs which to some extent make them look alike.

1.1 Benefits of object-orientation

It is difficult to discuss the benefits of object-orientation without first defining it. Before introducing the BETA approach, however, we shall briefly discuss what the benefits of object-orientation are considered to be. There are three main benefits: *real world apprehension*, *stability of design* and *reusability* of both designs and implementations. When people disagree about what object-orientation is, it is often because they attach different levels of importance to these aspects. We consider all three aspects to be important, though perhaps not equally so.

Real world apprehension

One of the reasons that object-oriented programming has become so widely accepted is that object-orientation is close to our own natural perception of the real world. (Krogdahl and Olsen, 1986) (translated from Norwegian) put it this way:

> 'The basic philosophy underlying object-oriented programming is to make the programs as far as possible reflect that part of the reality they are going to treat. It is then often easier to understand and to get an overview of what is described in programs. The reason is that human beings from the outset are used to and trained in the perception of what is going on in the real world. The closer it is possible to use this way of thinking in programming, the easier it is to write and understand programs.'

In (Coad and Yourdon, 1990) it is stated in the following way:

> 'Object-oriented analysis is based upon concepts that we first learned in kindergarten: objects and attributes, classes and members, wholes and parts.'

Both of these quotations stress that one important aspect of program development is to understand, describe and communicate about phenomena and concepts of the application domain. Object-oriented programming has turned out to be particularly well suited for doing this.

Stability of design

The principle behind the Jackson System Development (JSD) method, (Jackson, 1983) also reflects one of the benefits of object-orientation. Instead of focusing on the functionality of a system, the first step in the system's development according to JSD is to make a *physical model* of the real world with which the system is concerned. This model then forms the basis for the different functions that the system may have. Functions may later be changed, and new functions may be added without changing the underlying model.

As we shall see later, the notion of a physical model as introduced by JSD is central to object-orientation as described in this book. The concepts and techniques used by the JSD method to develop a physical model, and to subsequently implement it on a computer are, however, quite different from the concepts and techniques of object-oriented programming as presented in this book. As mentioned above, object-oriented programming provides a natural framework for modeling the application domain.

Reusability

One well known problem with software development is being able to reuse existing software components when developing new ones. The functionality of an existing component is often very similar to one needed for a new system. There may, however, be important differences which make it impossible to reuse the existing component. For this reason, the new component is often implemented by copying and modifying the existing component, but this means that it must be tested again. More problematic, however, is that the relations between the old and new components may be lost: if an error is detected in one, it must be corrected in both. Also, changes to common parts of the system may have to be performed in both components.

One of the benefits of object-oriented programming languages is that they have strong constructs for supporting incremental program modification. It is possible to define a new component as an incremental extension of an existing one, thus preserving the relations between the two components. Most object-oriented languages are based on the class/subclass mechanism (inheritance) which first appeared in Simula. One of the main contributions of Smalltalk was that these language constructs were combined with the flexibility of Lisp systems.

Even without the flexibility of Smalltalk, the ability to create programs by means of incremental extension is considered to be the main advantage of object-oriented programming by many programmers. The disadvantage of incremental modification is that the library of components reflects the historic development of those components. In addition, the relations between components are mainly dictated by maximal code sharing, often conflicting with the modeling requirements discussed above. These potential conflicts between requirements will be discussed later.

1.2 Object-oriented programming and BETA

To program is to understand: The development of an information system is not just a matter of writing a program that does the job. It is of the utmost importance that development of this program has revealed an in-depth understanding of the application domain; otherwise, the information system will probably not fit into the organization. During the development of such systems it is important that descriptions of the application domain are communicated between system specialists and the organization.

The approach to object-oriented programming presented in this book emphasizes the modeling capabilities. Most treatments of object-oriented programming are concerned with language constructs, and those familiar with the literature will know that concepts like inheritance and message passing are important considerations. There is, however, more to object-oriented programming than language constructs (this should be true for any programming language). The underlying conceptual framework or semantics is just as important as the language.

Other programming perspectives are based on some mathematical theory or model, giving them a sound theoretical basis, but object-oriented programming lacks a profound theoretical basis. For object-oriented programming, the initial observation of how people understand the world has to be formulated in a theory or conceptual framework. For the benefit of designing a programming language, and for the benefit of conveying an understanding of these basic concepts as part of a book on the language, this model does not have to be formal. In fact, the model underlying object-orientation is by its very nature informal, although part of the model has been formalized in terms of programming languages. This is necessary in order to create descriptions that may be executed on a computer. BETA may be seen as a formal notation for describing those parts of the application domain that can be formalized: BETA is formal in the sense that descriptions made in it have a precise meaning when executed on a computer. Often, a programming language is defined in terms of a mathematical model, yet such a model has not been constructed for BETA, although it might be useful for the purpose of consistency checking and formal verification.

This book attempts to go beyond language mechanisms and contribute a conceptual framework for object-oriented programming. This framework, however, needs further development.

We shall introduce the notions of **physical modeling**, to capture modeling of parts of the world based upon the identification of phenomena and concepts, and the notion of the **physical model**, to denote the models that are created in this process.

The use of informal concepts in the system development process is important, however, there is a tendency to put a greater emphasis on the concepts that can be formulated in terms of a programming language. The reason is clear, since the system development process eventually has to result in a description that can be executed on a computer. This book also emphasizes concepts that can be described in BETA. Below we briefly summarize the role of BETA in the system development process. Traditionally, system development is organized into *analysis*, *design* and *implementation*, and the concepts of object-orientation may be applied to all of these activities.

- *Analysis.* The primary goal of analysis is to *understand* the application domain. In this activity, relevant concepts and phenomena from the application domain must be identified and described, usually involving the system to be developed. For this reason, it is important that the concepts and phenomena identified can be communicated. In this process it is useful to use a high number of informal descriptions, since it would otherwise be quite difficult to communicate those descriptions to non computer specialists. The informal descriptions may consist of a mixture of text, graphics, and sometimes also incomplete program fragments. The use of graphics in system descriptions is important, particularly in analysis as it might be important to use graphical notation for part of the descriptions.

- *Design.* The design activity is concerned with *constructing* a precise description that can be refined into an executable program. Here the informal concepts developed in the analysis activity have to be made into formal concepts that can be described by a programming language like BETA. At this level the object-oriented program will be a description of phenomena and concepts from the application domain. Such a program will be fairly abstract, since it will include a number of elements that need further refinement before it can be executed. It is, however, important that the description is relevant for the application domain.

  Graphical notation may also be useful in the design activity. Most programming languages like BETA have a textual syntax, but it may often be advantageous to use graphical notations for part of the program instead of textual representation. Later we shall discuss how the same underlying language principles may be presented both graphically and textually.

  Analysis and design are similar in the sense that the descriptions must be meaningful in terms of the application domain. They are different with respect to their use of informal and formal descriptions.

- *Implementation.* This is concerned with *implementing* the design description on a computer, i.e. elements representing concepts and phenomena from the application domain must be described in terms of concepts that can be executed on the computer. These computer concepts do not represent concepts and phenomena from the application domain, i.e. the program is extended with details that are meaningless in the application domain. The basic principles of the two levels are the same; it is programming, but at different levels.

  Design and implementation are similar in the sense that a programming language is used for the descriptions. They differ in the sense that the elements of a design description must be meaningful in terms of the application domain, whereas this is not the case for an implementation description.

System development methods

The above description of analysis, design and implementation may give the impression that these activities are ordered in time (i.e. first analysis, then design, and finally implementation), but this is not the case. In some situations these activities may be intermixed, and the developer may not be conscious of them. There are various methods of organizing the system development process which differ in a number ways. The object-oriented framework presented in this book is not associated with any specific method, although it is not completely independent (we return to this in Chapter 18).

Logical *versus* physical system structure

BETA is a language for describing a system (program execution) consisting of objects and patterns, some of which represent phenomena and concepts from the application domain, and others which are for implementation purposes. The BETA objects and patterns provide the *logical structure* of a system; the BETA language provides mechanisms for describing this logical structure.

A BETA program (or BETA description) is usually constructed in the form of text in one or more files. The program may exist in a number of variants for different computers, and it may exist in various versions. Part of it may consist of modules included from a library; part may be used in many different programs. The BETA language does not have mechanisms for describing the physical organization of a BETA program in terms of files, variants, and versions, etc., because the *physical structure* of the program text is considered to be independent of the logical structure of the program. Some languages provide language elements for handling the physical structure, e.g. modules are often divided into interface and implementation modules. Such mechanisms are not a part of BETA. Instead, a language-independent technique for organizing the physical structure of a program text has been developed. This technique is based on the context free grammar of the language, where any correct sequence of terminal and nonterminal symbols (a so-called **sentential form**) of the grammar can be a module. This technique can be used for languages other than BETA. Chapter 17 describes techniques for organizing the physical structure of a BETA program.

There are aspects of the physical structure other than organization of the program text. A BETA system consists of a number of objects executing actions, and the actions executed by objects may take place concurrently.

Some of the objects of a BETA system are *transient* in the sense that they only exist while the program is executing. Other objects are *persistent* in the sense that they may be stored on secondary storage such as a disk and survive the program that created them. They may then be read and used by other programs. The separation of objects into transient and persistent objects is not part of the BETA language, but is handled by the Mjølner BETA System. An object-oriented database system supporting client and servers is currently being developed on top of the persistent object store of the Mjølner BETA System.

Modern computer hardware often consists of a large number of processors connected through some communication media, an example being a set of workstations connected through a local area network. The concurrency described in a BETA program may be realized through time sharing on a single processor, or by distributing the active BETA objects on a number of processors. BETA has constructs for describing the logical structure of concurrent objects, and the physical structure of mapping concurrent objects onto several processors is considered independent of the language. The Mjølner BETA System contains some support for distributed computing in BETA.

For the physical structure, only modularization is described in this book. The mapping of a BETA system onto a process generator (computer hardware) in terms of splitting objects into transient and persistent objects, and the distribution of objects onto several processors, is not dealt with in this book (see the Mjølner BETA System manuals for the current status of this).

Although the main emphasis in this book is on the logical structure of a system, the design and implementation of the physical structure is equally important. During design and implementation, the programmer must be explicit about the physical organization of the program text, as described in Chapter 17, and should be concerned with the organization of persistent and distributed objects.

BETA

BETA is a modern language in the Simula tradition. It supports the object-oriented perspective on programming and contains comprehensive facilities for procedural and functional programming. Research is going on with the aim of including constraint-oriented constructs.

BETA replaces classes, procedures, functions and types by a single abstraction mechanism called the **pattern**. It generalizes virtual procedures to virtual patterns, streamlines linguistic notions such as nesting and block structure, and provides a unified framework for sequential, coroutine and concurrent execution. The resulting language is smaller than Simula in spite of being considerably more expressive.

The Mjølner BETA System is a software development environment supporting the BETA language which includes an implementation of the BETA language as described in this book. In addition, the system includes a number of other tools, and a large collection of libraries and frameworks that greatly enhance BETA's usability by providing a large number of predefined patterns and objects. (The libraries and frameworks are not described in this book, though a short introduction is given in Appendix B. For a detailed description see the Mjølner BETA System manuals.)

The Mjølner BETA System was originally developed as part of the Nordic Mjølner project, which has also produced a large number of other results. (Knudsen *et al.*, 1992) is a collection of the project's main results.

1.3 Notes

In the early 1960s, the Simula I language was introduced with the purpose of writing simulation programs. In the late 1960s, a general programming language, Simula 67, was defined, the important contribution of which was the introduction of the class and sub-class concepts and the notion of virtual procedures. These constructs have become the core of most object-oriented languages. Whereas Simula I was a simulation language, Simula 67 is a general programming language that supports simulation by means of a general set of classes. This demonstrated the power of the Simula concepts. Instances of Simula classes behave like coroutines, making it possible to simulate concurrency, which was heavily used in the simulation package. Despite the usefulness of coroutines and quasi-parallel sequencing for modeling real-life phenomena, these concepts have not yet found their way into most object-oriented languages. For a further description of the history of Simula, see (Nygaard and Dahl, 1981).

Simula has been used by a relatively small community for many years. In the early 1970s, the class/sub-class concepts were used in the design of the Smalltalk language, leading in turn to a major breakthrough for object-oriented programming. The Smalltalk style of programming has particularly caught on in Lisp communities, resulting in a number of substantial contributions like Flavors (Cannon, 1982), and Loops (Bobrow and Stefik, 1983).

The object-oriented ideas have also started to impact on traditional software construction, the most influential seeming to be C++. Another contribution is Eiffel.

In the 1970s, much attention was given to the notion of **structured programming**. The discussions of object-oriented programming in the literature may be compared to that of structured programming. Structured programming was often associated with avoiding goto's when programming, yet there is clearly more to structured programming than avoiding goto's, just as there is more to object-oriented programming than inheritance and message passing.

The label 'object-orientation' is attached to many things. People talk about object-oriented programming, object-oriented design, object-oriented implementation, object-oriented languages, object-oriented databases, etc. Object-orientation has started to be applied to these activities, i.e. concepts such as object-oriented analysis, object-oriented design and object-oriented implementation have arrived. Often, object-oriented programming is associated with object-oriented implementation. The reason for this is that object-orientation originated from programming languages such as Simula and Smalltalk. In this book, object-oriented programming is meant to cover object-oriented analysis, object-oriented design and object-oriented implementation.

Object-orientation has also generated particular interest in the area of database systems. A book on object-oriented databases should cover the same material as this book, since the basic principles are the same. A database book might pay more attention to the handling of large sets of information. Database design and programming are both related to modeling/representing real world phenomena.

A programming language is often characterized as an object-oriented language, a functional language, a procedural language, etc. Also, the term **multi-perspective** (or **multi-paradigm**) **language** is used for languages supporting more than one perspective. Often the term 'object-oriented language' is used exclusively for languages that only support object-orientation. In this book, an **object-oriented language** is a programming language that supports object-oriented programming, and a **pure object-oriented language** is a programming language that only supports object-orientation. The same definitions apply to other perspectives.

Chapter 2

Introduction to Basic Concepts

In this chapter we briefly and informally introduce some of the basic concepts underlying object-oriented programming. They are further explained during the introduction of the BETA language in subsequent chapters, and a more detailed treatment is given in Chapter 18.

A computer executing a program generates a process consisting of various phenomena (an example of a phenomenon is an *object* representing a bank account of some customer). Such an object represents certain properties of the real bank account, like its balance, and a list of deposits and withdrawals performed on the account. The objects reside in the computer's memory.

In the real world, customers and bank clerks perform *actions* that change the *state* of the various bank accounts. At a certain point, the balance of a given account may be DKK 5000, but a deposit of DKK 105 will change its balance to DKK 5105. A deposit is one example of an action performed in a bank; other examples are the withdrawal of money, the computation of interest, opening and closing of accounts, etc. It is important to be aware of the fact that actions are ordered in time – in most banks you have to deposit some money before you can carry out a withdrawal.

The process generated by the computer has phenomena representing these actions and states. The state of a bank account is represented by the object representing the bank account, and actions changing the state of the bank account are represented by actions executed by the computer.

For a set of objects representing a bank system, we may be interested in measuring part of the state of several accounts, which could, for instance, consist of computing the balance of all a given customer's accounts.

A process generated by a computer executing a program is called a *program execution.* Program executions belong to a class of processes called *information processes.* The production process of cars in a factory, the processing of customer orders in a company, and the money flow between banks may be viewed as information processes.

The study of informatics or computer science is concerned with the study of information processes. This book will develop a conceptual framework for understanding and describing information processes, in particular being concerned with program executions. In Chapter 18 we return to the more general notion of information processes.

BETA is a *programming language* for describing program executions, and the main part of this book is about BETA.

2.1 Perspectives on programming

To understand object-oriented programming it is necessary to understand how it relates to other perspectives on programming. The purpose of this section is to give a short introduction to some of the most generally accepted perspectives, though it is not intended to be a complete description of the subject. Readers are encouraged to consult other references for this purpose.

In the literature, a large number of programming perspectives, such as process, type system and event perspectives are discussed, because programmers have different perspectives on programming (in principle, each programmer may have his own perspective). Also, the definitions of perspectives given below might not coincide with what other people understand by these perspectives.

2.1.1 Procedural programming

When computers were invented they were viewed as programmable calculators and many people still hold this view.

Consider a simple calculator. It may consist of a register for storing a value, and a number of operations such as add, sub, mult and div. It is possible to enter a number into the register and then modify this value using the operations. The following is a list of possible operations for a simple calculator:

```
enter V
add V
sub V
mult V
div V
result
```

The operations **enter, add, sub, mult, div** and **result** correspond to buttons on the calculator; `V` corresponds to a number entered through a number pad. We are not concerned with the physical layout of the calculator here as we are only interested in its functionality.

Instead of one register the calculator may have several registers, thus intermediate results of a calculation may be stored in these registers – with only one register the user would have to write down intermediate results on paper. Assume that our calculator is extended with registers `R0, R1, R2, ... Rn`, and that the previous operations operate on `R0`. We have the following new operations:

```
enter V Ri
add Ri Rj
sub Ri Rj
mult Ri Rj
div Ri Rj
copy Ri Rj
```

The operands `Ri` and `Rj` correspond to buttons for selecting a register.

A calculator with a fixed number of registers and operations has a limited scope of applications. Often the user has to carry out the same procedure over and over again on different data, perhaps carrying out the same sequence of operations. This lead to the idea of a *programmable calculator*. In addition to data registers and operations, a programmable calculator has a store where a sequence of operations may be stored:

```
define Pi Op1; Op2; ... end
call Pi
```

The `define` and `call` operations correspond to buttons for defining and calling procedures. `Pi` could be a number or another unique identification of the procedure being defined. Our programmable calculator could be used in the following way:

```
define P1:  copy R0 R1; mult R0 2; add R0 R1 end
enter 100
call P1
return
```

The store used for storing procedures may also be used for storing values, i.e. it is possible to move a value from a register to the store, and vice versa. In this way, it is possible to save a large number of intermediate results.

In the above examples it was possible to define a procedure by means of a sequence of operations, but for many types of calculations this is too primitive. The operations may be extended with control flow operations, making it possible to select from between sub-sequences of operations and to repeat the execution of a sub-sequence. The following is an example of possible control flow operations:

```
L:
goto L
if Ri=0 goto L
```

The first computers were just advanced programmable calculators with a large number of registers, a large store for saving procedures and a suitable set of basic operations.

With programmable calculators it is possible to solve large calculations; with computers, even larger ones can be solved.

One problem with our programmable calculator is that the programmer must keep track of which part of the store is used for values and which part for procedures. To help, a *symbolic assembler* may be used, where it is possible to declare a number of variables by means of names. The assembler allocates a memory cell corresponding to each variable, so the programmer can then refer to a variable/register by name instead of by a number.

It is, however, difficult and time consuming to write procedures using the simple language of the computer. Instead, a high-level programming language may be used. A compiler is used to translate a program written in the programming language into the language of the computer. The first programming languages had facilities for defining variables and procedures (variables are simply registers). Instead of a fixed number of registers, the programmer may define the number of variables needed, which is, of course, limited by the size of the store. We do not go into further detail about programming languages here, since this will be dealt with in the rest of the book.

Despite the fact that there is a huge difference between simple calculators and modern computers, a computer is still viewed by most programmers as an advanced calculator. When writing a program, the programmer thinks of defining a set of variables and a set of procedures for manipulating these variables. This *perspective* on programming is called *procedural* (or *imperative*) *programming.* In summary, procedural programming may be defined as follows:

Procedural programming. A program execution is regarded as a (partially ordered) sequence of procedure calls manipulating variables.

As mentioned above, procedural programming is still the most common perspective on programming, supported by languages like Algol (Naur, 1962), Pascal (Jensen and Wirth, 1975), C (Kernighan and

Ritchie, 1978) and Ada (US Department of Defense, 1980). It is in no way obsolete, still being useful for writing small procedures and, as we shall see later, it may be used together with object-oriented programming.

2.1.2 Functional and constraint programming

Since the mid-1960s, a large research effort has been directed towards giving a mathematical definition of programming languages. One main result of this is the notion of *functional* or (*applicative*) *programming.* When trying to give a mathematical definition of programming languages, it turned out that the notions of 'variable' and 'assignment' were the main bottlenecks. In practice, many programmers have realized that when writing large programs it is difficult to handle the large number of variables. One response to this is functional programming, in which a program is viewed as a mathematical function. A program is then a combination of mathematical functions.

A language supporting functional programming must, then, include facilities for defining mathematical functions, including higher order functions, i.e. functions that may have functions as parameters and return functions as results. In addition, such a language should include data types corresponding to mathematical domains.

Lisp is an example of a language with excellent support for functional programming. However, Lisp is not a pure functional programming language as it supports other perspectives as well, including procedural and object-oriented programming. ML and Miranda are examples of pure functional languages.

The most prominent property of the functional perspective is that there are no variables and no notion of state. A variable may only be bound once to a value, and it is not possible to assign a new value to a variable.

To summarize, functional programming may be defined as follows:

Functional programming. A program is regarded as a mathematical function, describing a relation between input and output.

Like procedural programming, functional programming should be seen as a supplement to procedural and object-oriented programming. It is useful for describing state transitions where the intermediate results are irrelevant.

The notion of functional programming has been generalized further. A function is a relation which is unique in its first element. Instead of just viewing a program as a functional relation, it might as well be viewed as a general relation (or a set of equations). This is the idea of so-called *logic programming*, *rule-based programming*, or as we shall call it here, *constraint programming*:

Constraint programming. A program is regarded as a set of equations describing relations between input and output.

This constraint-oriented perspective is supported by, for example, Prolog.

We shall not go into further details on functional- and constraint-oriented programming (readers are encouraged to consult (Wikstrøm, 1987; Leler, 1987). It is important to stress that different perspectives should not exclude each other – they are each useful for different purposes, and a programmer should have the possibility of using a given perspective when relevant. The ideal programming language should integrate the different perspectives. It is important to be aware that this should not be done by designing a language consisting of features from various procedural, functional and object-oriented languages. A programming language should be based on a conceptual framework, and the language constructs should be designed with respect to this framework.

2.2 Object-oriented programming

This section gives an informal introduction to object-oriented programming, defined as follows:

Object-oriented programming. A program execution is regarded as a physical model, simulating the behavior of either a real or imaginary part of the world.

The notion of a physical model should be taken literally. Most people can imagine the construction of physical models by means of, for example, Lego bricks. In the same way, a program execution may be viewed as a physical model. Other perspectives on programming are made precise by some underlying model defining equations, relations, predicates, etc. For object-oriented programming, however, we have to elaborate on the concept of physical models.

Physical models are not just relevant for computers. In the following we give examples of physical models where computers are not involved.

2.2.1 Manual systems

In many areas it is common to make a physical model of some construction so as to observe some properties before the 'real thing' is constructed. This is the case with buildings: before constructing a large building, a

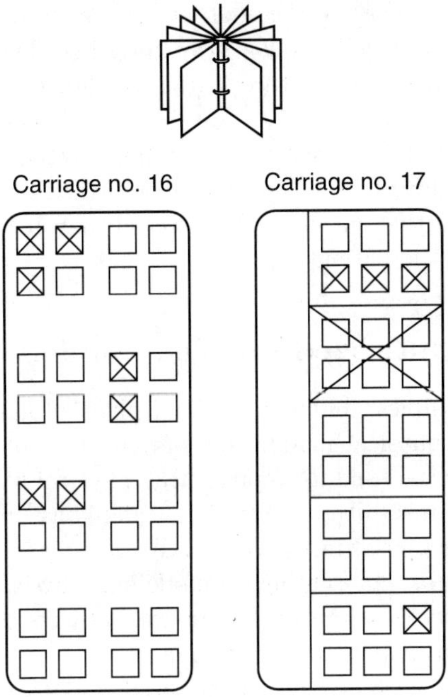

Figure 2.1 Manual seat reservation system.

model is usually made to check various properties of the design. This is also the case for bridges, cars, trains, aeroplanes, etc.

When building a railway system it is common to model it using a model train set. Such a model may simulate many of the properties of the 'real' train system. The following is a description of how manual train seat reservation was handled in Norway (and probably in other countries as well) before computers were invented. Manual train seat reservations were based on a number of sheets representing the wagons in the train. The upper part of Figure 2.1 shows the collection of sheets, and the lower part shows examples of two such sheets. The seats could be checked, or the part of the trip where the seat was occupied could be indicated. Travelers were given small tickets indicating the details of their reservation.

Such a train reservation system is an example of what we consider to be a physical model. Each wagon in a train is represented by a sheet, which includes those properties of the wagon that are essential for seat reservation. The system was flexible in terms of the kinds of services which could be supplied, e.g. the reservation of a seat next to another seat, the reservation of a seat close to the door, etc., were all possible. Entries were of course written in pencil to allow easy updating. The reservation sheets were kept at the train's departure station so they could be sent with the guard.

Hospitals provide another such example. At a hospital a medical record corresponding to each patient keeps track of the relevant information related to that patient. This record may be considered to be a representation of the patient.

2.2.2 Computerized physical models

In the above examples, different kinds of physical material are used for constructing the physical model. In computerized physical models, objects are the material used for representing physical phenomena from the application domain. Objects are thus considered as similar to cardboard, sheets, Lego bricks, etc., in the sense that objects are physical material that may be used for representing (or modeling) physical phenomena. Objects are *computerized material.* In this way, objects differ from material such as cardboard, paper, Lego bricks, etc.

An *object* is a piece of physical material that may be used to *represent* (or model) a real or imaginary phenomenon from the application domain. Sometimes we say that an object *represents* a phenomenon from the application domain, and sometimes we say that an object *models* a phenomenon.

In the following we present examples of different kinds of properties used to characterize phenomena, and explain how they are represented as objects.

Object attributes

Objects are characterized by various *attributes*, which represent/model a property of the phenomenon being modeled. There are different kinds of attributes which may be associated with objects. In the following some examples are given.

In a flight reservation system there will typically be an object representing each reservation. The properties of a reservation may include the date for the flight, a reference to the customer, the source and destination of the flight, etc. An object representing a reservation will then have attributes corresponding to these properties. An object corresponding to a medical record will typically include attributes representing properties such as the temperature and blood pressure of the patient, etc. Properties like these are called *measurable properties.*

A measurable property may vary with time. The temperature of a patient may be different at different points in time. An object must thus be able to represent this variation, i.e. at different points in time the attribute modeling measurable properties must result in different values. An object is said to have a *state.* The state of an object varies with time.

Object actions

Many real world systems are characterized by consisting of phenomena that perform their sequences of actions *concurrently.* The flight reservation system consists of several concurrent phenomena, e.g. flights and agents. Each agent performs its task concurrently with other agents. Flights will register the reservation of seats and ensure that no seats are reserved by two agents at the same time. Note that this kind of concurrency is an inherent property of the reality being modeled; it is not concurrency used to speed up computations.

Complex tasks such as those of the agents are often considered to consist of several more or less independent activities. This is so even though they constitute only one sequence of actions, and do not include concurrency. As an example, consider the activities 'tour planning', 'customer service' and 'invoicing', where each of these consists of a sequence of actions.

A single agent will not have concurrent activities, but *alternates* between different activities. The shifts will not only be determined by the agents themselves, but will be triggered by, for example, communication with other objects. An agent will, for instance, shift from tour planning to customer service (prompted by the telephone ringing), and resume tour planning when the customer service is completed.

The action sequence of an agent may often be decomposed into *partial action sequences* which correspond to certain routines carried out several times as part of an activity. As an example, the invoicing activity may contain partial action sequences, each for writing a single invoice.

Concepts and abstraction

In the real world we create concepts to capture the complexity of the world around us – we make abstractions. We all perceive the world in terms of concepts: for people we use concepts like person, male, female, boy and girl; in biology we use concepts like animal, mammal, predator, fish and dog.

A concept is a generalized idea of a collection of phenomena, based on knowledge of common properties of instances in the collection. Concepts are used to concentrate on those properties which are shared by a set of phenomena in the application domain, and to ignore the differences between them.

When talking about concepts, it is useful to identify the following characteristics:

- The *extension* of a concept is the collection of phenomena covered by the concept.
- The *intension* of a concept is a collection of properties that in some way characterize the phenomena in the extension of the concept.
- The *designation* of a concept is the collection of names by which the concept is known.

The extension of the concept predator contains all lions, tigers, cats, etc. The intension includes a property such as 'eating meat.'

We use the term *pattern* for a concept belonging to a computerized model. A pattern is thus a representation of a concept in our computerized model.

Organization of knowledge

People constantly use the following three fundamental methods of knowledge organization for understanding the real world:

- *Identification of phenomena and their properties* As a first step in understanding a complex collection of phenomena, individual phenomena and their properties are recognized. An object may be observed to consist of certain parts, have a certain size and weight, a certain color, etc. Similarities between different phenomena may not be realized, just as a systematic understanding of the individual phenomena may not be obtained.
- *Classification* Classification is the means by which we form and distinguish between different classes of phenomena. Phenomena and concepts with similar properties are grouped into classes corresponding to extensions of concepts. This process leads to *classification hierarchies.*

  In Figure 2.2, a hierarchy of concepts relating to biology is shown. The concept of an animal may be viewed as more general than the concepts of mammal, fish, bird and reptile, since all mammals, fishes, birds and reptiles are also animals. The concept animal is said to be a *generalization* of mammal, fish, bird and reptile. Similarly, mammal is a more general concept than predator and rodent, so mammal is a generalization of rodent and predator. A concept like mammal is also said to

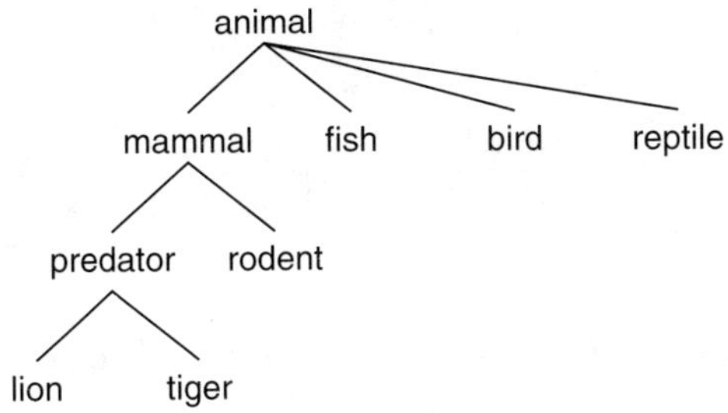

Figure 2.2 Part of a classification hierarchy for animals.

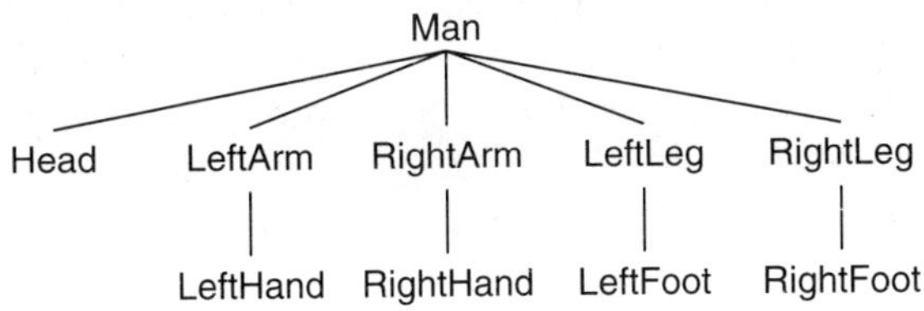

Figure 2.3 Whole/part hierarchy for a stick figure.

be a *specialization* of animal. Similarly, predator is a specialization of mammal.

Classification hierarchies are useful for understanding the relevant properties of a set of phenomena. For the concept animal we may associate properties common to all animals. We may associate the properties common to all mammals for the concept mammal as for the other concepts. Since a mammal, fish, bird or reptile is also an animal, we have isolated their common properties with the concept of animal.

- *Composition* In many situations it is useful to consider a phenomena or concept as a composition of other phenomena and concepts. One example of composition is to consider a *whole* as constructed from *parts*. The parts may again consist of smaller, simpler parts. The notion of a *whole/part composition* is an important means of understanding and organizing complex phenomena and concepts.

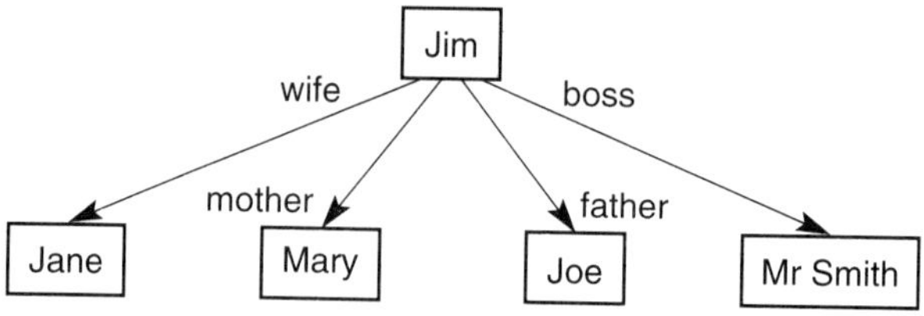

Figure 2.4 Example of reference composition.

Figure 2.3 shows an example of a whole/part hierarchy for a stick figure consisting of parts like head, body, arms and legs. In turn, the legs consist of lower leg, foot, etc. A car may similarly be viewed as consisting of a body, an engine, four wheels, etc.

An object representing a person may also have properties such as spouse, father, boss, etc. Such properties are not physical parts of a person. Instead, we may view a person object as composed of *references* to other objects. This form of composition is called *reference composition*, illustrated in Figure 2.4.

As mentioned before, the conceptual framework is discussed further in Chapter 18.

2.3 Exercises

(1) Design a calculator corresponding to the abstract calculator described above.

(2) Give other examples of physical models not involving computers.

(3) Develop a classification hierarchy for vehicles.

(4) Develop a whole/part hierarchy for a tree.

(5) Design a simple train reservation system.

2.4 Notes

The conceptual framework for object-oriented programming presented here and in Chapter 18 is a result of the BETA project, and has formed the basis for the design of BETA. It evolved over many years, and was influenced by several sources, including Simula,

(Holbæk-Hanssen *et al.*, 1975), (Knudsen and Thomsen, 1985), and a large number of student theses carried out in Aarhus and Oslo. The Norwegian train example is from (Sørgaard, 1988), and the stick figure example is from (Blake and Cook, 1987).

Other important contributions to a framework for object-oriented programming may be found in (Stefik and Bobrow, 1984), (Booch, 1986), (Shriver and Wegner, 1987), (ECOOP 1987–1992) and (OOPSLA 1986–1992).

Chapter 3

Objects and Patterns

The most fundamental elements of BETA are objects and patterns. This chapter introduces language constructs for describing objects and patterns.

3.1 Overview

A BETA program execution consists of a collection of objects and patterns. An object is some computerized material characterized by a set of attributes and an action part. Some objects in a program execution will represent phenomena from the application domain, whereas other objects are just part of the implementation.

An object representing a bank account may be described in the following way:

```
(# balance: ... ;
   Deposit: ... ;
   Withdraw: ... ;
#)
```

The bank account object is characterized by the attributes `balance`, `Deposit` and `Withdraw`. The attribute `balance`[1] represents the current balance of the account, `Deposit` represents the actions performed when money is placed in the account, and `Withdraw` represents the withdrawals performed. The dots ... indicate some details that have been left out of the description. All other parts of the description have a meaning in BETA. The syntactic construct `(# ... #)` is called an *object-descriptor*, which describes the *structure* of an object. Part of the structure of an object is its attributes like `balance`, `Deposit` and `Withdraw`. Later we shall see that the structure of an object may include more than its attributes.

[1]See also Section 18.7 for a discussion of how to represent properties like `balance`.

Singularly defined objects

A person programming his own private financial system may have only one bank account. In this case, there is only a need to represent one bank account in the system, described as follows:

```
myAccount: @
  (# balance: ... ;
     Deposit: ... ;
     Withdraw: ... ;
  #);
```

The above description has three parts:

(1) `myAccount` is the name that may be used to refer to the object representing the account,

(2) the symbol `@` shows that `myAccount` is the name of an object, and

(3) the object-descriptor `(# ... #)` describes the structure of the object.

The `myAccount` name may be used to denote the attributes of the bank account object. The *remote-name*[2] `myAccount.balance` denotes the balance attribute. The other attributes may be denoted in a similar way.

The `myAccount` object is called a *singular object*, since the object descriptor `(# ... #)` is only used for describing a single object.

Patterns

In a banking system there is clearly a need to represent several bank accounts, thus the system includes a `pattern` representing the concept of a bank account. The objects representing the actual bank accounts may then be described as instances of this pattern. The pattern representing the concept of a bank account may be described as follows:

```
Account:
  (# balance: ... ;
     Deposit: ... ;
     Withdraw: ... ;
  #);
```

The pattern description has two elements:

(1) `Account` is the name of the pattern, and

[2] See also Section 3.2.5.

(2) the object-descriptor `(# ... #)` describing the structure of each of the bank account instances.

The difference between the description of the `myAccount` object and the `Account` pattern is the use of the symbol `@` after `:`. The presence of `@` after `:` means that an object is described. When there is no symbol between `:` and `(# ... #)`, a pattern is described.

Pattern-defined objects

The `Account` pattern may, for instance, be used to describe three bank accounts:

```
account1: @Account;
account2: @Account;
account3: @Account;
```

The description of each bank account has three elements that are similar to those for the description of `myAccount`. The difference is the use of the `Account` pattern instead of `(# ... #)` to describe the structure of the account objects. The names `account1`, `account2` and `account3` may all be used like `myAccount`. It is, for example, possible to denote the balance of `account1` using the remote-name `account1.balance`.

The distinction between describing a *singular object* such as `myAccount` and describing a pattern representing a concept like `Account` is important. In the former, one is dealing with a situation where there is only one single object to consider. In the latter, there is a whole class of similar objects which may naturally be classified using a concept. From a technical point of view, it is convenient to avoid inventing a pattern name when there is only a singular object.

When making descriptions in BETA there is a large number of patterns available for describing objects. The `integer` pattern is one example. Instances of the `integer` pattern describe objects that may represent integer numbers. In the bank account example, the attribute `balance` could be represented as an instance of the `integer` pattern:

```
balance: @integer
```

Declarations

The syntactic element for describing attributes is called a *declaration*. The following are examples of declarations used above:

```
Account: (# ... #);
account1: @Account;
balance: @integer
```

In general, the syntactic construct : signals a declaration of some kind, i.e. a name being associated with some entity.

Description of actions

The Deposit and Withdraw attributes represent the depositing and withdrawing actions, respectively, performed on an account. These attributes may be described as follows:

```
Account:
  (# balance: @integer;

     Deposit:
       (# amount: @integer
       enter amount
       do balance+amount->balance
       exit balance
       #);

     Withdraw:
       (# amount: @integer
       enter amount
       do balance-amount->balance
       exit balance
       #);
  #)
```

Deposit and Withdraw are patterns. Deposit represents a concept covering all possible deposit actions. The execution of an instance of Deposit represents an actual deposit action. An instance of Deposit is an object consisting of one amount attribute representing the amount of money to be put into the account. The deposit action is described by enter amount do ... exit balance.

An action representing a deposit into the account1 account may be described as follows:

```
500->&account1.Deposit->newBalance
```

This describes that an instance of account1's Deposit attribute is generated (described by &account1.Deposit). The value 500 is assigned to the amount attribute (described by enter amount), then the value of amount is added to balance (described by do balance+amount->balance), and finally, the value of balance is returned (described by exit balance) and assigned to the object newBalance.

The symbol `&` means `new`, and the expression `&account1.Deposit` means that a new instance of the pattern `account1.Deposit` is created and executed. Creation of an instance of a pattern and executing it is often called *procedure invocation.*

`Withdraw` works like `Deposit`.

Imperatives

An *imperative* is a syntactic element for describing an action, of which the following are examples:

```
balance+amount->balance;
500->&account1.Deposit->newbalance
```

Complete programs

Until now, various elements of BETA descriptions have been shown. The example in Figure 3.1 shows how to combine some of these elements into one compound description in the form of an object-descriptor having `Account`, `account1`, `account2` and `account3` as attributes. In addition, the attributes `K1`, `K2` and `K3` have been added. The do-part of the object-descriptor consists of a sequence of actions performing various deposits and withdrawals on the accounts. This object-descriptor may be compiled and executed by a BETA processor.[3] An object-descriptor that may be executed is often called a *program.*

An abbreviated syntax for declaring `account1`, `account2` and `account3` has been used.

A text enclosed by the brackets { and } is a *comment.*[4]

State and state transitions

The *state of an object* at a given point in time is the value of its attributes, and execution of actions may change the state of an object. The *state of a program execution* at a given point in time is the objects existing at that point in time and their states.

In Figure 3.2, the state of the execution of the program from Figure 3.1 is shown. The comments `{L1}`, `{L2}` and `{L3}` indicate three points corresponding to the states shown in the figure. At `{L1}` the value of all integer objects is 0 (zero). (All integer objects will initially have the value 0.) At `{L2}` the state diagram shows that values have been deposited

---

[3]The Mjølner BETA System may be used for this. See the relevant manuals for further information.

[4]Note that { and } cannot be used in the Mjølner BETA System. Instead, `(*` and `*)` must be used.

```
(# Account:
     (# balance: @integer;
        Deposit:
          (# amount: @integer
          enter amount
          do balance+amount->balance
          exit balance
          #);
        Withdraw:
          (# amount: @integer
          enter amount
          do balance-amount->balance
          exit balance
          #);
    #);
   account1, account2, account3: @Account;
   K1,K2,K3: @integer;
do {L1}
   100->&account1.Deposit;
   200->&account2.Deposit;
   300->&account3.Deposit;
   {L2}
   150->&account1.Deposit->K1;
   90->&account3.Withdraw->K3;
   90->&account2.Deposit->K2;
   80->&account3.Withdraw->K3;
   {L3}
#)
```

Figure 3.1 Account program.

in the three accounts. Finally, at {L3} the final state of the program execution is shown.

3.1.1 Summary

We can now summarize the syntactic elements for describing objects and patterns.

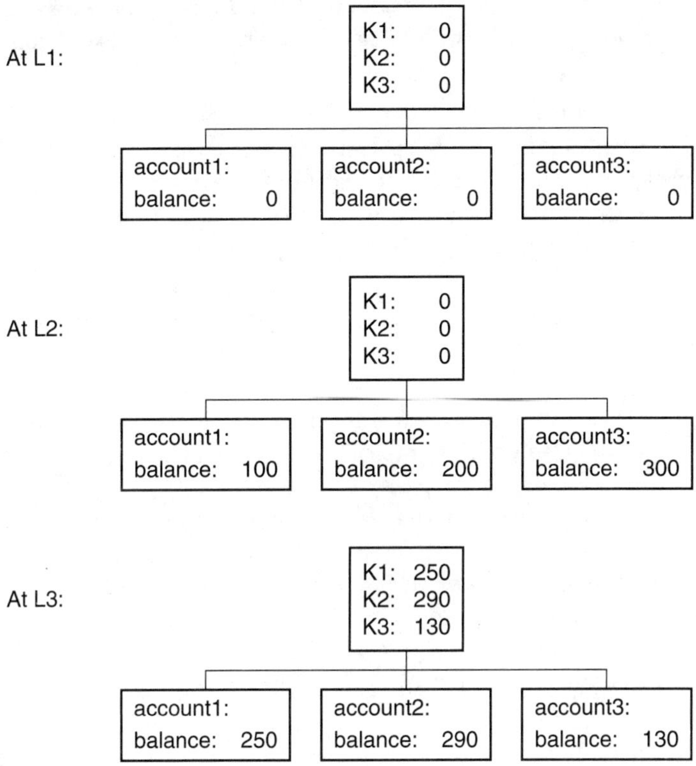

Figure 3.2 Snapshots of states during execution of the account program.

Object-descriptor

The syntactic element for describing an object is called an *object-descriptor*, and has the form:

```
(# Decl1; Decl2; ...; Decln
enter In
do Imp
exit Out
#)
```

The elements of an object-descriptor have the meanings:

- `Decl1; Decl2; ... ;Decln` is a list of attribute declarations that describes the *attribute-part* of the object. The possible kinds of attributes are further described below.

- `In` is a description of the *enter-part* of the object. The enter-part is a list of *input parameters* which may be entered prior to execution of the object.
- `Imp` is the *do-part* of the object. The do-part is an imperative that describes the actions to be performed when the object is executed. An object may, for instance, be executed as a procedure, a coroutine, or as a concurrent process. In Chapters 13–15, the use of objects as coroutines and concurrent processes is described.
- `Out` is a description of the *exit-part* of the object. The exit-part is a list of *output parameters* which may be produced as a result of execution of the object.

The enter-, do- and exit-parts are together called the *action-part* of the object. An object-descriptor may have additional parts, which will be introduced in subsequent chapters.

The object-descriptor is the basic syntactic construct in BETA. It may be used to describe a pattern like `Account`, and it may be used to describe a single object like `myAccount`. An object-descriptor is often part of a larger description, and a BETA program is an object-descriptor. Chapter 17 describes how a large number of object-descriptors may be combined into a complete program that can be compiled and executed.

Singular objects

A singular object may be described directly using an object-descriptor:

```
S: @(# Decl1; Decl2; ...; Decln
     enter In
     do Imp
     exit Out
     #)
```

The object `myAccount` described at the beginning of this chapter is an example of a singular object.

Pattern declaration

In BETA, a concept is represented by a *pattern*, a pattern being defined by associating a name with an object-descriptor:

```
P: (# Decl1; Decl2; ...; Decln
   enter In
   do Imp
```

```
exit Out
#)
```

Patterns serve as templates for generating objects (instances). The objects generated as instances of P will all have the same *structure*, i.e. the same set of attributes, the same enter-part, the same do-part and the same exit-part.

The intension of the concept being modeled is given by the object descriptor, while the objects that are generated according to this descriptor constitute the extension. The pattern name is part of the designation of the concept. By means of virtual patterns (see Chapters 7 and 9) and renaming, the pattern may also be designated by other names.

Pattern-defined objects

An instance of a pattern may be described as follows:

```
aP: @P
```

3.2 Reference attributes

The attribute `balance` of `Account` is an example of a *reference attribute*. A reference denotes an object, and may be either dynamic or static. A static reference constantly denotes the same object, whereas a dynamic reference is a variable which may denote different objects. The `balance` attribute is a static reference.

3.2.1 Static references

A *static reference* is declared in the following way:

```
X: @T
```

where `X` is the name of the reference and `T` is a pattern. An instance of `T` is generated as part of the generation of the object containing the declaration: the static reference `X` will constantly denote this `T`-object. An object generated in this way is called a *static object*, or also a *part-object*, since it is a permanent part of the object containing the declaration.

A *singular* static/part-object is declared in the following way:

```
Y: @(# ... #)
```

Static objects are useful for modeling part hierarchies, i.e. objects which consist of part-objects.

The following example describes objects that represent points (e.g. on a screen). Such objects may have two `integer` attributes:

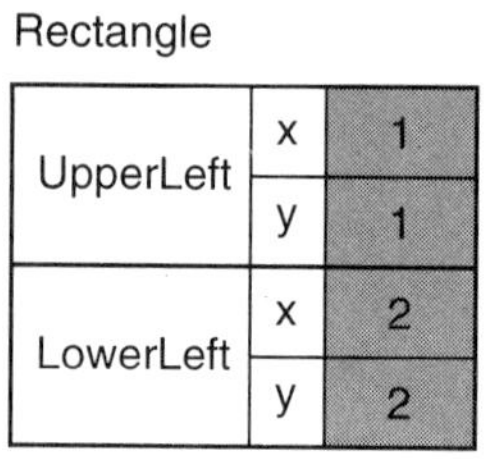

Figure 3.3 Diagrammatic representation of a `Rectangle object`.

```
Point: (# x,y: @integer #)
```

The `Point` pattern has empty enter-, do- and exit-parts and a single declaration that uses the predefined `integer` pattern. Given this pattern, two `Point`-objects may be generated by the following attribute declaration:

```
P1,P2: @Point
```

The `Point` pattern may in turn be used to describe attributes of other objects. Consider the following pattern declaration:

```
Rectangle:  (#  UpperLeft, LowerRight: @Point #)
```

The generation of an instance of the `Rectangle` pattern implies the generation of two instances of the `Point` pattern, one denoted by `UpperLeft` and one by `LowerRight`. The two `Point` instances will be a permanent part of this `Rectangle` object. Figure 3.3 illustrates a `Rectangle` object.

3.2.2 Dynamic references

A static reference is constant since it always denotes the same static object. It is necessary to be able to model that an object may have references to other objects which are not part of itself. In addition, it must be possible to model that such references are variable in the sense that they may denote different objects at different points in time. Both may be done by means of a *dynamic reference* (or *variable reference*), as declared in the following way:

```
A: ^T
```

where `A` is the name of the reference and `T` is a pattern name. A dynamic reference may at different points in time denote different objects. Initially, it denotes `NONE`, which represents 'no object.'

Consider the two attributes:

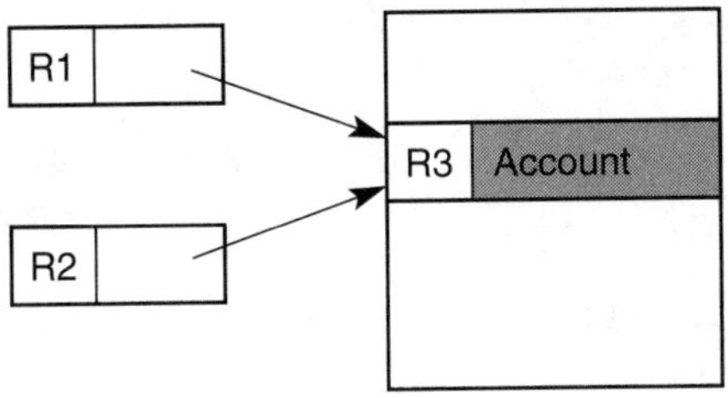

Figure 3.4 Illustration of dynamic references.

```
A1,A2: ^Account
```

`A1` and `A2` are dynamic references which may denote instances of the `Account` pattern. A dynamic reference may be given a value by means of a *reference assignment.* Consider the static reference:

```
A3: @Account
```

A reference assignment of the form:

```
A3[]->A1[]
```

implies that the object denoted by `A3` will also be denoted by `A1`. A similar assignment:

```
A1[]->A2[]
```

implies that the object denoted by `A1` is also denoted by `A2`. After this `A1`, `A2` and `A3` will all refer to the same object, illustrated in Figure 3.4.

A dynamic reference will initially have the value `NONE` , which means that it refers to *no object.* A dynamic reference may also explicitly be assigned the value `NONE`:

```
NONE->A1[]
```

Since a `NONE` reference refers to no object, it has no meaning to attempt to access an object using a `NONE` reference. If `A1` has the value `NONE`, then an evaluation of the form:

```
120->&A1.Deposit
```

is illegal, and execution of the program is terminated.[5]

[5]This is an example of a *run-time error.*

3.2.3 Dynamic generation of objects

It is possible to create objects dynamically by the execution of actions. The following evaluation creates an instance of the `Account` pattern, and the result of the evaluation is a reference to the newly created object:

```
&Account[]
```

As for procedure invocation, the symbol `&` means `new`. The symbol `[]` means that a reference to the object is returned as the result of the evaluation.

A dynamic generation may be part of a reference assignment:

```
&Account[]->A1[]
```

The result of this assignment evaluation is that a new instance of `Account` is created and a reference to this new object is assigned to `A1`.

The difference between `&P` and `&P[]` is very important: the expression `&P` means 'generate a new instance of `P` and execute it'; the expression `&P[]` means 'generate a new instance of `P` without executing it and return a reference to the new object.' This is discussed further later. An object generated in one of these ways is called a *dynamic object*.

Dynamic generation of objects is needed to describe systems where new objects are generated during program execution, as is often the case when modeling real life phenomena. From a technical point of view, recursive procedures and recursive data structures give rise to the dynamic generation of objects.

3.2.4 Example of using dynamic references

In a banking system, each account should have an identification of the owner of the account. For this reason we add an owner attribute to the `Account` pattern. The owner should not be a part of the account since several accounts may have the same owner. We therefore represent the owner of an account as a dynamic reference to an object representing the owner. Consider the following revised description of `Account`:

```
Account:
  (# owner: ^Customer;
     balance: ... ;
     Deposit: ... ;
     Withdraw: ... ;
  #);
```

`Owner` is a dynamic reference to an instance of the `Customer` pattern. Instances of the `Customer` pattern have attributes representing various properties of a customer such as name and address:

```
Customer:
  (# name: ...;
     address: ...;
  #)
```

We shall not go into `Customer` in further detail.

The following object generates two customers and three accounts. Two of the accounts have the same owner. The resulting objects are depicted in Figure 3.5:

```
(# A1: ^Account;
   C1: ^Customer;
   A2: ^Account;
   C2: ^Customer;
   A3: ^Account;
do &Customer[]->C1[]; &Customer[]->C2[];
   &Account[]->A1[]; C1[]->A1.owner[];
   &Account[]->A2[]; C1[]->A2.owner[];
   &Account[]->A3[]; C2[]->A3.owner[];
#)
```

3.2.5 Qualified references and remote access

A reference is *qualified* (typed) by means of a pattern name. The qualification of a reference restricts the set of objects that may be denoted by the reference. A reference declared as:

```
R1: ^Rectangle
```

may only denote instances of the `Rectangle` pattern. `Rectangle` is called the *qualification* or the *qualifying pattern* of `R1`.

Attributes in objects may be denoted by *remote access*, which has the form:

```
reference.attribute
```

The qualification of a reference determines which attributes may be denoted by remote access. For a reference like `R1`, the attributes `UpperLeft` and `LowerRight` may be denoted:

```
R1.Upperleft   R1.LowerRight
```

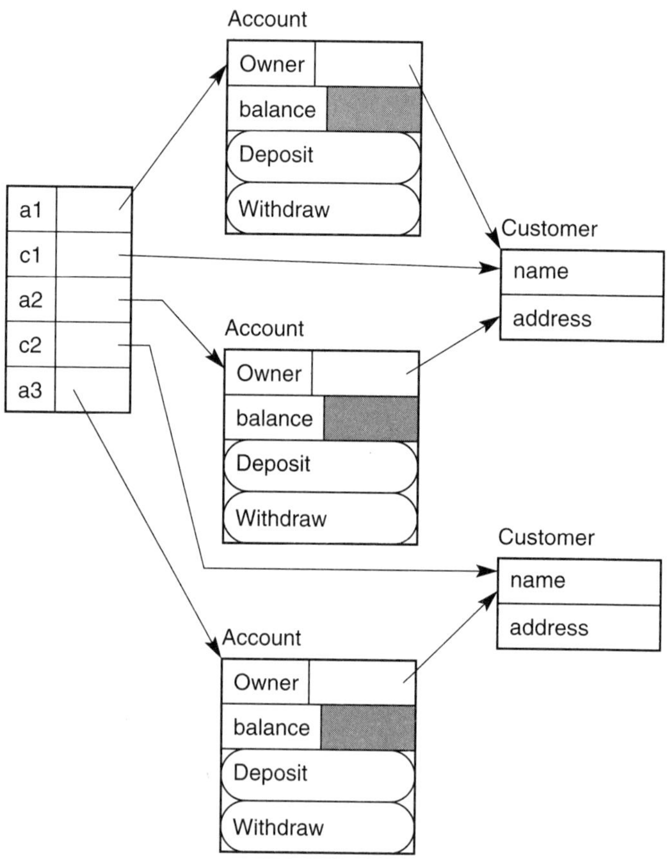

Figure 3.5 Account objects and customer objects.

Since `R1` is qualified by `Rectangle`, `R1` cannot be assigned a reference to an instance of the `Point` pattern. Also, it is not possible to refer to non-existing attributes. Illegal assignments and access of non-existing attributes give rise to many errors in languages without qualified references. In a typed language like BETA, such errors may be detected by the compiler. The disadvantage of qualified references is less flexibility for the programmer. In Smalltalk and most object-oriented extensions of Lisp, such errors are first caught at run-time. However, when constructing industrial software, it is a great advantage to have the compiler catch as many errors as possible. Note that a static reference will automatically denote an instance of the qualifying pattern.

3.3 Pattern attributes

The declaration of a pattern attribute has the form:

```
P: (# ... #)
```

The meaning of a pattern attribute has been described in Section 3.1. Several examples of pattern attributes have already been shown, including `Account`, `Deposit` and `Withdraw`.

In the next version of the `Point` pattern, a pattern attribute `Move` has been added. `Move` describes how `Point` objects may be moved around:

```
Point:
  (# x,y: @integer; {two reference attributes}

     Move:                      {a pattern attribute}
       (# dx,dy: @integer
       enter(dx,dy)
       do x+dx->x;
          y+dy->y
       #)
  #)
```

A `Point` object `P1` may be 'moved' by executing an instance of `P1`'s `Move`-attribute:

```
(11,22)->&P1.Move
```

which describes an execution of `P1.Move` with parameters `(11,22)`. A `Point` object has two reference attributes and a pattern attribute, but no enter-, do- or exit-parts.

The do-part is invoked by invoking a pattern name as in `&P1.Move`, which invokes the do-part of the `Move`-pattern in `P1` as a procedure. `&P1.Move` describes that an instance of the `Move`-pattern will be created, and causes the do-part of this instance to be executed. The symbol `&` reads `new`.

It is important that each instance of `Point` has its own set of attributes. Figure 3.6 represents the objects `P1` and `P2`. The `Move` attributes denote objects representing the structure of pattern `Move`. Such a *structure object* has a reference pointing back to the object of which the

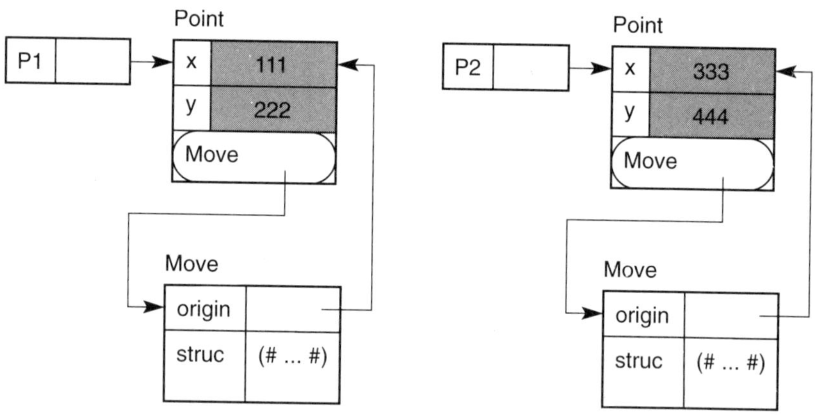

Figure 3.6 Diagrammatic representation of `Point` objects.

pattern is an attribute. This reference is called the **origin** of the pattern. Each instance of `P1.Move` will have a copy of the origin reference of the structure object corresponding to the `Move` attribute of `P1`, and the same is true for instances of `P2.Move`. Figure 3.7 shows instances of `P1.Move` and `P2.Move`. Notice the difference between the structure objects in Figure 3.6 describing the **pattern attributes** `Move` and the objects in Figure 3.7 representing **instances** of `Move`.

The origin reference is used when an object-descriptor refers to a non-local (global) attribute. In `Move` the global attributes `x` and `y` are referred. An evaluation like:

```
x+dx->x
```

is then interpreted as:

```
origin.x+dx->origin.x
```

If `P1.Move` is executed, the origin reference of the `Move` object will refer to `P1`. If `P2.Move` is executed, the origin reference of the `Move` object will refer to `P2`.

3.3.1 Self-reference

It is often useful to be able to refer directly to an enclosing object. This is possible using the construct:

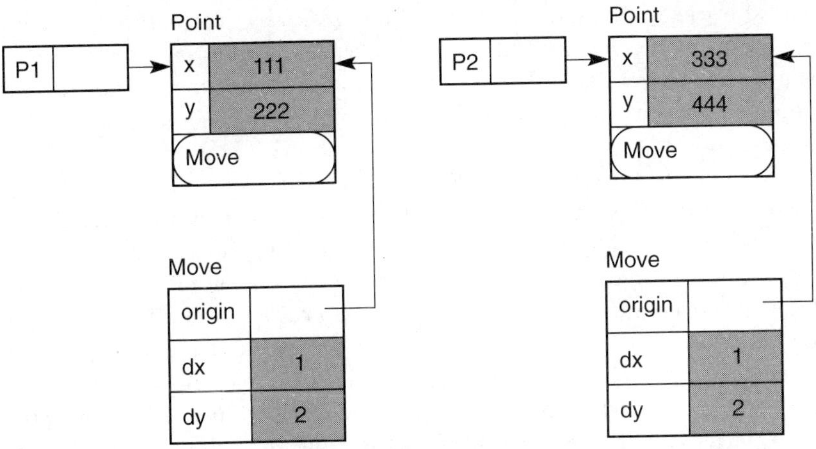

Figure 3.7 `Point` objects and `Move` objects.

```
this(P)
```

which is legal in the object-descriptor for `P`, i.e. `this(P)` may only appear inside a `P` pattern:

```
P: (#  ... this(P) ... #)
```

`this(P)` is an explicit name for the enclosing `P` object. The pattern `Point` can be described using `this(P)` in the following way:

```
Point:
  (# x,y: @integer; {two reference attributes}

      Move:                         {a pattern attribute}
        (# dx,dy: @integer
        enter(dx,dy)
        do this(Point).x+dx->this(Point).x;
           this(Point).y+dy->this(Point).y
        #)
  #)
```

Explict use of `this(P)` may make it easier to read a program when referring to global names.

The construct `this(P)` is often used to obtain a reference to an enclosing `P` object:

```
this(P)[]
```

We shall see examples of this later.

3.3.2 Procedure, function and class patterns

The above examples have shown two fundamentally different ways of using a pattern: (1) The `Account` pattern has been used as a template for generating objects that have a state which changes over time; (2) the `Deposit` pattern has been used as a template for generating an action-sequence.

In general, a pattern is a generalization of abstraction mechanisms such as *class*, *type*, *procedure*, *function*, etc. The fact that BETA has only one abstraction mechanism does not mean that it is not useful to distinguish between different kinds of patterns. In the following we shall refer to concepts like *class pattern*, *procedure pattern* and *function pattern* for patterns that are used as classes, procedures and functions, respectively. In later chapters some additional concepts will be introduced. Note, however, that technically there is no distinction in BETA between such pattern kinds. In the rest of this section we shall elaborate further on some of the most useful pattern kinds.

Procedure patterns

The `Deposit` pattern is used for generating an action-sequence. To represent temporary state information during this action-sequence, an instance of `Deposit` is generated. Such a pattern is usually called a *procedure*. Assume that `Deposit` is a traditional (Pascal) procedure. A procedure invocation of `Deposit` gives rise to the generation of an activation record, which is used for storing parameters and local variables of the invocation. The instance of the BETA pattern `Deposit` being generated plays the role of the procedure activation.

From a modeling point of view, the `Deposit` procedure and the `Deposit` pattern are used to generate action-sequences. The activation record and the object are only generated to represent temporary state information. However, from an implementation point of view these objects must be considered, since they take up space during the program execution.

The `Deposit` pattern is used as a procedure in the following way:

```
500->&account1.Deposit->newBalance
```

As described above, an instance of `account1.Deposit` will be created and executed.

Since patterns may be used as procedures, it is possible to express procedural programming in BETA as in Pascal, Modula-2, Ada or C. This style of programming is not recommended in general, but often a minor part of a system may be expressed more elegantly by using procedural programming rather than object-oriented programming.

Function patterns

Patterns may also be used as functions: the `Interest` pattern is an example of a function pattern. `Interest` computes the interest on a given sum of money:

```
Interest:
   (# sum,interestRate,res: @integer
   enter(sum,interestRate)
   do  (sum*interestRate) div 100->res
   exit res
   #)
```

`Interest` may be used in the following way:

```
(1100,3)->&Interest->V
```

The value of `V` is then 3% of 1100.

What is actually meant by a function pattern? Here a function pattern means a pattern intended for computing a value on the basis of a set of input parameters. The input values are entered through the enter-part, and the computed value is returned via the exit-part. The computed value depends solely on the input values. In addition, the computation of the value does not change the state of any other object (there are no side-effects).

Consider instead the following pattern, which computes the sum of the balances of three accounts:

```
TotalBalance:
  (# sum: @integer
  do account1.balance->sum;
     sum+account2.balance->sum;
     sum+account3.balance->sum;
  exit sum
  #)
```

Here the value computed by `TotalBalance` depends on the state of the objects `account1`, `account2` and `account3`, i.e. different calls of `TotalBalance` may return different values.

Class patterns

The `Account` pattern is used as a template for generating objects that have a state which changes over time. An instance of `Account` models a real physical object in the form of a bank account. A pattern describing

```
Link: {Link describes a linked list}
  (# succ: ^Link; {tail of this Link}
     elm: @integer; {content element of this Link}

     Insert: {Insert an element after this Link}
       (# E: @integer; R: ^Link;
       enter E
       do &Link[]->R[]; {R denotes a new instance of Link}
          E->R.elm; {E=R.elm}
          succ[]->R.succ[]; {tail of this Link = tail of R}
          R[]->succ[]; {R=tail of this Link}
       #)
  #)
```

Figure 3.8 Class pattern describing a recursive data structure.

such objects has traditionally been called a *class*. `Account` is thus an example of a *class pattern*.

Figure 3.8 shows another example of a class pattern which describes a linked list of integers. Elements may be inserted in the list by means of the procedure pattern `Insert`. The following object creates a list of four numbers:

```
(# head: @Link
do 1 ->head.Insert;
   2 ->head.Insert;
   6 ->head.Insert;
   24->head.Insert;
   {head = (0 24 6 2 1) }
#)
```

The object denoted by `Head` is just used for representing the head of the list, i.e. it is not part of the list.

Some class patterns like `Rectangle` only include reference attributes. A pattern used in this way is similar to a record type in Pascal, i.e. a pattern may also be used as a record type.

3.3.3 Basic patterns

A number of predefined *basic patterns* for commonly used data types such as `integer`, `boolean`, `char` and `real` and their operations are available.

For the `integer` pattern, the functional patterns `+`, `-`, `*`, `div` and `mod` are available, corresponding to the usual arithmetic functions. `Div` is integer division with truncation; `Mod` is the modulus function computing the remainder of an integer division. Consider the following declaration of three `integer`-objects:

```
I,J,K: @integer
```

The standard infix notation for `integer` expressions can be used:

```
1+I->I; (I*J)+12->K
```

In principle, it corresponds to the following evaluation using function calls:

```
(1,I)->+->I; ((I,J)->*,12)->+->K
```

It is, however, **not** possible to use the above function call syntax. Only the infix notation can be used.

For the `real` pattern, the arithmetic operations `+`, `-`, `*` and `/` are defined. For the `boolean` pattern, the functional patterns `and`, `or` and `not` are defined. In addition, the patterns `false` and `true` describe objects representing the boolean values false and true.

The `char` pattern is a representation of the ASCII character set. Each character in the ASCII character set has an associated value in the interval $[0, 255]$. The printable ASCII characters may be denoted in the following way:

```
'a' 'b' ... '0' '1' ... '!' '@' ...
```

The value of a `char` object is the integer corresponding to the char in the ASCII character set, meaning that it is possible to perform integer operations on chars. The evaluation:

```
'a'+1->b
```

will assign the ASCII value of `'a'` plus one to the variable `b`. Since the ASCII value of `'a'` is `97` and the ASCII value of `'b'` is `98`, `b` will have the ASCII value of `'b'`.

The `real` pattern is a representation of floating point numbers.[6]

[6]In the current implementations of the Mjølner BETA System, a 64-bit representation of floating numbers is used. For details consult the Mjølner BETA System manuals.

Relational operators The functional patterns `=`, `<>`, `<`, `<=`, `>` and `>=` corresponding to the standard relational functions equal, not equal, less than, less than or equal, greater than and greater than or equal are available for integer, boolean, char and real objects. For boolean, the `false` pattern describes objects which are less than and not equal to objects described by `True`. For char objects, the ASCII ordering is used.

Initial values Instances of basic patterns will have a default value: `Integer` objects will have the value 0; `char` objects will have the value 0 corresponding to the `null` character; `boolean` objects will have the value `false`; and `real` objects will have the value `0.0`.

Restrictions In the Mjølner BETA System there are a few pragmatic restrictions on the usage of basic patterns. It is not possible to declare dynamic references to instances of such patterns. Also, a basic pattern cannot be used as a super-pattern (see Chapter 6). BETA is a very general language, and sometimes this generality makes it hard to obtain an efficient implementation. The above restrictions are imposed for efficiency reasons. There is no logical motivation for these restrictions.

3.4 Exercises

(1) Use the Mjølner BETA System to execute the account program in Figure 3.1.

(2) Define the `name` and `address` attributes of the `Customer` pattern in Section 3.2.4. An address should consist of street, street number, city, zip code and country.

(3) Define patterns representing a point, line, segment, polygon, rectangle, square and rhombus. A segment is a list of lines where the end point of one line is the starting point of the next line.

It should be possible to create objects of these patterns, move the objects, change one of the coordinates of a point, change the start (or end) point of a line, change the start (or end) point of a line in a segment or polygon, add a new line to a segment, and add a segment to a segment (consider what this could mean).

3.5 Notes

A pattern is a unification of abstraction mechanisms like class, type, procedure, function, generic package, etc. It is a further generalization of the Simula class construct.

Patterns may also be compared to classes in Smalltalk. Pattern attributes of a pattern correspond to interface operations in Smalltalk classes, and reference attributes correspond to instance variables. The do-part of an object has no counterpart in Smalltalk, and is used when the object is executed as a procedure, coroutine or process. Compared to Smalltalk, the do-part of an object represents a very important extension of the notion of objects that allows patterns to be executed as procedures, and to be used in modeling ongoing processes and in system simulation.

A dynamic reference is similar to a reference in Simula and an instance variable in Smalltalk. It resembles Simula in the sense that a BETA reference is qualified. Instance variables are not qualified in Smalltalk. The advantage of qualified references is (1) the compiler may detect illegal access of attributes, (2) the compiler may generate more efficient code, and (3) the qualification improves the readability of the code. The price for this is, of course, less flexibility for the programmer. For implementing industrial software, a typed language like BETA will lead to more robust and safe programs.

Generation of dynamic objects with subsequent assignment of the reference to a dynamic reference variable `&P[]->R[]` corresponds to `R ← P New` in Smalltalk.

The framework for BETA presented in Chapter 2 makes a distinction between phenomena and concepts, and this is reflected in the language: objects model phenomena and patterns model concepts – a pattern is not an object. In contrast to this distinction between objects and patterns, Smalltalk-like languages treat classes as objects. Concepts are thus both phenomena and they are used to classify phenomena. In the BETA framework, patterns may be treated as objects, but that is in the *programming process*. The objects manipulated in a programming environment will be fragments (e.g. patterns) of the program being developed.

There are object-oriented languages that do not have a notion corresponding to patterns; such languages are called *classless* or *prototype-based*. Instead of generating objects as instances of patterns (classes), an object is generated as a *clone* of another object. The object being cloned is considered as a prototype to be used for generating similar objects. The generated object will have the same properties as the object from which it is generated, but it may modify some of the properties and add new ones. The most well known example of such a language is *Self* (Ungar and Smith, 1987).

BETA is a language belonging to the Algol family with respect to block structure, scope rules and type checking. In Algol and Simula a procedure or block may have local procedures and/or blocks. With respect to scope rules, BETA also follows the Algol tradition, since all names in textually enclosing object descriptors are visible. In addition to the Algol scope rules, most languages supporting classes have a rule that protects certain attributes of an object from being accessed remotely. In Simula this is handled by the hidden/protected mechanism; in Smalltalk, instance variables cannot be accessed from outside the object. BETA contains no such protection mechanism; instead, the modularization described in Chapter 17 is used.

Chapter 4

Repetitions

It is possible to declare a repetition of static or dynamic references. A repetition of static references is declared in the following way:

```
A: [eval] @P;
```

`A` is the name of a repetition of static references and `P` is a pattern describing the static instances. `eval` is an evaluation resulting in an integer number called the *range* of the repetition. The range of a repetition may be denoted by `A.range`. This repetition describes the following set of static references:

```
A[1], A[2], ..., A[A.range]
```

An element in the repetition may be denoted by an expression `A[exp]`, where `exp` is an integer evaluation that must result in a value in the interval `[1,A.range]`.

The example in Figure 4.1 illustrates the use of a repetition of static references. A repetition of integers has been added to the `Account` pattern. The repetition `transactions` keeps track of the sequence of transactions that have been made on the account. When 50 transactions have been made,[1] a statement of the transactions is sent to the customer (only indicated by a comment), the repetition is cleared, and the recording of transactions is begun again.

A repetition may also consist of dynamic references:

```
A: [eval] ^P
```

Here each element in the repetition is a dynamic reference.

The example in Figure 4.2 illustrates the use of a repetition of dynamic references. The object `BankSystem` includes two repetitions of dynamic

[1]For a description of the `if`-imperative see Chapter 5.

```
Account:
  (# ...
     transactions: [50] @integer; Top: @integer;

     Deposit:
       (# amount: @integer
       enter amount
       do balance+amount->balance;
          amount->&SaveTransaction
       exit balance
       #);
     Withdraw:
       (# amount: @integer
       enter amount
       do balance-amount->balance;
          -amount->&SaveTransaction
       exit balance
       #);
     SaveTransaction:
       (# amount: @integer
       enter amount
       do (if (top+1->top)>transactions.range // true then
                {Send statement of transactions to the customer}
                1->top
          if);
          amount->transactions[top]
       #)
  #)
```

Figure 4.1 Recording of transactions.

references for keeping track of all accounts and customers handled by the bank. The bank may have at most 200 accounts and 100 customers. The integer object `noOfAccounts` keeps track of the current number of existing accounts. The references `AccountFile[1]`, `AccountFile[2]`, ..., `AccountFile[noOfAccounts]` are the currently existing accounts. The pattern `NewAccount` generates a new account and adds it to the file. Customers are handled in a similar way.

If `aCustomer` is a reference to a customer, then a new account for this customer may be generated using `NewAccount`, as in:

```
aCustomer[]-> BankSystem.NewAccount->anAccount[]
```

```
BankSystem: @
   (# Account: (# ... #);
      Customer: (# ... #);

      AccountFile: [200] ^Account;
      noOfAccounts: @integer;

      CustomerFile: [100] ^Customer;
      noOfCustomers: @integer;

      NewAccount:
         (# C: ^Customer; rA: ^Account
         enter C[]
         do noOfAccounts+1->noOfAccounts;
            &Account[]->rA[]->AccountFile[noOfAccounts][];
            C[]->AccountFile[noOfAccounts].owner[]
         exit rA[]
         #)
      NewCustomer: (# ... #)
   #)
```

Figure 4.2 Banking system.

The reference anAccount will then refer to the new account.

4.1 Reallocation, assignment and slice

The banking system in Figure 4.2 may hold at most 200 accounts and 100 customers. In practice, it is not acceptable that such limitations are hard-coded into a program: it must be possible to dynamically expand the size of a repetition. In BETA it is possible to extend the range of a repetition. Consider a declaration:

```
R: [16] @integer
```

Execution of the imperative

```
10->R.extend
```

extends the size of R by 10 elements. Since R.range=16 before the assignment, R.range=26 after the assignment. The elements R[1], R[2], ... R[16] have the same values as before the assignment. The elements

`R[17]`, `R[18]`, ... `R[26]` have the default value for `integer` objects (which is zero).

It is also possible to make a complete new allocation of a repetition. Execution of

```
25->R.new
```

will allocate a new repetition of 25 elements. The previous elements are inaccessible; the new elements will have the default value of the element pattern `integer`.

The `extend` and `new` operations are defined for all repetitions.

Assignment is defined for repetitions in general. Consider declarations:

```
R1: [18] @integer;
R2: [12] @integer
```

An assignment

```
R1->R2
```

has the following effect:

```
R1.range->R2.new;
R1[1]->R2[1]; R1[2]->R2[2]; ...;
R1[R1.range]->R2[R2.range]
```

Or expressed using the `for`-imperative:[2]

```
R1.range->R2.new;
(for i: R1.range repeat R1[i]->R2[i] for)
```

Since the range of a repetition may be changed by using assignment, `new` and `extend`, one should always use the `range` attribute to refer to the range. Instead of

```
(for i: 12 repeat sum+R2[i]->R2[i] for)
```

it is usually better to use:

```
(for i: R2.range repeat sum+R2[i]->R2[i] for)
```

It is possible to assign part of a repetition to another repetition by using a *repetition slice*, which has the form:

```
R2[3:9]
```

Such a slice can be used in an assignment like:

---

[2]See Chapter 5.

```
R2[3:9]->R1
```

which is similar to `R2->R1` except that the source repetition only has `9-3+1=7` elements. The bounds in a slice can be arbitrary evaluations yielding an integer value:

```
R2[e1:e2]->R1
```

which means

```
e2-e1+1->R1.new;
R2[e1]->R1[1]; R2[e1+1]->R1[2]; ...; R2[e2]->R1[R1.range]
```

4.2 The text pattern

A predefined pattern for representing a text concept is available, though it is not a basic pattern like `integer`, `boolean`, `char` and `real`. The restrictions for the basic patterns mentioned in Section 3.3.3 do not apply to `text` objects. It is thus possible to create dynamic references to `text` objects and to use the `text` pattern as a super-pattern (see Chapter 6). There are, however, a few built-in language features that are special for the `text` pattern. The following is an example of using the `text` pattern:

```
(# T1,T2: @text; T3: ^text
do 'Hello'->T1; 'World'->T2; T2[]->T1.append;
   &text[]->T3[]; T1->T3;
#)
```

A `text` object may be generated and used as any other object. As may be seen, a `text` object may be assigned a text constant (like `'Hello'`), and one `text` object may be assigned to another `text` object (as in `T1->T3`). A `text` object has a number of attributes (like `append`) which are not predefined, but are part of the basic library defined for the Mjølner BETA System.

Basically, a `text` object is represented by a repetition of `char` objects:

```
text:
  (# R: [16] @char;
       ...
  #)
```

It is possible to assign a text constant to a char repetition:

```
'Hello'->R
```

The effect of this is that:

```
R[1]='H', R[2]='e', R[3]='l', R[4]='l', R[5]='o'
```

and that:

```
R.range = 5
```

The assignment has the effect that the previous content of the repetition is overwritten.

A `text` object can hold an arbitrary number of `char` objects. This is implemented by means of `R.extend` whenever the size of the `text` object needs to be enlarged.

4.3 Exercises

You may have to read Chapter 5 to solve the exercises below.

(1) Complete the `text` pattern by giving a complete implementation and defining a suitable set of operations. A `text` object should be able to hold a text of an arbitrary length.

Discuss the strategy for extending the size of the text. Should a `text`-object be extended with a fixed size every time, `n%` of its current size or double its size?

(2) Complete the banking system in Figure 4.2.

Use the `Customer` pattern developed in Exercise 2 in Chapter 3. Add procedure patterns for removing accounts and customers.

Change the recording of transactions to keep track of the latest 50 transactions. For each 50 transactions send out a statement to the customer.

Modify the `Account` pattern such that an account may have several owners.

The bank system should not be restricted to handle a limited number of customers and accounts.

4.4 Notes

The repetition construct (often called an *array*) has been known since the early days of programming languages, and is present in languages such as FORTRAN and Algol 60. Algol 60 introduced the notion of dynamic arrays where the size of the array is computed at run-time. After an array is created its size cannot be changed. One of the successors to Algol 60, Pascal, imposed the limitation on arrays that their size must be known at compile-time, which means that only constants may be used to specify the size of Pascal arrays. The motivation for this restriction was efficeincy.

The possibility of extending the size of an array after it has been created is known from a number of other languages, including Algol 68. Extending the size of an array is an expensive operation, since it usually implies allocation of a new array object and copying of the old values to the new area.

Chapter 5

Imperatives

The do-part of an object is a sequence of imperatives that describes actions to be executed. Until now we have seen various examples of imperatives:

```
x+dx->x;              {assignment}
(11,22)->&P1.Move;    {procedure invocation}
R1[]->R2[];           {reference assignment}
&Rectangle[]->R1[];   {dynamic generation and}
                      {reference assignment}
```

The first four imperatives are examples of the evaluation imperative, which will be further described in the next sub-section. In addition, BETA has a few imperatives for controlling the flow of executions, called *control structures*, which will also be described below.

5.1 Introduction to evaluations

The basic mechanism for specifying sequences of object execution steps is called an *evaluation*. An evaluation is an imperative that may cause changes in state and/or produce a value when it is executed. The notion of an evaluation provides a unified approach to assignment, function-call and procedure-call. Examples of evaluations are:

```
(11,22)->&P1.Move;
x+dx->x
```

The evaluation:

```
x+dx->x
```

specifies an ordinary assignment (the assignment of `x+dx` to `x`). An evaluation may specify *multiple assignment*, as in:

```
(#
   Power: {Compute X^n where n>0}
     (# X,Y: @real; n: @integer;
     enter(X,n)
     do 1->Y;
          (for inx: n repeat Y*X->Y for)
     exit Y
     #);

   Reciproc: {Compute (Q,1/Q)}
     (# Q,R: @real
     enter Q
     do (if Q // 0 then 0->R
          else (1 div Q)->R
        if)
     exit(Q,R)
     #);

   A,B: @real
do (3.14,2)->&Power->&Reciproc->(A,B);
   {A=3.14*3.14, B=1/A}
#)
```

Figure 5.1 Example of using patterns as procedures/functions.

```
3->I->J
```

where 3 is assigned to I and the value of I is assigned to J. The evaluation:

```
(11,22)->&P1.move
```

specifies a procedure-call. The value (11,22) is assigned to the enter-part of P1.Move, and P1.Move is then executed with these enter parameters. Note that the pattern P1.Move is invoked as an instance.

As shown above, an evaluation may specify multiple assignment of values. The multiple assignment form may also be used to combine execution of objects. Consider the example in Figure 5.1. The program contains the declaration of two patterns, Power and Reciproc, and two objects of the pattern real, A and B. The do-part of the program consists of the *evaluation-imperative*:

```
(3.14,2)->&Power->&Reciproc->(A,B)
```

The execution of this evaluation-imperative takes place as follows: The values 3.14 and 2 are assigned to the input parameters `X, n` of `Power` (described by `enter(X,n)`), the do-part of `Power` is executed, the output parameter `Y` of `Power` (described by `exit Y`) is assigned to the input parameter `Q` of `Reciproc`, the do-part of `Reciproc` is executed, and finally, the output-parameters `Q, R` of `Reciproc` are assigned to `A,B`.

The do-part of `Power` consists of two imperatives: an evaluation-imperative assigning `Y` the value 1; and a for-imperative. The index-variable `inx` steps through the values `1,2, ... ,n`. The do-part of the `Reciproc` pattern consists of an if-imperative.

Note that a function-pattern may return a list of values like the `Reciproc` pattern. The result of a pattern returning a list may be entered directly into another pattern that has a compatible enter-part. Assume that the pattern `Max` has an enter-part consisting of two reals. `Reciproc` and `Max` may then be combined in the following way:

```
exp->&Reciproc->&Max->M
```

The previous examples have shown examples of evaluations describing the generation of objects as instances of patterns. It is also possible to use singular objects in the action part, as shown in the following example:

```
(# Y,V,W: @real
do ...;
   {Singular object:}
   (# X: @real
   do Y->&Reciproc->(V,W);
      (V,3)-> &Power->V;
      (W,5)-> &Power->W;
   #);
   ...
#)
```

The action part of the above object descriptor includes a singular object. Singular objects in the action part are useful when there is a need for declaring some local objects (like `X` above) which are only needed for intermediate computations. In general, it is possible to arbitrarily nest object-descriptors, including singular objects and patterns (see Section 5.9).

5.2 For-imperative

The iteration control structure of BETA is called a *for-imperative* and has the following form:

```
(for Index: Range repeat Imperative-list for)
```

where `Index` is the name of an `integer`-object and `Range` is an `integer`-evaluation. `Range` is evaluated prior to the execution of the for-imperative, and determines the number of times that `Imperative-list` is executed. `Index` will step through the values `[1, 2, ..., Range]`. The name `Index` is only visible in the `Imperative-list`. It is not possible to assign to `Index`. The following example illustrates the for-imperative:

```
(# V: [100] @integer
do (for i: V.range repeat i->V[i] for);
   0->sum;
   (for i: V.range repeat sum+V[i]->sum for)
#)
```

The for-imperative describes that the imperative:

```
i->V[i]
```

is executed `V.range` number of times, i.e. 100 times. The index variable `i` will step through the values `[1,2,...,100]`. The for-imperative thus describes an execution of:

```
1->V[1];
2->V[2];
...
100->V[100]
```

Often it is desirable to step through an index set which does not start with `1`, and which uses `1` to increment the index variable. An example of such an index set is `[-4, -2 ,0, 2, 4]`. In Chapter 6 an example will be given of how to define new control structures using patterns. BETA has only a few predefined control structures – the idea is that most control structures should be defined using patterns.

5.3 If-imperative

The selection control structure is called an *if-imperative* and has the following form:

```
(if E0
 // E1 then I1
 // E2 then I2
    ...
 // En then In
 else I
if)
```

where E_0, E_1, E_2, ..., E_n are evaluations and I1, I2, ..., In and I are imperatives. The else part (else I) is optional. E_0 is first evaluated, and that value is tested for equality with E_1, E_2, ..., E_n in an arbitrary order. If $E_0 = E_j$ then I_j may be selected for execution. If one or more alternatives are selectable, then one of these is chosen randomly. If no alternative can be selected, then the possible else part is executed; otherwise, the execution continues after the if-imperative.

In the following example the integer object x is tested for equality with some integer evaluations:

```
(if x
 // 17 then ...
 // 33 then ...
 // y+3 then ...
 else ...
if);
```

The next example shows how to select on the basis of a boolean value. The false case may also be handled by an else part:

```
(if (x>0) and (y<0)
 // True then ...
 // False then ...
if)
```

The next example shows how to select on the basis of a number of boolean conditions:

```
(if true
 // (x<0) and (y=0) then ...
 // (x=0) and (y=0) then ...
 // x>=0 then ...
if)
```

It is also possible to select by comparing references. Assume that R0, R1, R2 and R3 are references to Point objects. The following if-imperative tests whether or not R0 denotes the same object as one of R1, R2 and R3:

```
(if R0[]
 // R1[] then ...
 // R2[] then ...
 // R3[] then ...
if)
```

In the above example, `R0` and `R1` may denote different `Point` objects, but the `x` and `y` attributes of these objects may still be identical. In this case, the two objects have the same state or value. In BETA there is clear distinction between *reference equality* and *value equality*. In the if-imperative above the references are tested for reference equality. It is also possible to test whether the two point objects are identical with respect to the values of their attributes `x` and `y`. In BETA, value equality is not just a bit by bit comparison of the two objects; the description of a pattern must explicitly describe how value equality is carried out. Assuming that this has been done, an if-imperative testing for value equality of the `Point` objects may look as follows:

```
(if R0
 // R1 then ...
 // R2 then ...
 // R3 then ...
if)
```

Here it is tested whether or not the state of the object denoted by `R0` is identical to the state of some of the other objects.

Note that it is the presence of the symbol `[]` which indicates reference equality instead of value equality. This is the same usage of `[]` as for dynamic generation and reference assignment (Section 3.2.3).

5.4 Labels and jump imperatives

A *labeled imperative* has one of the following forms:

```
L: Imperative
```

```
(L: Imp1; Imp2; ... Impn :L)
```

where `L` is a name. In the first case, the scope of the label is the `Imperative` to which the label is attached, i.e. `L` may only be referred to within the `Imperative`. In the second case, the scope of the label is the imperatives `Imp1; Imp2; ... Impn`. The execution of a labeled imperative may be terminated by executing a *leave*- or *restart-imperative* within it: if **leave** `L` is executed, the execution continues after the imperative labeled by `L`; if **restart** `L` is executed, the execution continues at the imperative labeled by `L`, i.e. the execution of the labeled imperative is repeated.

Consider the following example:

```
(L: (if ... if);
    M: {2}
       (for ... repeat
            (if ...
             // ... then leave L
             // ... then restart M
            if)
       for);
    X->Y
:L) {1}
```

An execution of **leave** L implies that execution continues at {1}. An execution of **restart** M implies that execution continues at {2}.

5.5 A large example

The Register pattern in Figure 5.2 describes a category of objects. Each Register-object consists of the attributes Table, Top, Init, Has, Insert and Remove. Table is an indexed collection of static references denoting 100 integer-objects.

The Register pattern may be used as follows:

```
(# R: @Register
do &R.Init;
   (for inx: 6 repeat
        inx*inx->&R.Insert
   for);
   (for elm: 100 repeat
        (if (elm->&R.Has) // True then
            {elm is in R} ...
   if)for)
#)
```

The imperative &R.Init has the effect of initializing R. Then the square of the numbers 1-6 are inserted into R. Finally, it tests which integers from 1 to 100 are members of R.

The operations of a Register object are defined by the pattern attributes Init, Has, Insert and Remove. The representation of a Register object is the reference attributes Table and Top. A Register object should only be accessed via its operations. The above description of the Register pattern does not prevent access to the representation – mechanisms for doing this are described in Chapter 17.

```
Register:
  (# Table: [100] @integer; Top:  @integer;
     Init: (#do 0->Top #);
     Has: {Test if Key in Table[1:Top]}
       (# Key: @integer; Result: @boolean;
       enter Key
       do False->Result;
          Search:
            (for inx: Top Repeat
                 (if ((Table[inx]=Key)->Result) // True
                  then leave Search
            if)for)
       exit Result
       #);
     Insert: {Insert New in Table}
       (# New: @integer
       enter New
       do (if (New->&Has) {Check if New is in Table}
           // False then {New is not in Table}
              Top+1->Top
              (if (Top<=Table.Range) {Table.Range=100}
               // True then New->Table[Top]
               // False then {Overflow}
       if)if)#);
     Remove: {Remove Key from Table}
       (# Key: @integer
       enter key
       do Search:
            (for inx: Top repeat
                 (if Table[inx] // Key then
                     (for i: Top-inx repeat
                          Table[inx+i]->Table[inx+i-1]
                     for);
                     Top-1->Top;
                     leave Search
       if)for)#);
  #)
```

Figure 5.2 Pattern Register.

5.6 Assignment and equality

One of the fundamental concepts in programming is the distinction between the address of a memory location and the content (state) of a memory location – it is a common programming error to confuse these two issues. In object-oriented programming this distinction is the difference between the reference to an object and the state of an object. In some languages this difference is not made explicit in the syntax, implying that the programmer may not be aware of whether a reference or the state of an object is being manipulated. In the BETA syntax there is an explicit distinction between manipulation of a reference and manipulation of the state of an object. Consider the following object:

```
(# R1,R2: @Point;
   R3,R4: ^Point
do &Point[]->R3[]; &Point[]->R4[];
   (1,1)->(R1.x,R1.y); (2,2)->(R2.x,R2.y);
   (3,3)->(R3.x,R3.y); (4,4)->(R4.x,R4.y);
   L1:
   R3[]->R4[]; R1[]->R3[];
   L2:
   (100,200)->&R1.Move
   L3:
#)
```

Figure 5.3 shows the state of the object at the points `L1`, `L2` and `L3`, respectively.

`R1` and `R2` denote part objects, whereas `R3` and `R4` denote separate objects. At `L2` it can be seen that execution of the reference assignments implies that `R1` and `R3` denote the same object. At `L3` it can be seen that the imperative `(100,200)->&R1.Move` also affects the object denoted by `R3`.

Next we consider assignment of integer objects:

```
(#  a,b,c: @integer
do 111->a; 222->b; 333->c;
   L1:
   a->b;
   L2:
   c->b;
   L3:
#)
```

Figure 5.4 shows the state of the above object at `L1`, `L2` and `L3` respectively. Note that `a`, `b` and `c` are not references to values, but are objects having a state corresponding to the values `111`, `222` and `333`. At `L2` it can be seen that `a` and `b` have the same value (state); at `L3` it can be seen that `a` is not affected by a new assignment to `b`.

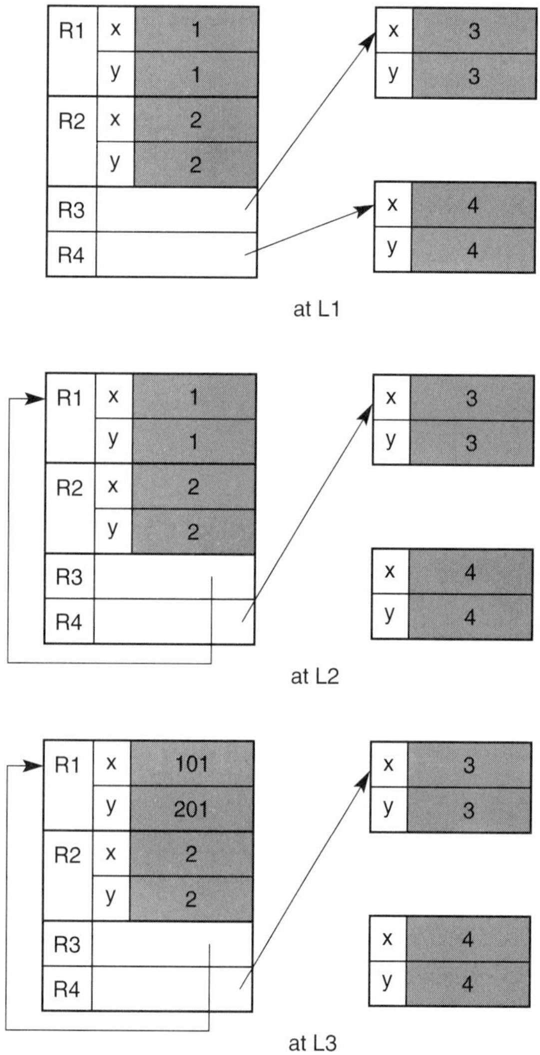

Figure 5.3 Illustration of reference assignment.

This example shows that integer objects and the assignment of integer objects behave like ordinary variables and assignment in traditional procedural programming languages, i.e. assigning object `a` to object `b`

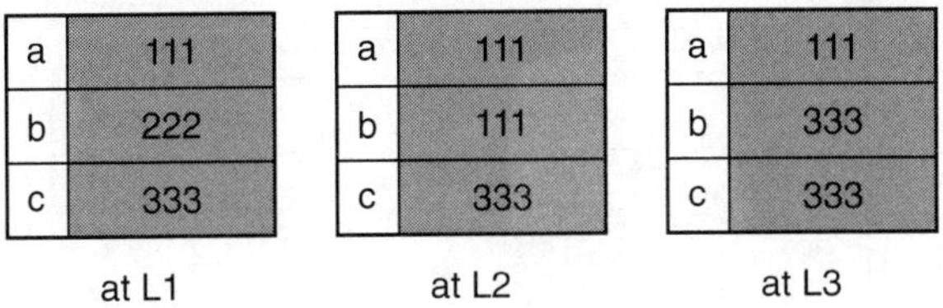

Figure 5.4 Basic value assignment.

consists of copying the state of `a` to `b`. This form of assignment is called *value assignment.*

It is also possible to define value assignment for patterns like `Point`. The `Point` pattern may be redefined such that value assignment of `Point` objects is possible, as in the following object:

```
{Note:the current definition of the Point pattern must}
{be revised in order for this example to be legal!}
{For purposes of discussion only.}
(# R1,R2: @Point;
   R3,R4: ^Point
do &Point[]-> R3[]; &Point[]->R4;
   (1,1)->R1; (2,2)->R2; (3,3)->R3; (4,4)->R4;
   L1:
   R1->R3; R2->R4;
   L2:
   R3->R2; (5,5)->R1
   L3:
#)
```

The meaning of the above assignments may be interpreted as follows: an assignment like:

```
(1,1)->R1
```

assigns the value 1 to `x` and `y`. An assignment of the form:

```
R1->R3
```

assigns the `x` and `y` attributes of `R1` to the `x` and `y` attributes of `R3`. Figure 5.5 shows the state of the above object at `L1`, `L2` and `L3`, respectively. The difference from Figure 5.3 may be observed.

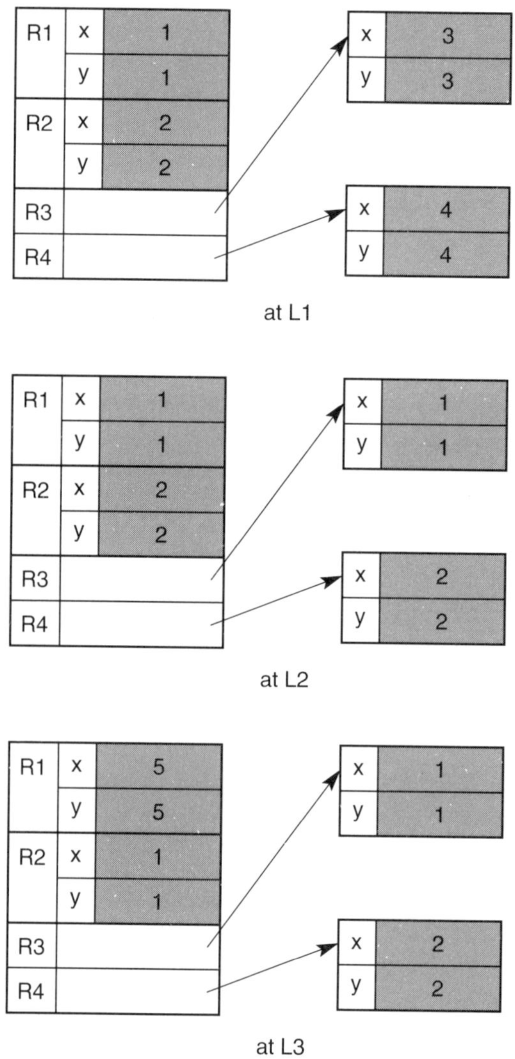

Figure 5.5 Illustration of value assignment.

Value assignment for non-basic objects could be defined as a pure copy of the state of the object. This would be sufficient for the above example. Most languages define value assignment as a pure copy. The state of an object is, however, a representation of an abstract value capturing the interesting properties of the object's state. It is often the case that two or more different states represent the same abstract value. For this reason, the programmer should be able to define the meaning of assignment and equality.

The first example shows how assignment may be defined for the `Point` pattern:

```
Point:
  (# x,y: @integer
  enter(x,y)
  exit(x,y)
  #)
```

Assignment (and as we shall see later, equality also) is defined by means of the enter and exit parts. Consider the following assignments:

```
(11,22)->R1;    {1}
R1->R2;         {2}
```

In line 1, the values 11 and 22 are assigned to the enter part of `R1`, i.e. `x` and `y` are assigned. In line 2, the elements of the exit-list of `R1` are assigned to the corresponding elements of the enter-list of `R2`. As can be seen, there is technically no difference between assignment and parameter transfer in a procedure invocation. The `Point` pattern may have a do-part, as in the following example:

```
Point:
   (# x,y,count: @integer
   enter(x,y)
   do count+1->count
   exit(x,y)
   #)
```

As for procedure invocation, the do-part will be executed each time a `Point` object is assigned from and/or to. The number of times this happens for each object is counted in the `Count` variable. By making `Count` global to `Point`, the total number of accesses to `Point` objects could be counted.

5.6.1 Equality

As there is a distinction between reference assignment and value assignment, there is also a distinction between *reference equality* and *value equality*. Consider the following example:

```
(# a,b: @integer;
   R1, R2: ^Point;
   B1,B2,B3: @boolean
do ...
   (a = b)->B1;            {1}
   (R1[] = R2[])->B2;      {2}
   (R1 = R2)->B3           {3}
#)
```

In line 1, a value comparison between two integer objects is described. Value equality for the basic pattern, like `integer`, works in the usual way. Line 2 describes a reference comparison: the comparison is true if the two references denote the same object.

Line 3 describes a value comparison between two point objects: this comparison is true if the 'value' of the two objects is the same. Value equality here means that elements of the exit list of `R1` are compared to corresponding elements of the exit list of `R2`, i.e. the exit part is also used for describing what to compare in a value equality.

If a do-part is present it will be executed prior to comparison of the exit lists. The `Count` variable in `Point` will also count the number of comparisons.

It should now be possible to understand the details of all the examples of if-imperatives from Section 5.3 involving value equality.

Further details of assignment and equality are described in Section 5.8.

5.6.2 Basic patterns

Reference assignment and equality are not available for basic patterns like `integer`. In principle, there is no reason for this restriction; the restriction is only dictated by efficiency reasons. If it was possible to have general references to, say, integer objects, then memory management would be more expensive. However, in practice there does not seem to be any need for this.

5.7 Computed references and computed remote name

Consider the banking example in Figure 4.2 with the following procedure pattern added. It finds the account of a given customer, and if the customer does not have an account, a new one is created.

```
GetAccount:
  (# C: ^Customer; rA: ^Account
```

```
enter C[]
do (for i: noOfCustomers repeat
        (if C.name[]->CustomerFile[i].name.equal
         //true then AccountFile[i][]->rA[]
        if)
   for);
   (if rA[]//NONE then C[]->NewAccount->rA[] if)
exit rA[]
#)
```

This pattern may be used as:

```
Joe: ^Customer; acc: ^Account; bal: @integer
...
Joe[]->BankSystem.getAccount->acc[];
acc.balance->bal
```

If we are simply interested in the balance of Joe's account, we may use a *computed reference* to access the balance and avoid introducing the reference variable acc:

```
(Joe[]->BankSystem.getAccount).balance->bal
```

The result of the evaluation Joe[]->BankSystem.getAccount is a dynamic reference to an Account. The evaluation is said to be a *computed reference*, since it is the result of an evaluation of a proceure pattern. A procedure pattern computes a reference if its exit-list has one element which must be a dynamic reference. A computed reference may be used in a *computed remote name*, which has the form:

```
(ComputedReference).name
```

The result of ComputedReference must be a reference R. Let R be qualified by T. The name must be an attribute of T. The computed remote name (ComputedRemote).name denotes the attribute name of the object referenced by R.

Since Joe[]->BankSystem.getAccount computes a reference to the Account object of Joe, the computed remote name:

```
(Joe[]->BankSystem.getAccount).balance
```

denotes the balance account of Joe's account.

5.8 Detailed description of evaluations

In Chapter 2, different kinds of properties that may be used to characterize phenomena were briefly mentioned. Among these were *measurable properties* of phenomena. A measurable property may be obtained by observing the state of one or more objects. To perform such an observation it is necessary to perform a *measurement*, which is an action-sequence that results in a measurement.[1] A measurement may be described by a value and/or compared to other measurements. A value is an abstraction which classifies measurements. In the following we shall say that a measurement produces a value.

In BETA a measurable property is reflected by an object that produces a value as a result of executing the object. The representation of a value is described by the exit-part of the object being executed. Since measuring involves a computation, the resulting value may depend upon the state of several objects.

The notion of assignment is dual to measurement. Assignment means enforcing a value upon the state of one or more objects.

An evaluation is the basic mechanism for specifying an action sequence that may cause state changes and/or produce a value. The notion of an evaluation is a unified approach to assignment, function-call and procedure-call. An evaluation may specify either an imperative, a measurement, an assignment or a transformation:

- An *evaluation-imperative* (or just *evaluation*) describes an action sequence.
- An evaluation specifying a *measurement* describes an action sequence that computes a *value.*
- An evaluation specifying an *assignment* describes an action sequence that enforces a value on the state of some objects.
- An evaluation specifying a *transformation* describes an action sequence that enforces a value on the state of some objects and computes a value. A transformation is thus a combination of an assignment and a measurement.

Consider the following object:

```
X: @
   (#
   enter E0
```

[1]Note that measurement here is both used as an action and as the result of an action. According to Webster: 1. The act of measuring or condition of being measured. 2. Extent, size, etc. as determined by this.

```
do   E1->E2->E3
exit E4
#)
```

The whole evaluation E1->E2->E3 describes an evaluation imperative, E4 and E1 describe measurements, E2 describes a transformation, and E3 and E0 describe assignments. This will be further elaborated below.

An evaluation may be described as an object, an evaluation list, or as an assignment evaluation. In the following, the meanings of these three evaluation forms are described.

5.8.1 Object evaluation

An evaluation may be described as an object evaluation. The object may be obtained by means of a reference or a generation using a pattern. It may specify an evaluation in one of the following ways:

- **Imperative** The result of executing the do-part of the object.
- **Measurement** The result of executing the do-part of the object followed by evaluating the exit-part of the object. The value produced is the measurement produced by the exit-part.
- **Assignment** The object may be assigned a value. The value is assigned to the enter part of the object followed by executing the do-part of the object.
- **Transformation** A value is enforced upon the assignment described in the enter-part of the object, followed by executing the do-part of the object, followed by evaluating the measurement described in the exit-part of the object.

In the following, example X is the object defined above:

- **Imperative** An object evaluation used as an imperative may be specified as follows:

  ```
  X
  ```

  The result of this is that E1->E2->E3 is executed.
- **Measurement** An object evaluation used as a measurement may be specified as follows:

  ```
  X->...
  ```

The result of this is that `E1->E2->E3` is executed followed by the execution of `E4`. The value produced by `E4` will be assigned to whatever the dots (...) stand for.

- **Assignment** An object evaluation used as an assignment may be specified as follows:

```
...->X
```

The result of this is that the value produced by whatever the dots stand for is assigned to `E0`, whereafter `E1->E2->E3` is executed.

- **Transformation** An object evaluation used as a transformation may be specified as follows:

```
...->X->...
```

The result of this is that the value produced by the left-most dots is assigned to `E0`, then `E1->E2->E3` is executed, and finally `E4` is executed, and the value produced is assigned to the right-most dots.

5.8.2 Evaluation list

An evaluation list has the form:

```
(E1,E2,...,En)
```

An evaluation list may specify an evaluation in one of the following ways:

- **Imperative** The n imperatives `En` are evaluated in some order.
- **Measurement** Describes a compound value `(M1,M2,...,Mn)`, where each `Mi` is described by `Ei`.
- **Assignment** Describes assignment of a compound value `(M1,M2,...,Mn)`, where each `Mi` is assigned to `Ei`.
- **Transformation** Describes a transformation of a compound value `(M1,M2,...,Mn)` into another compound value `(Q1,Q2,...,Qn)`, where each transformation `Ei` describes the transformation from `Mi` to `Qi`.

Consider the following example:

```
(# x,y,z: @integer;
   A,B: @
      (# i,j,k: @integer
      enter(i,j,k)
```

```
        do i+2->i; j+3->j; k+4->k
        exit(k,j,i)
        #)
do 111->x; 222->y; 333->z;
   (x,y,z);          {1}
   (x,y,z)->A;       {2: A.i=113, A.j=225, A.k=337}
   A->(x,y,z);       {3: A.k=x=341, A.j=y=228, A.i=z=115}
   A->(x,y,z)->B;    {4: A.k=345=x, B.i=347,
                         A.j=231=y, B.j=234,
                         A.i=117=z, B.k=121}
#)
```

- **Imperative** {1} above is an example of an evaluation list used as an imperative. This example is not interesting, since execution of `x`, `y` and `z` has no effect.
- **Measurement** {2} is an example of an evaluation list used as a measurement: the evaluation `(x,y,z)` describes a measurement producing the compound value `(111,222,333)`, which is assigned to `A`.
- **Assignment** {3} is an example of an evaluation list used as an assignment: the compound value produced by `A` (`(341,228,115)`) is assigned to `(x,y,z)`.
- **Transformation** {4} is an example of an evaluation list used as a transformation: the compound value `(345,231,117)` is assigned to `(x,y,z)`, which is subsequently assigned to `B`.

5.8.3 Assignment evaluation

An assignment evaluation has the form:

```
E1->E2->...->En
```

It may specify an evaluation in one of the following ways:

- **Imperative**
  - `E1` describes a measurement producing the value `M1`
  - `E2` describes a transformation being assigned the value `M1` and producing the value `M2`
  - ...
  - `En` describes an assignment being assigned the value `Mn-1`
- **Measurement** Identical to imperative, except that `En` describes a transformation which, in addition to being assigned `Mn-1`, also produces `Mn`.

- **Assignment** Identical to imperative, except that E1 describes a transformation which is assigned some measurement M0 and produces M1.
- **Transformation** Identical to imperative, except that E1 describes a transformation which is assigned some value M0 and En describes a transformation producing some value Mn

Consider the following example:

```
(# a,b,c,d,e,f,g: @integer
enter a->b        {1}
do b->c->d->e     {2}
exit f->g         {3}
#)
```

- **Imperative** {2} is an example of an assignment evaluation used as an imperative.
- **Measurement** {3} is an example of an assignment evaluation used as a measurement.
- **Assignment** {1} is an example of an assignment evaluation used as an assignment.
- **Transformation** c->d within {2} is an example of an assignment evaluation used as a transformation.

Note that the recursive definition of assignment means that the do-part of objects being assigned during a value-transfer are also executed.

5.8.4 Value relations

Values (measurements) can be compared using the relational operators =, <>, etc. In addition, the if-imperative makes use of value equality.

Let E1 and E2 be two evaluations specifying measurements. E1 and E2 are equal if the two measurements M1 and M2 produced by evaluating E1 and E2, respectively, are identical.

For the basic patterns integer, char, boolean and real we have that integer-objects are assignable to integer-objects, etc. As described in Section 3.3.3, it is also possible to assign char objects to integer objects, etc.

It is also possible to assign integer objects to real objects, and vice versa:

```
I: @integer; X: @real
...
I->X;   X->I; 13->X; 3.14->I
```

Such assignments imply the usual conversion between integer numbers and floating point numbers.

As also mentioned in Section 3.3.3, it is also possible to compare instances of the basic patterns using relational operators.

As mentioned in Section 4.2, it is possible to assign a text constant and a text object to another text object. It is, however, not possible to compare `text` objects using the relational operators. The `text` pattern defined in the Mjølner BETA System has various attributes for comparing `text` objects, including an operation that tests for the equality of two `text` objects:

```
T1[]->T2.equal
```

5.9 Block structure and scope rules

The difference between the *declaration of a name* and the *application of a name* is a fundamental issue. Consider the following object:

```
(#  R1: @Point;  {1}
    R2: ^Point   {2}
do  R1[]->R2[]   {3}
#)
```

Line 1 contains a declaration of the name `R1` and an application of the name `Point`. The application of `Point` refers to a declaration of `Point` somewhere else in the program. Line 2 has a declaration of `R2` and an application of `Point`. The names used in line 3 are both applications referring to the declarations in lines 1 and 2.

Most programming languages have a unit in which all declarations of names must be different, i.e. the same name may not be declared more than once. In addition, each declared name has a *scope*, which is that part of the program text where applications of the same name refer to the declaration.

In BETA, all names declared in the attribute part of an object descriptor must be unique. The scope of a declared name is the object descriptor in which it is declared. Since object descriptors may be textually nested, a declaration in an internal object descriptor may hide a declaration in the enclosing object descriptor. Also, the index variable of a for-imperative and the label of a labeled imperative may hide names declared in the enclosing program text. In the following example, an identifier of the form `a_1` refers to the `a` declared in line 1, etc.:

```
(#  a: ...; b:...; i:...;            {1}
    P: (# a:...; c: ...              {2}
```

```
          do (for i: ... repeat          {3}
                 {Visible names:
                  b_1,a_2,c_2,i_3}
               for)
          #)
   do (# b: ...                          {8}
          {visible names a_1,i_1,b_8}
      #)
   #)
```

The above scope rules are the traditional block structure rules from Algol 60 and Pascal, but they do not cover remote identifiers like `R1.Move`. Consider the declaration:

```
R: @T
```

Any attribute, say `a`, declared in `T` may be accessed using a remote identifier of the form:

```
R.a
```

In BETA, object descriptors may be textually nested. The examples so far have shown up to three levels of textually nested object descriptors: the program, a pattern (like `Point`) and operations (like `Move`). In fact, object descriptors may be textually nested to an arbitrary depth: this is known as *block structure.*

Block structure is an important mechanism for structuring individual components of a large program, and is a means for providing locality of declarations. For more examples of using block structure, see Chapter 8.

We have previously mentioned the `origin` attribute used to access global attributes. In fact, all objects have an `origin` attribute referring to its enclosing block. Consider the following example:

```
(# a: @integer;
   P: (# b: @integer;
         T: (# c: @integer
            do a+b->c;
            #)
      do a * 2->b
      #);
do 1->a; &P
#)
```

The use of global attributes is handled by using `origin` as follows:

```
(# a: @integer;
   P: (# b: @integer;
         T: (# c: @integer
            do origin.origin.a+origin.b->c;
            #)
      do origin.a * 2->b
      #);
 do 1->a; &P
 #)
```

The above scope rules will later be extended to cover sub-patterns and virtual patterns, as introduced in Chapters 6, 7 and 9.

5.10 Object kinds and construction modes

This section introduces the notions of *object kind* and *construction mode*. Object kind is used to classify objects as either sequential or multi-sequential (coroutines or concurrency). Construction mode defines the different ways for constructing and generating objects.

5.10.1 Object kinds

In this chapter it has been shown how to generate objects corresponding to class objects, and procedure objects, etc. These objects all relate to program executions consisting of one sequential action sequence. It is possible to generate objects which may be executed as coroutines and as concurrent processes. For this purpose there is a distinction between different *object kinds*. BETA has two kinds of objects: *component* and *item*. The kind of an object specifies how the object can be executed.

- A component object (coroutine) may be executed concurrently or alternately with other components.
- An item object is a partial action sequence contained in a component or item.

In this chapter objects of the item kind have been described. Objects of the component kind are described in Chapters 13–15.

5.10.2 Construction modes and inserted objects

In the preceding sections two different modes for generating objects have been shown. Objects may be created statically by declaration, or created dynamically by a 'new'-imperative. These different ways of creating objects are called *construction modes*. The construction mode gives rise to two sorts of objects, respectively called *static* and *dynamic objects*. There is a third construction mode called *inserted object*, described in the next section.

As mentioned previously, the invocation of a pattern as a procedure gives rise to the generation of an object for representing the action-sequence being generated by execution of the procedure. This leads to the generation of a large number of small objects. These objects have to be generated and removed by the storage management system, which may be quite expensive. For this reason it is possible to describe that such procedure objects be generated as a permanent part of the object invoking the procedure pattern.

As shown previously, a pattern `P` may be used to generate a procedure object as follows:

```
E->&P->A
```

The generation of an inserted item is done as follows:

```
E->P->A
```

The `P` object (called an *inserted item*) will be an integral part of the enclosing object. This inserted item will then be executed when control reaches the evaluation imperative. The state of this `P` item will be undefined prior to each execution of it. The notion of an inserted item is similar to an in-line procedure call.

Apart from the allocation, the execution of an inserted item is like the execution of any other object. In the above case, the execution assigns the output of `E` to the enter-part of the inserted `P` item, and causes the instance to be executed. Finally, the exit-part of the inserted `P` instance is assigned to `A`.

The evaluation:

```
(11,22)->P1.Move
```

specifies an inserted item for the pattern `P1.Move`. This temporary instance is actually allocated as part of the object executing `P1.Move`. In this way, `P1.Move` describes an *in-line* allocation of a `Move` instance.

As already mentioned, inserted objects are allocated in-line in the calling object. The motivation for inserted objects is a matter of efficiency, since the compiler may compute the storage requirements of the calling object. Inserted objects are analogous to static objects in the sense that they are allocated as part of the enclosing object.

With this semantics of inserted items, it follows that inserted items cannot be used to describe recursive procedures, since this will lead to an infinite recursion. This is analogous to static items, which cannot be used for describing recursive data structures.

5.10.3 Summary of construction modes

As mentioned in the previous section, objects may be of two different kinds. The objects described in this chapter are of the item kind; below we summarize the construction modes for objects of this kind:

- **Static items** The following declarations describe the generation of static items:

  ```
  E: @P;                {1}
  F: @P(# ... #);       {2}
  G: [...] @P;          {3}
  H: [...] @(# ... #) {4}
  ```

  where P is a pattern name, E and F are static references, and G and H are indexed collections of static references. The static items generated by lines 1 and 3 are pattern defined, whereas the static items generated by lines 2 and 4 are singular.

- **Dynamic items** The following imperatives describe the generation of dynamic items:

  ```
  e1->&P->e2;             {1}
  e3->&P(# ... #)->e4; {2}
  &P[]->R1[];             {3}
  &(# ... #)[]->R2[]    {4}
  ```

  Lines 1 and 2 describe the generation of dynamic items which are immediately executed as procedure objects. Lines 3 and 4 describe the generation of dynamic items, where references to the new objects are assigned to dynamic reference attributes. Lines 1 and 3 describe the generation of pattern defined objects, whereas lines 2 and 4 describe the generation of singular objects.

- **Inserted items** The following imperatives describe the generation of inserted items:

  ```
  e1->P->e2;            {1}
  e3->(# ... #)->e4;  {2}
  ```

```
(# P: (# I,J: @integer;
         enter(I,J)
         do I+J->I
         exit(J,I)
         #);
   E: @P; {declaration of a static (part) item}
   X: ^P; {declaration of reference to an item}
   N,M: @integer;
do {generation of a dynamic P-item and}
   {subsequent assignment of the reference X}
   &P[]->X[];

   {an evaluation using static, inserted and dynamic items}
   (3,4)->E->P->E->&P->X->P->(N,M)
#)
```

Figure 5.6 Example of dynamic items.

> Line 1 describes the generation of a pattern defined object, whereas line 2 describes the generation of a singular object.

In Figure 5.6, examples are given of the three different construction modes. The last evaluation involves two executions of the static item `E`, execution of two different inserted items (specified by the two `P`s), and execution of two different dynamic items, one denoted by `X` and an anonymous one generated during the evaluation by `&P`.

The notions of kind and construction mode are orthogonal, since objects of the kind component may also be created either statically, inserted or dynamically.

5.11 Exercises

(1) Write a pattern that transforms a UNIX path of the form:

```
/users/smith/src/beta
```

into the corresponding Macintosh form:

```
:users:smith:src:beta
```

and vice versa.

(2) Modify the banking example from Exercise 2 in Chapter 3. Include a pattern for computing the sum of the balance of all accounts for a specific customer, and one for deleting all accounts for a specific customer.

(3) Write a pattern that computes all prime numbers less than 100 using the sieve of Eratosthenes. Construct a list of objects containing the numbers $2, \ldots, 100$. For each `i` where `2 <= i <= 100`, eliminate all elements of the list containing a number that is divisible by `i`. The remaining list will have all prime numbers less than 100.

Write the pattern in such a way that it is easy to use a value other than 100, i.e. the value 100 should be a parameter to the pattern.

Make a solution where the list is represented using a repetition, and one where it is a linked list using references. The prime pattern should be independent of the actual representation of the list.

(4) Write patterns for standard data structures like stack, queue, deque and tree.

(5) Design and implement a simple soda machine which 'dispenses' two kinds of drinks, cola and juice. The soda machine should have the following properties:

1. One or more coins may be inserted.
2. If enough money has been inserted, the appropriate drink plus change may be obtained.
3. The machine should keep track of the current total amount of money, and the current number of colas and juices.
4. The customer may reset the machine and get back the money he/she has inserted.
5. It will be possible to refill the machine and take out the money.
6. It will be possible to adjust the price for the drinks. The price for a cola and a juice may be different.

5.12 Notes

Imperatives such as assignment, for-imperative, if-imperative and labels and jump-imperatives have been around since the early programming languages. In most languages, the BETA assigment:

```
exp->V
```

is expressed like

```
V := exp
```

For BETA it was felt that it is more natural to express an assignment in the order of evaluation. This is especially the case for multiple assignments and combinations of function calls. In BETA it is possible to combine arbitrary function calls in an evaluation. Consider the following Algol-like assignment statement, where `F`, `G` and `H` are functions:

```
var := F(G(exp1),H(exp2,exp3))
```

This may be expressed in BETA in the following way:

```
(exp1->G,(exp2,exp3)->H)->F->var
```

In some languages there is a distinction between a procedure and a function, in the sense that a function may return a value and be used in an expression. In most languages, a function may return exactly one value and not a list of values, as in BETA. The BETA pattern is, among other things, a unification of procedures and functions, and a procedure/function pattern may return a list of values. As mentioned in Section 3.3.2, the important distinction between a procedure pattern and a function pattern is that the latter should not have side-effects.

We have mentioned the similarities between inserted items and in-line procedure calls, and between dynamic items and Algol-like procedure activation records. We also note that a static item may be used as a static subroutine.

The register example in Figure 5.2 is similar to Hoare's small integer set (Hoare, 1972).

Chapter 6

Sub-patterns

As described in Chapter 3, patterns may be used to represent concepts. The forms of patterns used so far are sufficient as long as the extensions of the concepts being modeled are disjoint, i.e. the set of objects generated from different patterns are disjoint. In practice, there are numerous situations where this is not the case. Consider the classification hierarchy for animals illustrated in Figure 2.2 in Chapter 2. The extensions for lion and tiger are clearly disjoint, but the extension for predator includes the extensions for lion and tiger. In this chapter, language constructs for representing classification hierarchies like these are introduced.

6.1 Specialization by simple inheritance

Consider a travel agency which handles reservations of several kinds, including flight and train reservations. When designing a computer system for handling reservations, it is thus natural to formulate concepts such as train reservation and flight reservation. Patterns for representing the concepts of flight reservation and train reservation may be described in the following way:

```
FlightReservation:
   (# Date: ...
      Customer: ...
      ReservedFlight: ...
      ReservedSeat: ...
   #);
TrainReservation:
   (# Date: ...
      Customer: ...
      ReservedTrain: ...
      ReservedCarriage: ...
```

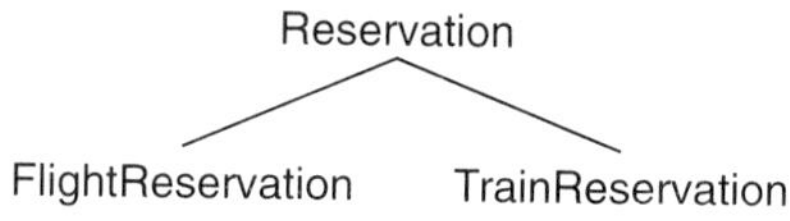

Figure 6.1 Classification hierarchy for reservations

```
      ReservedSeat: ...
   #)
```

The above patterns include the properties we may want to model for flight reservations and train reservations.

Flight and train reservations have some common properties such as the date of the reservation and the customer who has made the reservation. They also differ in various ways: a flight reservation includes a reference to the flight and information about reserved seat, etc.; a train reservation includes information about the train, the carriage and the seat. In addition to the flight reservation and train reservation concepts, it is useful to define a general concept of reservation covering the common properties of flight and train reservations. This gives rise to a simple classification hierarchy for reservations, as illustrated in Figure 6.1.

Suppose that we also want to model the concept reservation, which includes the common properties of flight reservations and train reservations. This could be described as:

```
Reservation:
   (# Date: ...
      Customer: ...
   #)
```

There are, however, no relations between the pattern `Reservation` and the patterns `FlightReservation` and `TrainReservation`. The description does not include the property that `Reservation` is a generalization of `FlightReservation` and `TrainReservation`. The objects created as instances of the three patterns will form three disjoint sets (have disjoint extensions). Instances of `Reservation` bear no relation to instances of `FlightReservation`. Finally, the description of common attributes such as `Date` and `Customer` has been repeated three times.

In the real world we consider all flight reservations to be reservations. Likewise, in our program execution we also want to consider all instances of FlightReservation to be instances of Reservation. Similarly, all instances of TrainReservation should also be considered instances of Reservation.

For the purpose of representing such classification hierarchies, patterns may be organized in *sub-pattern* hierarchies. A sub-pattern is a pattern which is a specialization of another pattern.

The reservation concepts may be modeled in the following way using sub-patterns:

```
Reservation:
  (# Date: @DateType;
     Customer: ^CustomerRecord
  #);
FlightReservation: Reservation
  (# ReservedFlight: ^Flight;
     ReservedSeat: ^Seat;
  #);
TrainReservation: Reservation
  (# ReservedTrain: ^Train;
     ReservedCarriage: ^Carriage;
     ReservedSeat: ^Seat;
  #)
```

By prefixing the object descriptor for FlightReservation by Reservation, the object descriptor for FlightReservation inherits all the declarations from Reservation, meaning that the attributes Date and Customer will be inherited from Reservation. Objects generated according to FlightReservation will have the attributes Date and Customer (from Reservation), plus ReservedFlight and ReservedSeat.

Similarly, objects generated according to TrainReservation will have the attributes Date, Customer (from Reservation), ReservedTrain, ReservedCarriage and ReservedSeat.

This is an example of specialization by simple inheritance of attributes. We say that FlightReservation and TrainReservation are *sub-patterns* of Reservation, and that Reservation is the *super-pattern* of FlightReservation and TrainReservation.

The reason that a pattern like FlightReservation is called a sub-pattern of Reservation is that the set of all FlightReservation objects is a subset of all Reservation objects. Similarly, the set of all TrainReservation objects is a subset of all Reservation objects. In addition, the set of FlightReservation objects and the set of TrainReservation objects are disjoint, illustrated in Figure 6.2. The same may be expressed in terms of extensions of concepts: the extension of FlightReservation is a subset of the extension of Reservation.

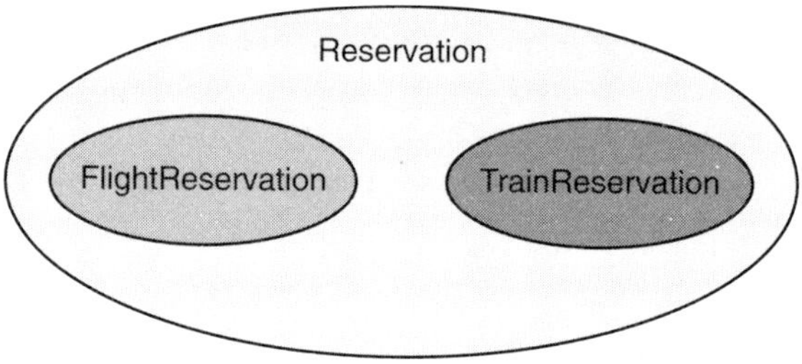

Figure 6.2 Subset relations for extensions of reservation patterns

The set of objects generated from a pattern constitutes its extension. The intension of a concept represented by a pattern is defined by its object-descriptor, which represents the properties of the object in terms of its attributes and action-part. For example, the `Reservation` pattern's object-descriptor states that elements in the extension (`Reservation` objects) all have a `Date` and a `Customer` attribute. For the `FlightReservation` pattern, additional properties are described: elements in the extension also have a `ReservedFlight` and a `Customer` attribute. When we define a sub-pattern, we define a pattern that has some additional properties in addition to those of the super-pattern. Adding new properties restricts the set of possible instances. This may be summarized as follows:

- The intension of a sub-pattern **extends** the intension of the super-pattern, since more properties are added.
- The extension of a sub-pattern is a **subset** of the extension of the super-pattern, since more properties must be fulfilled.

As already mentioned, the kind of properties that can be added are those that can be described by an object-descriptor. Examples of such properties include new attributes, the qualification of the attributes, whether or not it is a part object or a reference to a separate object, etc. Properties describing actions executed by an object are another example. Later in this chapter we present examples of specializing the action-part.

Object generation

The reservation patterns may be used to generate objects:

```
T1: @TrainReservation;
F1: @FlightReservation;
T2: ^TrainReservation;
F2: ^FlightReservation;
...
T1[]->T2[]; &FlightReservation[]-> F2[]
```

It is also possible to generate instances of `Reservation`:

```
R1: @Reservation;
R2: ^Reservation
...
&Reservation[]->R2[];
```

This may not be very useful since our reservation system will handle either train reservations or flight reservations. Patterns like `Reservation` that are just used as super-patterns, but never used for generating instances, are called *abstract super-patterns.*

In Section 3.2.5 the notion of a *qualified reference* was introduced. The references `R1,T1,F1 ...` are qualified by `Reservation`, `TrainReservation`, `FlightReservation`, ... The qualification of a reference restricts the set of objects that may be referred to by the reference. In addition, the qualification determines which attributes may be denoted by remote access. For `R1, T1, F1 ...` it is possible to access attributes like:

```
R1.Date T1.Date T1.ReservedTrain F2.ReservedFlight ...
```

whereas the following remote identifiers are not legal:

```
R1.ReservedSeat T2.ReservedFlight F1.ReservedTrain ...
```

Using super-patterns for qualifying references

Consider the following declarations:

```
R: ^Reservation;
F: ^FlightReservation;
T: ^TrainReservation
```

These declarations state that `R` may refer to `Reservation` objects, `F` may refer to `FlightReservation` objects, and `T` may refer to `TrainReservation` objects. From a conceptual point of view, `FlightReservation` objects are also `Reservation` objects, which means that `R` should be allowed to refer to `FlightReservation` objects, and that is also the rule. It is possible to perform the following reference assignment:

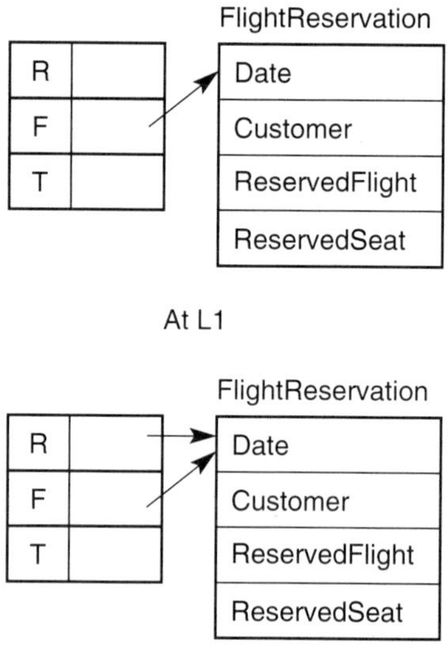

Figure 6.3 A `Reservation` reference may refer to instances of sub-patterns of `Reservation`.

```
L1:
   F[]->R[];
L2:
```

At the label `L1` it is assumed that `F` denotes an instance of `FlightReservation`; at the label `L2`, `R` will also refer to this instance of `FlightReservation`, illustrated in Figure 6.3.

Using `R` it is possible to refer to the attributes `Date` and `Customer` as described by the `Reservation` pattern. This means that `R.Date` and `R.Customer` are legal. `R` refers to a `FlightResevation` object, but since `R` is qualified by `Reservation`, we may only make use of the general `Reservation` properties. It is **not** possible to refer to the attributes `ReservedFlight` and `ReservedSeat`, even though it is known that `R` denotes a `FlightReservation` object, because the description of `R` states that `R` may denote arbitrary `Reservation` objects. This means that it is not known whether or not `R` denotes a `FlightReservation` object or a `TrainReservation` object.

Consider an assignment like:

```
R[]->F[]
```

If R denotes a FlightReservation object, then this is meaningful. If, however, R denotes a TrainReservation object, this is not meaningful, since F is supposed to denote only FlightReservation objects. In general, it is not possible to infer from the description of R and F and the assignment whether or not such an assignment is meaningful. When the program is executing it can be tested whether or not the assignment is meaningful. In BETA the above assignment is considered legal. It may, however, lead to a run-time error[1] if R does not refer to a FlightReservation object.

The use of general super-patterns for qualifying references provides great flexibility. More examples will be presented later.

Multi-level hierarchies

The classification hierarchy for reservations only includes two levels. It is possible to model classification hierarchies consisting of an arbitrary number of levels, as illustrated by the following example. All Record, Person, Employee, Student and Book objects may be viewed as Record objects, and they all have the attribute key. Similarly, Person, Employee and Student objects may be viewed as Person objects, and they all have the Person attributes key, name and sex. This sub-pattern hierarchy is illustrated in Figure 6.4.

```
Record: (# key: @integer #);
Person: Record(# name: @Text; sex: @SexType #);
Employee: Person
  (# salary:@integer; position: @PositionType #);
Student: Person(# status: @StatusType #);
Book: Record(# author: @Person; title: @TitleType #);
```

Example

Suppose that our travel agency wants to keep a register of all reservations. A simple version of such a register may be described as follows:[2]

```
ReservationRegister:
   (# {The reservations are stored in Table[1:top]}
      Table: [100] ^Reservation; top: @integer;
```

[1] In the Mjølner BETA System the compiler marks all assignments that require a run-time test.

[2] The example, like many other examples in this book, has been simplified to keep it small. In the Insert pattern, it should be tested that top does not exceed Table.range. Similarly, in GetElm it should be tested that 0<inx<=Top.

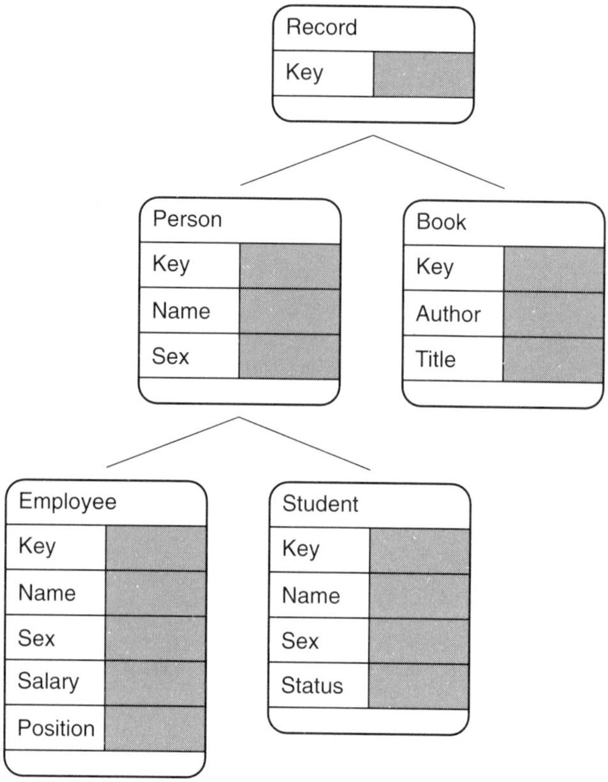

Figure 6.4 Illustration of sub-pattern hierarchy.

```
Insert: {Insert a reservation into the register}
   (# R: ^Reservation
   enter R[]
   do R[]->Table[top+1->top][]
   #);
NoOfElm:{Return no. of reservations in register}
  (# exit top #);
GetElm: {Get reservation no. 'inx'}
  (# inx: @integer
```

```
            enter inx
            exit Table[inx][]
            #);
      #);
   Reservations: @ReservationRegister
```

The Reservations register may contain instances of FlightReservation and TrainReservation. This means that reservations may be inserted into the register in the following way:

```
F: ^FlightReservation;
T: ^TrainReservation;
...
F[]->Reservations.Insert; ...
T[]->Reservations.Insert; ...
```

In the description of the ReservationRegister pattern it is not necessary to know whether it is a train reservation or a flight reservation that gets inserted. For this reason, all references in the ReservationRegister pattern are qualified by Reservation. Also, the ReservationRegister pattern will not need to be changed if a new kind of reservation is introduced. If our travel agency wants to extend its business to handle boat reservations, we could introduce a BoatReservation pattern as a sub-pattern of Reservation, and thus the ReservationRegister pattern would not need to be changed.

Suppose that we want to find all reservations made by Mr Olsen and insert these reservations into a special register containing all reservations made by Mr Olsen. This could be done as follows:

```
R: ^Reservation; Olsen: ^CustomerRecord;
OlsensReservations: @ReservationRegister
...
(for i: Reservations.NoOfElm repeat
      i->Reservations.GetElm->R[];
      (if R.Customer[] // Olsen[] then
          R[]->OlsensReservations.Insert
      if)
for)
```

In this example we do not care whether or not the reservations are train or flight reservations, we are only interested in reservations in general.

Testing pattern membership

Suppose, however, that we are interested in counting the number of flight reservations and the number of train reservations. Then we would need to know for each element in the register whether or not it is an instance of `TrainReservation` or `FlightReservation`. Thus we need to test the class membership of an object. This may be done as follows:

```
R: ^Reservation; Olsen: ^Customer; NTR,NFR: @integer
...
(for i: Reservations.NoOfElm repeat
     i->Reservations.GetElm->R[];
     (if R##
      // TrainReservation## then NTR+1->NTR
      // FlightReservation## then NFR+1->NFR
     if)
for)
```

The expression `R##` denotes the pattern of the object referred by `R`. Similarly, the expression `'TrainReservation##'` denotes the **pattern** `TrainReservation`. (Remember that the expression `TrainReservation` without `##` describes the generation of a `TrainReservation` object.)

The first branch of the if-imperative is taken if the expression:

```
R## = TrainReservation##
```

is true. This is the case if `R` refers to an instance of `TrainReservation`. Similarly, the second branch of the if-imperative is taken if `R` denotes an instance of the pattern `FlightReservation`. As we shall see later, it is rarely necessary to use this form of testing, and it should be avoided, as demonstrated in the next chapter on virtual patterns.

6.2 Specialization of actions

Patterns may also be used to model concepts where the extension consists of sequences of actions. We have previously referred to such patterns as **procedure** patterns. By means of sub-patterns it is possible to model classification hierarchies for action sequences. Consider the concept `HandleReservation`: an element in the extension of this concept is an action-sequence performed by an agent when making a reservation. This concept may have specializations like `HandleFlightReservation` and `HandleTrainReservation`. To model such classification hierarchies, it is necessary to be able to combine the action part of a super-pattern with the action part of a sub-pattern.

Consider the following example:

```
C: (# a,b: @integer
   do 11->a;
```

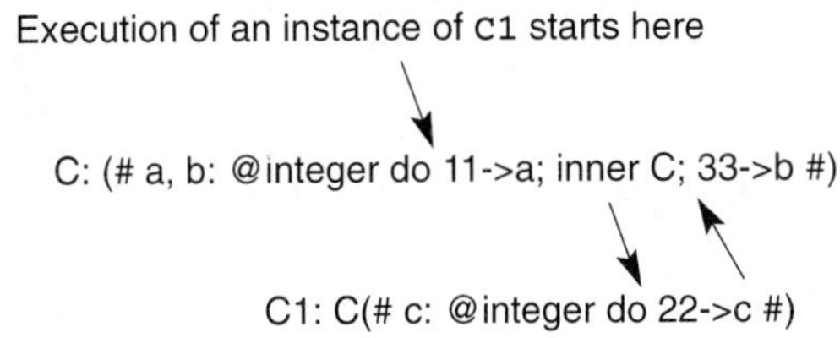

Figure 6.5 Illustration of inner.

```
        inner C
        33->b
    #);

  C1: C (# c: @integer  do 22->c #)
```

Instances of C1 have the attributes a, b, c. The execution of a C1 object starts by execution of the imperatives described in C. Each execution of inner C during the execution of these imperatives implies an execution of the imperatives described by C1. An execution of a C1 object implies execution of:

```
11->a,
22->c  and
33->b.
```

illustrated in Figure 6.5.

Executing an instance of the C-pattern will result in execution of 11->a, followed by 33->b, i.e. execution of inner C is the empty action.

The imperative inner C is only legal in the do-part of the pattern C.

The **inner** construct is the mechanism that is provided for specialization of actions, which may be obtained in two ways: as a specialization of the effect of the general action, or as a specialization of the partially ordered sequence of part-actions that constitute the general action. The inner mechanism supports the latter form of specialization.

Here is another example illustrating the usefulness of specialization of action-parts:

```
Cycle: (#do (Loop: inner Cycle; restart Loop :Loop) #)
```

The Cycle pattern repeatedly executes an inner-imperative, and may be used as a cycle control structure:

```
...; Cycle(#do Keyboard.get->Screen.put #); ...
```

This construct is an example of a singular inserted item. As mentioned in Section 3.1.1, a singular item (object) in the action part corresponds to an *anonymous procedure*. The execution of Cycle implies that inner Cycle is executed forever. Each execution of inner Cycle implies that Keyboard.get->screen.put is executed. Of course, it is possible to exit the body of such a cycle by executing a leave:

```
(# F,G: @File
do {Open the files F and G}
   L: Cycle {Copy F to G}
      (#
      do (if F.eos {end-of-stream}
            // true then leave L
         if);
         F.get->G.put
      #);
   {Close the files F and G}
#)
```

It is possible to further specialize Cycle:

```
CountCycle: Cycle
   (# inx: @integer
   enter inx
   do inner CountCycle;
      inx + 1-> inx ;
   #);
```

The CountCycle pattern is a sub-pattern of Cycle. This has the effect that when executing an instance of CountCycle, its do-part will also be repeatedly executed. The CountCycle pattern is used in the following evaluation:

```
 ...;
L: 1->CountCycle
         (# F: @integer
         do  (if inx //  10 then leave L  if);
             inx->& Factorial->F;
             {Factorial is computed for inx in [1,9]}
         #);
...
```

The effect of using `CountCycle` may be described by the following evaluation:

```
L: 1 ->
       (#  inx: @integer; F: @integer
        enter inx
        do
          (Loop:
              (if inx // 10 then leave L if);
              inx->& Factorial->F;
              inx + 1->inx;
              restart Loop :Loop)
        #)
```

The patterns `Cycle` and `CountCycle` are examples of using patterns for defining control structures. Such patterns will be referred to as *control patterns*.

Specialization of actions may be used for making general control structures tailored to specific data structures. Figure 6.6 describes a new version of the pattern `Register` from Chapter 3. The new version describes a register of `Record` objects, and a new pattern attribute, `ForAll`, has been added. `ForAll` is a control pattern which scans through the elements of the register, making it possible to step through all the elements of a `Register` and perform an operation upon each element, independently of how the register is represented.

Notice that `inner` is an imperative, and as such it may be used wherever an imperative may be used. There may also be more than one `inner` in a descriptor, in which case they will cause execution of *the same* actions.

The `ForAll` operation may be used in the following way:

```
...; R.ForAll (# do Current[]->DoSomething #);...
```

The construct `R.ForAll(# ... #)` is another example of a singular inserted item. It has the `Forall` pattern attribute of the object denoted by `R` as a super-pattern. `Current` will then step through the elements of `R` and each element will one-by-one be assigned to `DoSomething`. Sometimes there is a need for nesting control patterns. In this case, it is inconvenient that the name of the index variable always has to be `Current`, since this makes it impossible to refer to the index variable of the outer control pattern. This may be changed by adding the pattern attribute `Index` to `ForAll`:

```
ForAll:
  (# Current: ^Record;
```

```
Register:
  (# Table: [100] ^Record;
     Top: @integer;

     Init: (# ... #);
     Has: (# key: ^Record enter key[] do ... #);
     Insert: (# ... #);
     Remove: (# ... #);

     ForAll:
       (# Current: ^Record
       do (for  inx: Top repeat
                Table[inx][]-> Current[];
                inner ForAll
          for)
       #)
  #)
```

Figure 6.6 Iterator on the `Register` pattern.

```
     Index: (# exit Current[] #)
  do ... {As before} ...
  #)
```

`ForAll` may now be used as follows (assuming that `R1` and `R2` are references to `Register` objects):

```
R1.ForAll
(# I: @Index
do R2.ForAll
   (# J: @Index
   do (I,J)->DoMore
   #)
#)
```

The attribute `I` returns the value of `Current` corresponding to the outermost control pattern, and `J` returns the value of `Current` corresponding to the innermost control pattern.

Shorthand notation for `inner`

Instead of `inner P` it is possible to write just `inner`. In this case, `inner` refers to the immediate enclosing object-descriptor. Consider the following example:

```
PP:
  (#
  do (# P: (# ...
           do {1} inner PP; ...
              {2} inner P; ...
              {3} inner; ...
           #)
     do  {4} inner;
          Cycle(#do {5} inner PP; ... {6} inner; ... #)
     #)
  #)
```

The `inner` constructs at `1`,`2` and `5` are unambiguous, since they explicitly refer to an enclosing pattern/object-descriptor. The `inner` at `3` refers do the pattern/object-descriptor `P`; the `inner` at `6` refers to `Cycle(# ... #)`, since it is the nearest enclosing object-descriptor. This `inner` will have no effect, as there is no sub-pattern of this descriptor. **In general, `inner` has no effect in a singular object-descriptor.**

6.3 Enter/exit-parts for sub-patterns

The enter-part of a sub-pattern is a concatenation of the enter-part of the super-pattern, and the enter-part specified in the sub-pattern and similar for the exit-part. Consider:

```
P: (# ... enter(x,y,z) do ... exit u #);
PP: P(# ... enter a do ... exit b #);
PPP: PP(# ... enter(n,m) do ... exit(s,t) #)
```

The three patterns have the following enter- and exit-parts:

Pattern	enter-part	exit-part
`P`	`(x,y,z)`	`u`
`PP`	`(x,y,z,a)`	`(u,b)`
`PPP`	`(x,y,z,a,n,m)`	`(u,b,s,t)`

In the concatenation of enter/exit-lists an enter/exit list consisting of a single element is considered to be a list with one element. In the above example, `exit u`, `enter a` and `exit b` are interpreted as `exit(u)`, `enter(a)` and `exit(b)`.

Consider the specification of a pattern `Point`:

```
(# Point:
     (# X,Y: @integer;
        move:
```

```
            (# x1,y1: @integer
            enter(x1,y1)
            do x1->X; y1->Y; inner
            #)
       enter (X,Y)
       exit (X,Y)
       #);
     P1,P2: @Point;
do ...; P1->P2; ...; (3,14)->P1.move; ...
#)
```

Point objects are assignable, and when assigning one Point object to another, the values of X and Y are transferred.

Consider making a three-dimensional point as a specialization of Point: for such points to be assignable, the extra attribute Z should also be transferred in an assignment. This is accomplished by extending the enter- and exit-parts of Point by enter/exit of Z. In addition, a sub-pattern move3D of move has been added:[3]

```
(# ThreeDpoint: Point
     (# Z: @integer;
        move3D: move
          (# z1: @integer enter z1 do z1->Z; inner #)
     enter Z
     exit Z
     #);
   P1,P2: @ThreeDpoint;
do ...; P1->P2; ...; (111,222,333)->P1.move3D
#)
```

Instances of ThreeDpoint have an enter-part and an exit-part of the form (X,Y,Z). The enter-part of move3D is (x1,y1,z1).

6.4 The object pattern

There is a predefined pattern

```
Object: (# ... do inner #)
```

which is the most general abstract super-pattern. All patterns are sub-patterns of Object. In an object descriptor without a super-pattern, the Object pattern is implicitly assumed to be the super-pattern. An object descriptor of the form:

[3] A better alternative will be to define move as a virtual pattern (see Chapter 7).

```
(# Decl1; Decl2; ...; Decln
enter In
do Imp
exit Out
#)
```

is interpreted in the following way:

```
Object
(# Decl1; Decl2; ...; Decln
enter In
do Imp
exit Out
#)
```

The pattern `Object` has no attributes. Its action-part consists of an inner imperative. The main purpose of the `Object` pattern is to allow 'unqualified' references. It is possible to declare references like:

```
R: ^Object
```

A reference like `R` may refer to any object in a program execution. Such a reference cannot, of course, be used to access attributes of the object being referred. It may be used to execute the object and to pass object references around.

Restrictions on basic patterns

As mentioned in Chapter 3, there are certain restrictions on the use of the basic patterns `integer`, `boolean`, `char` and `real` in the Mjølner BETA System. One restriction is that these patterns are **not** sub-patterns of `Object`.

Another restriction is that it is not possible to obtain a dynamic reference to instances of the basic patterns. In the following example, code marked by `illegal` is not accepted by the compiler:

```
   X: @integer;   {legal}
   R: ^integer;   {illegal}
...
   X[] {illegal}->...
```

The reason for these restrictions is efficiency of implementation rather than any conceptual problem. It is, however, possible to get around these restrictions by using patterns of the form:

```
integerObject: (# V: @integer enter V exit V #)
```

The pattern integerObject is a sub-pattern of Object, and dynamic references can be obtained to such objects, as shown in the following example:

```
X: @integer;
Y: @integerObject;
Z1,Z2: ^integerObject
...
111->X;
222->Y;
Y[]->Z1[];
333->Z1;
&integerObject[]->Z2[];
444->Z2;
```

Be aware that an assignment like:

```
333->Z1
```

is only legal if Z1 is different from NONE.

The Mjølner BETA System includes predefined patterns like integerObject. This is conceptually not the best solution, but it works in practice.

6.5 Summary

In this section a summary of the sub-pattern mechanism will be given. An object descriptor may include a *super-pattern* (often called *prefix-pattern*, or simply *prefix*). This specifies that objects generated according to the description have all the properties described by the super-pattern.

Figure 6.7 shows two patterns, P and P1. P1 is an example of a pattern that has a super-pattern. The super-pattern of P1 is P; P1 is also said to be a *sub-pattern* of P. Any P1-object will have the same properties as P-objects in addition to those specified between (# ... #), called the *main-part* of P1.

A P1-object will have attributes corresponding to the declarations Decl1, ..., Decln and Decl'1, ..., Decl'm. The enter-part of a P1-object is a concatenation of In and In'. The exit-part of a P1-object is a concatenation of Out and Out'.

The action part of a P1-object is a combination of Imp and Imp'. This combination is controlled by means of the inner: the execution of a P1-object starts by execution of the imperative Imp in P. Each execution of an inner during the execution of Imp implies an execution of Imp'. If there is no inner in Imp, then Imp' will never be executed.[4]

[4]The Mjølner BETA System compiler will give a warning in this case.

```
P: (# Decl1; Decl2; ... Decln
   enter In
   do Imp
   exit Out
   #);

P1: P
    (# Decl'1; Decl'2; ... Decl'm
    enter In'
    do Imp'
    exit Out'
    #);
```

Figure 6.7 Sub-pattern Declaration.

In general, the notion of main-part is defined for patterns, object descriptors and objects: the *main-part of a pattern* is the part described between `(# ... #)` as stated above. The *main-part of an object descriptor* `P(# ... #)` is the part between `(# ... #)`. The *main-part of an object* `X` generated according to a descriptor `P(# ... #)` is the attributes and actions (including enter/exit parts) described by `(# ... #)`.

6.6 Qualifications and scope rules

We now extend the notions of qualification and scope rules introduced in Sections 3.2.5 and 5.9 to handle sub-patterns.

6.6.1 Qualification

We first extend the definition of super-pattern and sub-pattern slightly. Consider the pattern declaration:

```
B: A(# ... #)
```

- The pattern `A` is said to be a *direct super-pattern* of `B`.
- A pattern `P` is a *super-pattern* of `B` if it is a direct super-pattern of `B`, or if it is a super-pattern of the direct super-pattern of `B`.
- The pattern `B` is a *direct sub-pattern* of `A`.
- A pattern `P` is a *sub-pattern* of `B` if it is a direct sub-pattern of `B`, or if it is a sub-pattern of the direct sub-pattern of `B`.

Consider the patterns:

```
Record: (# ... #);
Person: Record (# ... #);
Employee: Person(# ... #);
```

Here Employee is a sub-pattern of both Person and Record. It is a direct sub-pattern of Person. Similarly, Record and Person are super-patterns of Employee, while Person is a direct super-pattern of Employee.

Reference attributes are *qualified* using pattern names. Consider a reference attribute, R, declared as follows:

```
R: @Record
```

or

```
R: ^Record
```

The attribute R is said to be *qualified* by Record.

The qualification of a reference restricts the set of objects which may be referred to by the reference.

A reference attribute may denote instances of its qualification or instances of sub-patterns of its qualification.

Consider:

```
R: ^Record;
P: ^Person;
E: ^Employee
```

The reference R is qualified by Record, and it may refer to instances of Record, Person and Employee. The reference P is qualified by Person, and it may refer to instances of Person and Employee. Finally, E is qualified by Employee; it may only refer to instances of Employee.

A reference qualified by Record may refer to objects of all the patterns Record, Person, Employee, Student and Book, while a reference qualified by Person may only refer to Person, Employee and Student objects.

6.6.2 Scope rules

The scope of an attribute declared in a pattern P includes all sub-patterns of P, i.e. a name declared in P is visible in sub-patterns of P.

```
A: (#  a:...; b:...; c: ...; #);
B: A(# d:...; e:...; f: ...
       {a,b,c,d,e,f are visible here}
   #)
```

Sub-patterns combined with a block structure must also be considered. The rule is that names inherited from the super-patterns may hide names declared in the enclosing object descriptors:

```
(# a: ...; d:...; x:...;                         {1}
   A: (#  a:...; b:...; c: ...; #);              {2}
   B: A(# d:...; e:...; f: ...                   {3}
        {x_1,a_2,b_2,c_2,d_3,e_3,f_3 are visible here}
     #)
#)
```

Given a reference declared as:

```
X: ^B
```

all attributes declared in B and in super-patterns of B can be accessed remotely, i.e. the following remote identifiers are legal:

```
X.a  X.b  X.c  X.d  X.e  X.f
```

Given a reference qualified by `Record`:

```
R: ^Record
```

then only the attributes of `Record`, i.e. `key`, are accessible by remote access:

```
R.key
```

This is still true even if `R` denotes a `Person` object, i.e. references to `Person` attributes `name` and `sex` of the form:

```
R.name;
R.sex;
```

are illegal.

6.7 Exercises

(1) Redo Exercise 3 in Chapter 3 using sub-patterns.

(2) Modify the banking system constructed in Exercise 2 in Chapter 5 to handle savings accounts and check accounts. For a savings account, the attributes should include the interest rate and calculation of interest. For checking accounts, the customer should be charged a fee for each check they write unless the balance exceeds a certain threshold, in which case writing checks is free.

Next, modify the banking system such that an owner may be a person, a company or an organization (e.g. a soccer club).

(3) Generalize the soda machine developed in Exercise 5 in Chapter 5 by defining a super-pattern called `VendingMachine`. Make a sub-pattern of `VendingMachine` called `CandyMachine`, which is like a `SodaMachine` except that instead of juice and cola it provides chewing gum, chocolate bars, etc. Attributes common to `SodaMachine` and `CandyMachine` should be defined in `VendingMachine`.

(4) Define a pattern `ForTo` that executes an `inner ForTo` for each element in an interval `[first,last]`. An integer variable `index` holds the current index value. The following imperative:

```
(3,8)->ForTo(#do index->&Factorial #)
```

should compute `3!,4!,...,8!`.

Make similar `DownTo` and `StepTo` patterns that may be used like:

```
(6,2)->DownTo(#do index->&Factorial #)
   {computes 6!,5!,...,2!}
(1,3,8)-StepTo(#do index->&Factorial #)
    {computes 1!,4!,7!}
```

6.8 Notes

Patterns and sub-patterns generalize the class and sub-class mechanism from Simula. Most object-oriented languages have a construct similar to the sub-class mechanism; the term *inheritance* is often used for this. The idea of specializing action-parts by means of `inner` also originates in Simula, where it is used for prefixing of classes. (Vaucher, 1975) proposes to extend this idea for prefixing of procedures. In (Thomsen, 1987) specialization of processes is further discussed.

One of the differences between BETA and Smalltalk is the notion of 'typing' object references. In Smalltalk an object reference has no type and may refer to any object. In BETA an object reference is qualified by means of a pattern name. The qualification specifies that the reference may only refer to objects that have been generated according to that pattern or its sub-patterns.

Testing for class pattern membership as described in Section 6.1 is, by some people, considered a bad programming style. In Simula and Smalltalk it is possible to perform these tests. In C++ they have been deliberately left out, since they are viewed as violating the advantages of object-orientation.

Multiple inheritance has come up as a generalization of single inheritance. With single inheritance a class may have at most one super-class, whereas multiple inheritance allows a class to have several super-classes. Inheritance is used for many purposes, including code sharing and hierarchical classification of concepts. In the BETA language, inheritance is mainly intended for hierarchical classification. BETA does not have multiple inheritance, due to the lack of a profound theoretical understanding, and also because the current proposals seem technically very complicated.

In existing languages with multiple inheritance, the code-sharing part of the class/sub-class construct dominates. Flavors has a name that directly reflects what is going on: mixing some classes, so the resulting class has the desired flavor, i.e. the desired attributes. For the experience of eating an ice cream cone it is significant whether the vanilla ice cream is at the bottom and the chocolate on top, or the other way around. Correspondingly, a class that inherits from the classes (A, B) is not the same as a class that inherits from the classes (B, A).

If, however, multiple inheritance is to be regarded as a generalization of single inheritance, and thereby as a model of multiple concept classification (and it should be in the model presented here), then the order of the super-classes should be insignificant. When classifying a concept as a specialization of several concepts, then no order of the general concept is implied, and that should be supported by the language.

Single inheritance is well suited for modeling a strict hierarchical classification of concepts, i.e. a hierarchy where the extensions of the specializations of a given concept are disjoint. Such hierarchies appear in many applications, and it is often useful to know that the extensions of, say, class predator and class rodent are disjoint.

In classifying objects by means of different and independent properties, several orthogonal strict hierarchies may be constructed. A group of people may be classified according to their profession, leading to one hierarchy, and according to their nationality, leading to another hierarchy. Multiple inheritance is often used for modeling the combination of such hierarchies. It may, however, be difficult to recognize if such a non-strict hierarchy is actually a combination of several strict hierarchies.

Chapter 7

Virtual Procedure Patterns

The pattern/sub-pattern mechanism makes it possible to group common properties of patterns into general super-patterns. This is sufficient as long as the general attributes and actions can be completely described in the super-pattern. By this we mean that attributes in a super-pattern can be described independently of the sub-patterns. In the travel agency example, the attributes `Date` and `Customer` do not depend on the sub-patterns `TrainReservation` and `FlightReservation`. This is, however, not always the case.

Consider a pattern `A` with sub-patterns `B` and `C`. The common attributes of `B` and `C` are located in `A`, and the special attributes for `B` and `C` are located in `B` and `C`, respectively. Suppose that both `B` and `C` have an attribute `f`, and that the semantics of `f` is similar for `B` and `C`. If the descriptions of `f` in `B` and `C` are identical then we can move the description of `f` to `A`. If, however, the descriptions of `f` in `B` and `C` are not identical, then we cannot move the description of `f` from `B` and `C` to `A`. Since `f` is a property of all `B` and `C` objects, we would, however, like to describe in `A` that all sub-patterns of `A` have an `f` attribute. In many cases, the descriptions of `f` in `B` and `C` have a common structure and we would like to move as much as possible of this common structure to `A`. This may appear fairly abstract. Consider the following example.

In case of the travel agency, it might be useful to display the attributes of a reservation on a computer screen or print them out on paper. For `TrainReservation` we might add a `Display` attribute that displays the values of the attributes `Date`, `Customer`, `ReservedTrain`, `ReservedCarriage` and `ReservedSeat`. For `FlightReservation` we might similarly have a `Display` attribute that displays the values of the attributes `Date, Customer, ReservedFlight` and `ReservedSeat`. The property of having a `Display` attribute is common to both patterns. In addition, both `Display` attributes display the values of `Date` and `Customer`. Ideally, such common properties should be described in the general `Reservation` pattern.

In this chapter the notion of *virtual patterns* will be introduced. By using virtual patterns it is possible to describe general properties of a pattern attribute in a super-pattern, and to specialize this description in sub-patterns. In this chapter we introduce virtual patterns used as procedures. In Chapter 9 the use of virtual class patterns is described. Note, however, that in the same way that patterns can be used either as classes or procedures, also virtual patterns can be used either as virtual classes or virtual procedures.

7.1 Motivation

In this section we analyze the example of adding a `Display` attribute to the reservation patterns. First we consider the situation where each of the patterns `TrainReservation` and `FlightReservation` has a `Display` attribute:

```
TrainReservation: Reservation
   (# ...
      Display:
        (#
        do Date.Display; Customer.Display;
           ReservedTrain.Display;
           ReservedCarriage.Display;
           ReservedSeat.Display
        #)
   #);
FlightReservation: Reservation
   (# ...
      Display:
        (#
        do Date.Display; Customer.Display;
           ReservedFlight.Display; ReservedSeat.Display
        #)
   #);
```

The dots (...) indicate the attributes `Date`, `Customer`, etc. in the same way as in the previous chapter. We assume that each of the attributes, `Date`, `Customer`, etc. has a `Display` attribute.

As mentioned above, the property that all `Reservation` objects have a `Display` attribute is not reflected in the description of `Reservation`. In addition, the two `Display` attributes both include the code for displaying `Date` and `Customer`.

Before introducing a solution using virtual patterns, we first describe a partial solution to the problem. Instead of one display attribute we have one for each pattern. This makes it possible to describe the general properties of the display attribute in `Reservation`. In this version of the `Reservation` patterns we have implemented a classification hierarchy of display patterns:

```
Reservation:
   (# ...
      DisplayReservation:
        (#
        do Date.Display; Customer.Display; INNER
        #)
   #);
TrainReservation: Reservation
   (# ...
      DisplayTrainReservation: DisplayReservation
        (#
        do ReservedTrain.Display;
           ReservedCarriage.Display;
           ReservedSeat.Display;
           INNER
        #)
   #);
FlightReservation: Reservation
   (# ...
      DisplayFlightReservation: DisplayReservation
        (#
        do ReservedFlight.Display; ReservedSeat.Display;
           INNER
        #)
   #)
```

The above patterns describe two parallel classification hierarchies, one consisting of the reservation patterns and one consisting of their display attributes, illustrated in Figure 7.1. The hierarchy of display patterns is an example of using the sub-pattern mechanism for specialization of actions, as described in Section 6.2.

Consider the references:

```
F: ^FlightReservation;
T: ^TrainReservation
```

We can invoke the corresponding display patterns in the following way:

```
F.DisplayFlightReservation  T.DisplayTrainReservation
```

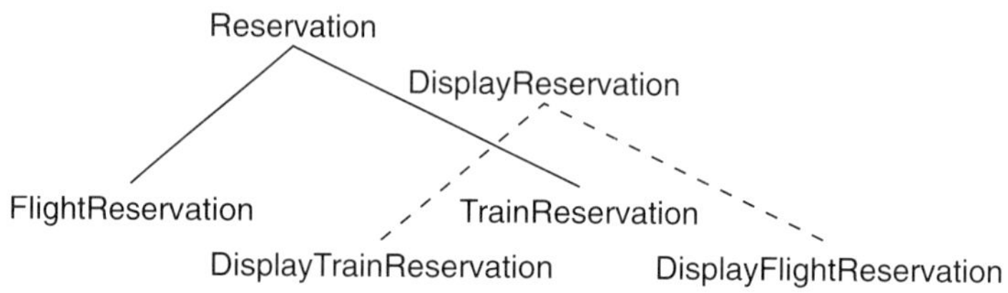

Figure 7.1 Parallel classification hierarchies.

As described in Section 6.2, an invocation of `F.DisplayFlightReservation` causes execution of the following actions:

(1) The super-pattern `F.DisplayReservation` is invoked. This implies execution of

  (a) `Date.Display`
  (b) `Customer.Display`
  (c) `INNER`
  Execution of `INNER` implies:

(2) The main part of `F.DisplayFlightReservation` is invoked. This implies execution of:

  (a) `ReservedFlight.Display`
  (b) `ReservedSeat.Display`
  (c) `INNER`, which here is the empty action.

At this point, all reservation objects have a display property. We have described the general structure of this property using the `DisplayReservation` attribute in the `Reservation` pattern, and we have described the specialized attributes `DisplayTrainReservation` and `DisplayFlightReservation` as sub-patterns of `DisplayReservation`. There are, however, some problems with this solution:

(1) We have to invent a new name for the display attribute for each sub-pattern.

(2) Consider a reference qualified by `Reservation`:

```
R: ^Reservation
```

Using this reference we may invoke the general display attribute:

```
R.DisplayReservation
```

This will result in the display of the general reservation attributes. Since `Reservation` is an abstract super-pattern, `R` should refer to an instance of `TrainReservation` or `FlightReservation`. If `R` refers to an instance of `FlightReservation`, the invocation `R.DisplayReservation` will only display the general attributes `Date` and `Customer`. The special flight reservation attributes `ReservedFlight` and `ReservedSeat` will not be displayed.

Instead, the display attributes of `Reservation` and its sub-patterns should have the following properties:

(1) Each of the patterns `Reservation`, `TrainReservation` and `FlightReservation` should have a pattern attribute called `Display`. When `Display` is invoked, the actions described by `DisplayReservation` and `DisplayTrainReservation` or `DisplayFlightReservation`, respectively, should be executed.

(2) An invocation

```
R.Display
```

should invoke the `Display` attribute of the object denoted by `R`. If `R` denotes an instance of `TrainReservation`, it should invoke the `DisplayTrainReservation` attribute described in the `TrainReservation` pattern. Similarly, if `R` denotes an instance of `FlightReservation`, it should invoke the `DisplayFlightReservation` attribute. (In the theoretical case that `R` denotes an instance of `Reservation`, it should of course just invoke the `DisplayReservation` attribute described in the `Reservation` pattern.)

7.2 Declaration of virtual pattern

The above properties may be obtained by declaring the `Display` attribute of `Reservation` as a virtual pattern, and by extending the description of `Display` in the sub-patterns `TrainReservation` and `FlightReservation`. The resulting reservation patterns may be described as follows:

```
Reservation:
   (# ...
      DisplayReservation:
        (#
        do Date.Display; Customer.Display; INNER
        #);
      Display:< DisplayReservation
   #);
TrainReservation: Reservation
   (# ...
      DisplayTrainReservation: DisplayReservation
        (#
        do ReservedTrain.Display;
           ReservedCarriage.Display;
           ReservedSeat.Display;
           INNER
        #);
      Display::< DisplayTrainReservation
   #);
FlightReservation: Reservation
   (# ...
      DisplayFlightReservation: DisplayReservation
        (#
        do ReservedFlight.Display; ReservedSeat.Display;
           INNER
        #);
      Display::< DisplayFlightReservation
   #)
```

The construct (called a *virtual pattern declaration*):

```
Display:< DisplayReservation
```

is a declaration of a virtual pattern attribute called `Display`. The pattern `DisplayReservation` is the *qualification* of the virtual pattern attribute. For a non-virtual pattern attribute, the complete structure of the pattern is described. For a virtual pattern attribute, its structure is only partially described. It is possible to extend the structure of a virtual pattern in sub-patterns.

A virtual pattern may be extended to any sub-pattern of its qualification, meaning that `Display` may be extended to sub-patterns of `DisplayReservation`. Such a *virtual pattern extension* may be described in a sub-pattern of `Reservation`. The declaration:

```
Display::< DisplayTrainReservation
```

states that the Display pattern is extended to be a DisplayTrainReservation. The qualification of Display in TrainReservation is DisplayTrainReservation. A virtual pattern extension is also called a *virtual pattern binding*, or just *binding*.

In the FlightReservation pattern, the Display is extended to DisplayFlightReservation by:

```
Display::< DisplayFlightReservation
```

Figure 7.2 illustrates the different bindings of the Display attribute.

Consider again the references T, F and R qualified by TrainReservation, FlightReservation and Reservation, respectively. Invocation of:

```
T.Display
```

will invoke DisplayTrainReservation of T. An invocation of:

```
F.Display
```

will invoke DisplayFlightReservation of T.

It is more interesting to consider an invocation of:

```
R.Display
```

Assume that R refers to an instance of TrainReservation. From the qualification of R we know that R has a Display attribute. Since R refers to an instance of TrainReservation, the Display attribute has been extended to be the DisplayTrainReservation pattern, meaning that R.Display will invoke DisplayTrainReservation.

If instead R refers to an instance of FlightReservation, R.Display will invoke DisplayFlightReservation.

Virtual pattern attributes provide great flexibility when describing systems. At the place in the program where an invocation like R.Display takes place, one need not know the exact type of the object being referred to, as that object selects the appropriate pattern attribute.

Consider the reservation register from the end of Section 6.1. Suppose that we want to display all the reservations made by Mr Olsen. This can be done in the following way:

```
(for i: Reservations.NoOfElm repeat
     i->Reservations.GetElm->R[];
     (if R.Customer[] // Olsen[] then R.Display if)
for)
```

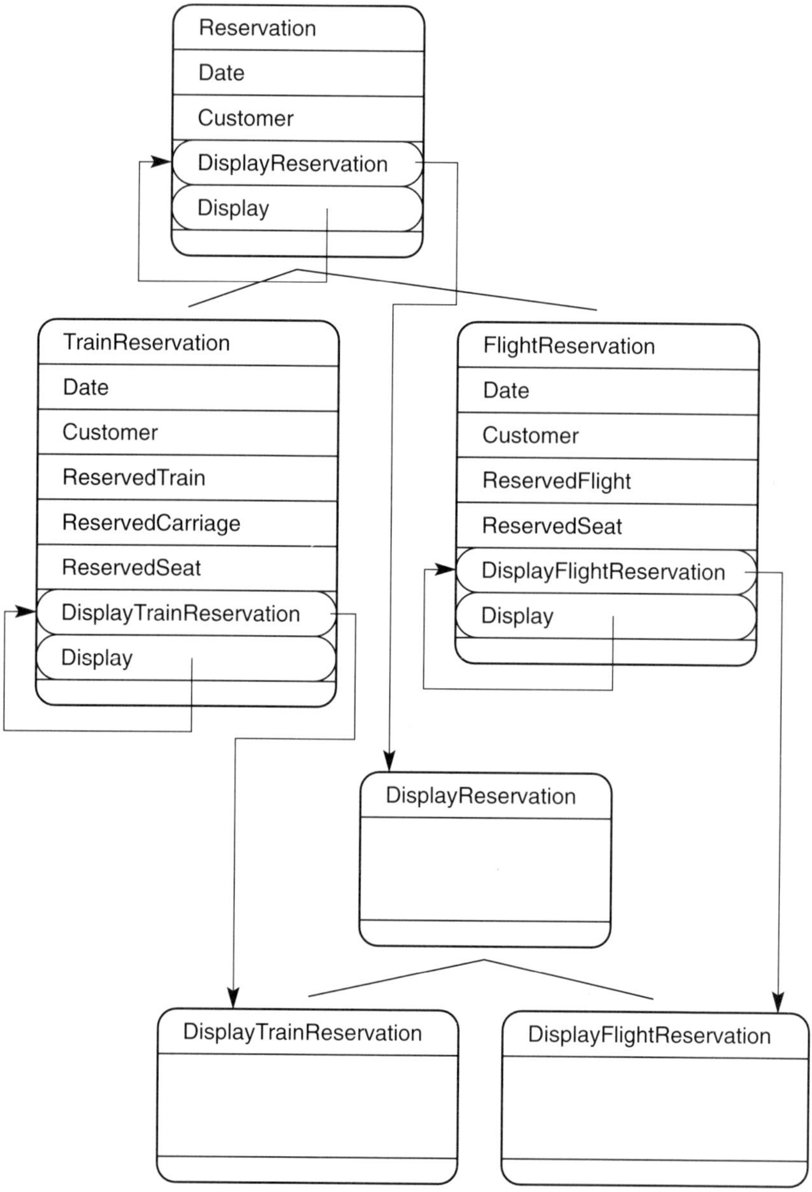

Figure 7.2 Reservation patterns with virtual `Display` attribute.

7.3 Direct qualification of virtual patterns

In the above example it may seem inconvenient to have to introduce names like DisplayTrainReservation. For this reason, it is possible to use *direct qualification* of a virtual pattern, which has the following syntax:

```
Reservation:
   (# ...
      Display:<
        (#
        do Date.Display; Customer.Display; INNER
        #)
   #);
TrainReservation: Reservation
   (# ...
      Display::<
        (#
        do ReservedTrain.Display;
           ReservedCarriage.Display;
           ReservedSeat.Display;
           INNER
        #)
   #);
FlightReservation: Reservation
   (# ...
      Display::<
        (#
        do ReservedFlight.Display; ReservedSeat.Display;
           INNER
        #)
   #)
```

The virtual declaration:

```
Display:<
  (#
  do Date.Display; Customer.Display; INNER
  #)
```

states that Display is qualified by an *anonymous pattern* associated with the given descriptor. The extension of Display in FlightReservation:

```
Display::<
  (#
```

```
do ReservedFlight.Display; ReservedSeat.Display;
   INNER
#)
```

states that Display is extended to a new anonymous pattern which is a sub-pattern of the anonymous pattern in Reservation. These anonymous patterns have the same structure as the DisplayReservation, DisplayTrainReservation and DisplayFlightReservation patterns.

7.4 Continued extension of a virtual pattern

The extension of a virtual pattern attribute can be continued at arbitrary levels of sub-patterns. Possible sub-patterns of, say, FlightReservation might extend the display attribute further. In the following example, we show how the description of a virtual pattern may be extended through several levels of sub-patterns. The example used is the classification hierarchy for records:

```
Record:
  (# Key: @integer;
     Display:< (#do {Display Key}; INNER #)
  #);
Person: Record
  (# Name: @text; Sex: @SexType;
     Display::< (#do {Display Name,Sex} ; INNER #)
  #);
Employee: Person
  (# Salary: @integer; Position: @PositionType;
     Display::< (#do {Display Salary,Position}; INNER #)
  #);
Student: Person
  (# Status: @StatusType;
     Display::< (#do {Display Status}; INNER #);
  #);
Book: Record
  (# Author: @Person; Title: @TitleType;
     Display::< (#do {Display Author,Title}; INNER #)
  #)
```

Consider references:

```
R: @Record;
P: @Person;
E: @Employee
```

Note that these references denote part objects. This means that instance `R` constantly denotes the same instance of `Record`:

- `R.Display` invokes the `Display` attribute described in `Record` resulting in execution of `Display Key`.
- `P.Display` invokes the combination of the `Display` in `Record` and the `Display` in `Person`. This means that `Display Key; Display Name and Sex` are executed.
- `E.Display` invokes the combination of `Display` as described in `Record`, `Person` and `Employee`. This means that `Display Key; Display Name and Sex; Display Salary and Position` are executed.

7.5 More examples of using virtual patterns

In this section we provide additional examples of virtual patterns.

7.5.1 Specialization of initialization patterns

Virtual patterns are useful for describing the initialization of objects. In the following example, the virtual pattern attribute `Init` may be used to initialize instances of the patterns. Each sub-pattern level extends the specification of `Init`.

Consider a pattern defining point objects:

```
Point:
  (# X,Y: @integer;
     Init:< (# do 0->X; 0->Y; inner #);
  #)
```

The specification of `Init` indicates that it is a virtual pattern.

A sub-pattern of `Point` may bind `Init` to a descriptor that is a sub-descriptor of the `Init` in `Point`:

```
ThreeDPoint: Point
  (#  Z: @integer;
      Init::< (# do 0->Z; inner #);
  #)
```

When executing the `Init` of `ThreeDPoint`, the actions of its super-pattern are performed, assigning `0` to both `X` and `Y`. Execution of the `inner` in `Init` of `Point` implies execution of the actions in a possible sub-pattern;

in this case, the assignment of `0` to `Z`. In the case of a `ThreeDPoint`-object, the **inner** following `0->Z` is an empty action, but in the case where `ThreeDPoint` is used further to define, for example, `FourDPoint`, then the **inner** would cause execution of the specialized initialization of `FourDPoint`.

7.5.2 Computation of salary for different job types

Consider a company which has employees working in four kinds of different jobs. In two of the job types the employees have permanent positions, whereas they work on an hour-by-hour basis in the other two job functions. Figure 7.3 shows a set of patterns representing the different job types. The most general pattern `Job` includes a set of attributes for computing salary, tax and deductibles for the employee performing that job. The computation of tax is the same for all jobs, i.e. 45% of the salary minus deductibles.

The computation of salary and deductibles are, however, different for the four job types. The patterns for computing salary and deductibles are therefore virtual patterns. Each employee has a standard deduction of 10 000 which is handled in the definition of `Deductible` in pattern `Job`. Note that `Value` is just an auxiliary pattern. In `NonPermanentJob` a new virtual pattern, `hourlyWage`, for computing the hourly wage of the employee, is defined.

Assume that the company has 100 employees. `Staff` is a repetition of references denoting various job objects corresponding to the employees, i.e. `Staff[1]` may denote an instance of `Job1`, `Staff[2]` may denote an instance of `Job4`, etc. The pattern `ComputeSalarySum` computes the sum of all salaries for all employees.

7.5.3 Geometric figures

Figure 7.4 shows a classification hierarchy of geometric figures. Suppose we want to develop a computer system for handling geometric figures. For all kinds of symbols it should be possible to draw the symbol on a screen, compute the area of the symbol, rotate the symbol, move the symbol, etc. Most of these functions cannot be described in a general super-class, but have to be declared as virtual patterns. We leave it as an exercise for the reader to fill in the details.

7.5.4 Defining control abstractions

We have previously seen how sub-patterns can be used to define control abstractions using **inner**. An example of this is the `ForAll` pattern in

```
Job:
  (# name: @text;
     Value: (# V: @integer do INNER exit V #);
     Tax: Value(#do (Salary-Deductible)*45 div 100 ->V #);
     Salary:< Value;
     Deductible:< Value(#do 10000->V; INNER#)
  #);
PermanentJob: Job(# #);
NonPermanentJob: Job
  (# noOfHours: @integer;
     Salary::< (# do noOfHours*hourlyWage->V #);
     Deductible::<(#do 3000+V->V; INNER #);
     hourlyWage:< Value
  #);
Job1: PermanentJob
  (# Salary::< (#do 35000->V #);
     Deductible::< (#do 2000+V->V #)
  #)
Job2: PermanentJob
  (# Salary::< (#do 45000->V #);
     Deductible::< (#do 2500+V->V #)
  #);
Job3: NonPermanentJob
  (# hourlyWage::< (#do 80->V #); (* 80 pr. hour *)
  #);
Job4: NonPermanentJob
  (# hourlyWage::< (#do 85->V #); (* 85 pr. hour *)
  #);

Staff: [100] ^Job;
ComputeSalarySum:
  (# Sum: @integer
  do 0->Sum;
     (for i: Staff.range repeat Staff[i].salary+sum->sum for)
  exit Sum
  #)
```

Figure 7.3 Job hierarchy.

Figure 6.6. This technique may be used to define abstractions that control execution of one action sequence as executed by **inner**, but other examples of abstractions need to control the execution of more than one action

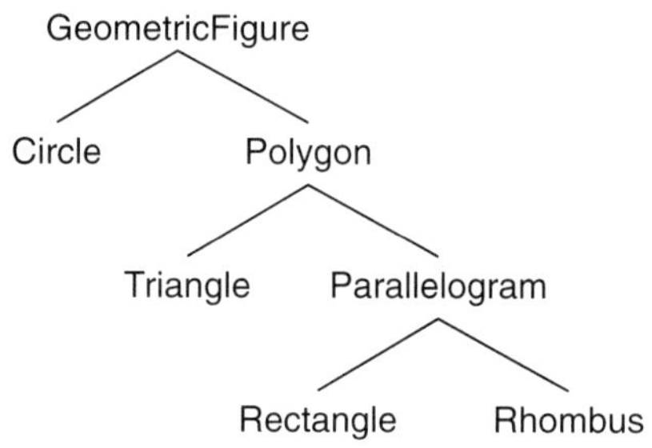

Figure 7.4 Classification hierarchy for geometric figures.

sequence. An example is a control abstraction `Find` for the `Register` pattern. `Find` searches for a given record in the register: if the record is found, one action sequence should be executed; if the record is not found, another action sequence should be executed. The `Find` pattern may be defined using a virtual pattern:

```
Find:
  (# Subject: ^Record;
     NotFound:< Object;
     index: @integer
  enter Subject[] {The Record to be searched}
  do 1->index;
     Search:
       (if (index<=Top) // True then
           (if table[index][] // Subject[] then
               INNER;
               leave Search
           if);
           index+1->index;
           restart Search
        else NotFound
       if)
  #)
```

This `Find` pattern may be added as an attribute to the `Register` pattern. `Find` will search for an element identical to `Subject`. If such an element is found an inner will be executed, otherwise the virtual pattern `NotFound` will be invoked.

`Find` may be used to implement the pattern `Has`:

```
(# Expression:
     (# value:< (# V: @integer do INNER exit V #);
     #);
   Const: Expression
     (# C: @integer;
        value::<(#do C->V #)
     enter C
     exit this(Const)[]
     #);
   BinOp: Expression
      (# E1,E2: ^Expression
      enter(E1[],E2[])
      exit this(BinOp)[]
      #);
   Plus: BinOp(# Value::<(#do E1.value+E2.value->V #) #);
   Mult: BinOp(# Value::<(#do E1.value*E2.value->V #) #);

   E: ^Expression
do {Assign (111+222)*2->E}
   ((111->Const,222->Const)->Plus,2->Const)->Mult->E[];
   E.value->putInt
#)
```

Figure 7.5 Patterns for representing arithmetic expressions.

```
   Has: Find
     (# Result: @boolean;
        NotFound::< (#do False->Result #)
     do True->Result
     exit Result
     #)
```

7.5.5 Arithmetic expressions

Figure 7.5 shows patterns for representing arithmetic expressions. An expression is composed of integer values and binary operations such as plus and mult. The virtual pattern `value` computes the value of an expression.

7.6 Benefits of virtual patterns

Sub-patterns and virtual patterns are powerful abstraction mechanisms. Consider the above example for computation of salaries and, in particular, the pattern ComputeSalarySum. This pattern is independent of the actual job objects. The evaluation:

```
Staff[i].Salary
```

invokes the Salary pattern corresponding to the actual job object denoted by Staff[i].

Suppose that we had to compute the salary without using virtual patterns. We would then need some mechanism to test the job type of a job object. One way of doing this is to add a job type attribute to pattern Job:

```
Job:
  (# name: @text;
     jobType: @integer;
     ...
  #)
```

When creating instances of Job1, Job2, Job3 and Job4 we could then give jobType the value 1, 2, 3 and 4, respectively. A (functional) pattern, ComputeSalary, for computing the salary could then be written as shown in Figure 7.6. In addition, a revised version of ComputeSalarySum is included. As can be seen, it is necessary to check the job type of each object in order to compute the corresponding salary. By using virtual patterns, the computation of salary is defined together with each job pattern. A (functional) pattern, ComputeDeductible, could be written in a similar way.

Instead of introducing the attribute jobType we could have used the mechanism for testing pattern membership as described in Section 6.1. The if-imperative of ComputeSalary would then have the following form:

```
(if R##
 // Job1## then ...
 // Job2## then ...
 // Job3## then ...
 // Job4## then ...
if)
```

The technique of using attributes like jobType has been shown, since this is often used in procedural programming languages like Pascal and C.

Perhaps the most important advantage of using virtual patterns appears when a new job type is added. Using virtual patterns, we could add a new job type by defining a new sub-pattern of, say, PermanentStaff:

```
ComputeSalary:
  (# R: ^Job; sum: @integer
  enter R[]
  do (if R.jobType
      // 1 then (* Job1 *) sum + 35000->sum
      // 2 then (* Job2 *) sum + 45000->sum
      // 3 then (* job3 *)
         (# S: ^Job3
         do R[]->S[]; S.noOfHours*80 + sum->sum
         #)
      // 4 then (* job4 *)
         (# S: ^Job4
         do R[]->S[]; S.noOfHours*85 + sum->sum
         #)
     if)
  exit sum
  #);
ComputeSalarySum:
  (# Sum: @integer
  do 0->Sum;
     (for i: Staff.range repeat
          (Staff[i][]->ComputeSalary)+sum->sum
     for)
  exit Sum
  #);
```

Figure 7.6 Functional pattern for computing salary.

```
Job5: PermanentStaff
  (# Salary::< (#do 50000->V #);
     Deductible::<(#do 1500->V #)
  #)
```

The `ComputeSalarySum` pattern need not be changed, since it is independent of the actual job patterns.

Without virtual patterns we would have to make changes to all patterns like `ComputeSalary` and `ComputeDeductible`. In general, we recommend using virtual patterns in such situations.

7.7 Summary

In this section a summary and further details of virtual patterns is given. A pattern attribute V of pattern P is declared as virtual using one of the forms:

```
V1:    P: (# V:< Q  #)

V2:    P: (# V:< Q0(# ... #) #)

V3:    P: (# V:< (# ... #) #)
```

where Q and Q0 are pattern names. Case V3 is identical to case V2 except that the object-descriptor for V is implicitly assumed to have Object as a super-pattern.

The pattern Q (case V1), the object-descriptor Q0(#...#) (case V2), and the object-descriptor (#...#) (case V3) is called the *qualification* of V.

In an object descriptor that has P as a super-pattern, the virtual pattern V may be extended to object descriptors that are sub-patterns of the qualification. In case V1 this implies that V may be extended to sub-patterns of Q; in case V2 V may be extended to sub-patterns of Q0(#...#); and in case V3, V may be extended to sub-patterns of (#...#).

So even though V may be defined differently in different sub-patterns of P, it is still known in P to be at least a Q, Q0(#...#) or (#...#). The extensions of a virtual pattern in different sub-patterns are thus enforced to be specializations of the definition in the super-pattern.

In P-objects and in instances of sub-patterns of P with no extensions of V, the qualification is the definition of V, so the qualification is also a default-binding.

The description of a virtual pattern V may be extended in sub-patterns of P by means of a *further binding*, which has one of the forms:

```
E1:    P1: P(# V::< Q1 #)

E2:    P1: P(# V::< Q1(# ... #)  #)

E3:    P1: P(# V::< (# ... #) #)
```

The cases E1, E2 and E3 correspond to the cases V1, V2 and V3 in the following way:

(1) Cases E1 and E2 can define a further binding of a virtual pattern defined as in case V1, provided that Q1 is a sub-pattern of Q. Q1 does not have to be a direct sub-pattern of Q.

(2) Case E3 can further bind a virtual pattern defined as in cases V1, V2 or V3. The descriptor `(#...#)` is automatically made a sub-pattern of the qualification of `V` in `P`.

`Q1`, `Q1(#...#)` and `(#...#)` corresponding to the cases E1, E2 and E3, respectively, are called the *extended descriptor*.

In instances of `P1`, the pattern `V` is bound to the extended descriptor. Let `X` be an instance of `P1`. Instances of `X.V` will be instances of the extended descriptor. This is also the case if the generation of `X.V` is specified in the super-pattern `P` of `P1`.

A further binding as shown above specifies that `V` is also a virtual pattern in `P1`. The qualification of `V` in `P1` is its extended descriptor. This means that `V` may be further extended in sub-patterns of `P1`:

```
P2: P1 (#  V ::< ... #)
```

It is possible to extend `V` by a so-called *final binding*, which has one of the forms:

```
F1:     P1: P(# V:: Q1 #)

F2:     P1: P(# V:: Q1(# ... #) #)

F3:     P1: P(# V::(# ... #) #)
```

A final binding has the same effect as a further binding, except that `V` is not virtual in `P1`. This implies that `V` may not be further extended in sub-patterns of `P1`.

7.8 Exercises

(1) Redo Exercise 3 in Chapter 3 using virtual patterns. Include patterns for describing the geometric figures in Section 7.5.3.

(2) Redo Exercise 3 in Chapter 6 using virtual patterns.

(3) Redo Exercise 2 in Chapter 6 using virtual patterns.

(4) Discuss the difference between specialization using sub-patterns and specialization using virtual patterns.

7.9 Notes

The concept of virtual procedures was originally introduced in Simula. Class, subclass and virtual procedure are often viewed as the most essential language constructs associated with object-oriented programming. In

Simula, C++ and Eiffel, a procedure attribute may either be non-virtual or virtual, corresponding to pattern attributes in BETA being either non-virtual or virtual. In Smalltalk, all procedure attributes (called methods) are virtual. In Chapter 9, further historical notes on the virtual concept are given.

Object-oriented programming does not necessarily imply late and unsafe binding of names, which is sometimes claimed to be a weakness of object-oriented languages. As mentioned above, pattern attributes of BETA objects and procedures in C++ objects may be specified as non-virtual, which means that late binding is not used when invoking them.

When a Smalltalk or Flavors object reacts to a message passed to it with 'message not understood', it has nothing to do with Smalltalk or Flavors being object-oriented, but with the fact that they are untyped languages.

The combination of qualified (typed) references and virtuals in BETA implies that it may be checked at compile-time that expressions like `aRef.aMethod` will be valid at run-time, provided of course that `aRef` denotes an object. A late binding determines which `aMethod` (of which sub-pattern) will be executed. Which `aMethod` to execute depends upon which object is currently denoted by `aRef`.

Consider a reference `SomeReservation` qualified by `Reservation`. This means that `SomeReservation` may denote objects generated according to the pattern `Reservation` or sub-patterns of `Reservation`. As `Display` is declared as a virtual in `Reservation`, it is assured that:

```
SomeReservation.Display
```

is always valid, and that it will lead to the execution of the appropriate `Display`. However, the use of untyped references in Smalltalk-like languages has the benefit that recompilation of a class does not have to take the rest of the program into consideration.

What makes late binding slow is not only the method look-up. If a method in Smalltalk has parameters, then the correspondence between actual and formal parameters must be checked at the time of execution. `Display` will, for instance, have a parameter telling how many copies to display. This will be the same for all specializations of `Display`, and should therefore be specified as part of the declaration of `Display` in `Reservation`.

In BETA this is obtained by *qualifying virtuals*. The fact that `Display` will have a parameter is described by a pattern `DisplayParameter`:

```
DisplayParameter:
   (# NoOfCopies: @integer
   enter NoOfCopies
```

```
do
  ...
#)
```

Qualifying the virtual `Display` with `DisplayParameter` implies that all specializations of `Display` in different sub-patterns of `Reservation` must be sub-patterns of `DisplayParameter`, and thus have the properties described in `DisplayParameter`. This implies that `Display` in all sub-patterns of `Reservation` will have an integer `NoOfCopies` input-parameter.

If object-oriented programming is to be widely used in real applications programming, then the provision of typed languages is a must. As Peter Wegner says in 'Dimensions of Object-Based Language Design' (Wegner, 1987):

> '..., the accepted wisdom is that strongly typed object-oriented languages should be the norm for application programming and especially for programming in the large.'

As demonstrated above, it does not have to exclude flexibility in specialization of methods or late binding.

Since inheritance has been introduced by object-oriented languages, object-oriented programming is often defined to be programming in languages that support inheritance. Inheritance may, however, also be supported by functional languages, where functions, types and values may be organized in a classification hierarchy.

In object-oriented languages inspired by Smalltalk, classes are special objects and inheritance is defined by a message-forwarding mechanism. Objects of sub-classes send (forward) inherited messages that are not defined by the object to the super-class 'object' in order to have them performed. This approach stresses *code sharing*: there shall be only one copy of the super-class, common to all sub-classes. With this definition of inheritance it is not strange that 'distribution is inconsistent with inheritance' (Wegner, 1987) and that 'This explains why there are no languages with distributed processes that support inheritance.'

In the model of object-oriented programming presented here, the main reason for sub-classing (specialization) is the classification of concepts. The way in which an object inherits a method from a super-class is – or rather should be – an implementation issue, and it should not be part of the language definition.

According to the definition of patterns and objects in BETA given above, patterns are not objects, and in principle every object of pattern P will have its own descriptor. It is left to the implementation to optimize by having different objects of P share the descriptor. Following this definition of patterns and objects, there is no problem in having two objects of the same sub-pattern act concurrently, and even be distributed. The implementation will in this case simply make as many copies of the pattern as needed, including a possible super-pattern. This does not exclude that a modification of the super-pattern will have an effect on all sub-patterns.

Chapter 8

Block Structure

Composition is a fundamental means for organizing objects and patterns in terms of components of other objects and concepts. There are a number of different forms of composition, one of these being *localization*. In BETA, localization is supported by means of *block structure*, which was first mentioned in Section 5.9. In this chapter the usefulness of block structure will be further explored. Composition is discussed in general in Section 18.5.2.

A programming language supports block structure if procedures, classes and blocks can be textually nested. BETA supports block structure since object-descriptors may be arbitrarily nested. This chapter contains a number of examples of using block structure in the form of nested patterns.

8.1 Simple block structure

Most object descriptors contain a simple form of block structure. One example is the pattern `Register`, which has the form

```
Register:
   (# ...
      Init: (# ... #);
      Has: (# ... #);
      Insert: (# ... #);
      Remove: (# ... #);
   #)
```

The object descriptors for `Init`, `Has`, `Insert` and `Remove` are nested within the object descriptor for `Register`.

A procedure pattern may have local procedure patterns, as in the following example:

```
HandleReservations:
   {Handle one or more reservations for a customer}
   (# GetReservation:
         {Get reservation request from customer}
         (# ... #);
      MakeReservation:
         {Perform temporary reservation}
         (# ... #);
      ReleaseReservation:
         {Release a temporary reservation}
         (# ... #)
      CompleteReservation:
         {Book desired reservations}
         (# ... #)
    do {Investigate one or more possible reservations  }
       {from customer using GetReservation and         }
       {MakeReservation. Release reservations not used }
       {and finalize desired reservations using        }
       {ReleaseReservation and CompleteReservation.    }
   #)
```

Here the procedure pattern `HandleReservations` has been decomposed into a number of simpler procedure patterns. This decomposition of procedure patterns into smaller procedure patterns is a useful structuring mechanism for large procedures. Block structure is useful to provide locality for these patterns.

All these examples show the nesting of procedure patterns. We next give examples of nested class patterns.

8.2 Class grammar

The first example of nested class patterns is a pattern representing the concept of a context free grammar. Instances of the `Grammar` pattern represent the context free grammar of programming languages such as Pascal and Simula. A grammar has the associated concept `Symbol`, i.e. a grammar defines the symbols of the language being defined by the grammar. Different concrete grammars have different symbols. Pascal symbols differ from Simula symbols. We would like to reflect this property in the definition of the `Grammar` pattern; this can be done using nested class patterns, as shown in Figure 8.1.

An instance representing a Pascal grammar can be declared as follows:

```
Pascal: @Grammar
```

```
Grammar:
   (# noOfRules: @integer;
      ... {Other attributes for representing a grammar}
      Parse:<
        (# input: ^text; output: ^AbstractSyntaxTree
        enter input[]
        do {Parse the input string according to the grammar}
           {and produce an abstract syntax tree}
        exit output[]
        #);
      Symbol:
        (# id: @integer; printName: @text; ...
           isTerminal: (# ... exit aBoolean #);
        #);
   #)
```

Figure 8.1 Grammar pattern.

For this instance it is possible to access the attributes as usual:

```
Pascal.noOfRules    someText[]->Pascal.Parse->anAST[]
```

The pattern `Symbol` may be used to declare Pascal symbols in the following way:

```
A,B: @Pascal.Symbol
```

Using `A` and `B`, it is possible to access attributes described in the `Symbol` pattern:

```
A.printName   B.isTerminal -> aBool
```

Consider another set of instances:

```
Simula: @Grammar; X,Y: @Simula.Symbol
```

`Pascal` and `Simula` are both instances of the same pattern `Grammar`. The objects `A,B` and `X,Y` are, however, not instances of the same pattern; `A,B` are instances of the pattern `Pascal.Symbol`, whereas `X,Y` are instances of the pattern `Simula.Symbol`. Intuitively, this is what we want, since `A,B` are Pascal symbols and `X,Y` are Simula symbols. The two classes of symbols are clearly different.

The difference between `Pascal.Symbol` and `Simula.Symbol` is the same as the difference between `Pascal.Parse` and `Simula.Parse`. The

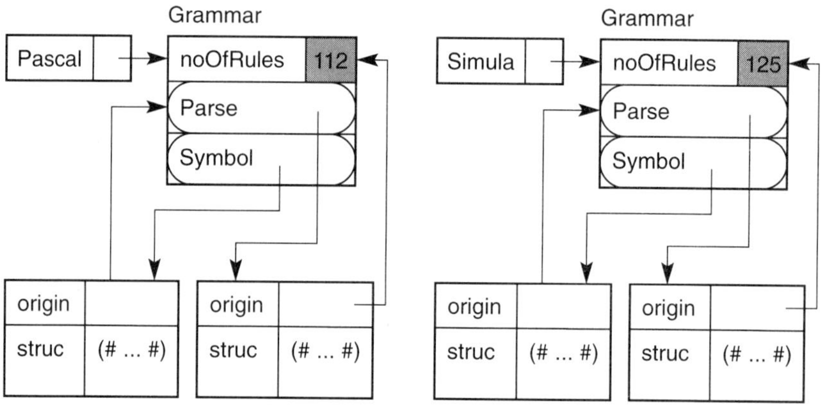

Figure 8.2 Diagrammatic representation of `Grammar` objects.

latter two expressions invoke different `Parse` instances, since they have different origins. Figure 8.2 shows a diagram representing the objects `Pascal` and `Simula`.

Figure 8.3 shows the objects `Pascal`, `Simula`, `A,B,X` and `Y`. Note that `A,B` and `X,Y` have different origins. The structure references for `Parse`, `Symbol` and `isTerminal` have been omitted.

By declaring `Symbol` local to the `Grammar` pattern, we have the possibility of distinguishing between symbols of different grammars. Also, since the class `Symbol` is local to `Grammar`, a symbol has no existence without a grammar. From a modeling point of view, this is what we want.

In the example above the static references `A,B,X` and `Y` denote static objects. It is, of course, also possible to declare dynamic references like:

```
C: ^Pascal.Symbol; Z: ^Simula.Symbol
```

The reference `C` may denote any instance of `Pascal.Symbol` and `Z` any instance of `Simula.Symbol`. Suppose that we want to declare a reference that can denote arbitrary symbols. This can be done by declaring a dynamic reference qualified by `Grammar.Symbol`:

```
S: ^Grammar.Symbol
```

Note the difference from the declaration of `A` using `Pascal.Symbol`, where `Pascal` is a reference to a `Grammar` object. In the declaration

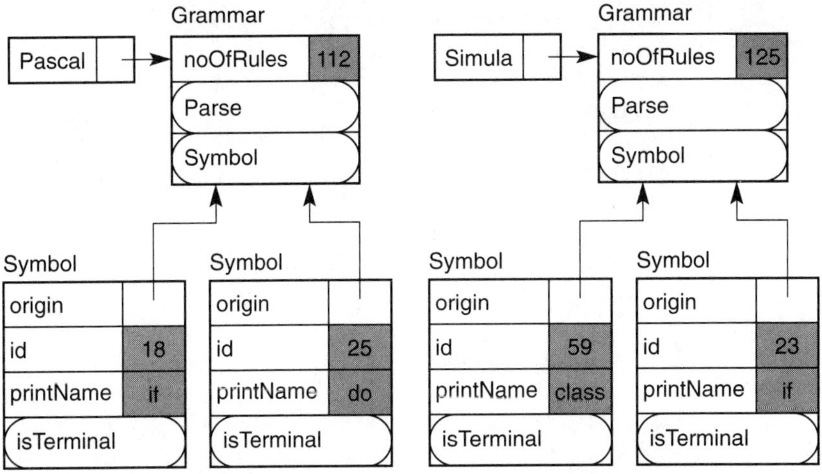

Figure 8.3 Diagrammatic representation of `Grammar` and `Symbol` objects.

of `S`, `Grammar` is a pattern name. `S` can refer to instances of either `Pascal.Symbol` or `Simula.Symbol`. In fact, the pattern `Grammar.Symbol` may be viewed as a generalization of the patterns `Pascal.Symbol` and `Simula.Symbol`. The `Grammar.Symbol` pattern is then a representation of the general concept of a symbol of a context free grammar.

8.3 Flight reservation example

In this section we make use of nested class patterns to further extend the travel agency example. The `FlightReservation` pattern contains an attribute declaration:

```
ReservedFlight: ^Flight
```

We now consider how to describe the pattern `Flight`, but before doing so we need to understand the concept of a flight.

Consider the flight table of Scandinavian Airline Systems (SAS). This table contains a description of various entries SK273, SK451, SK511, etc., corresponding to the various routes served by SAS. An entry like SK273 contains information about the source and destination of the route, and other properties such as departure, arrival and flying times are given. It

```
FlightType:
   (#   source, destination: ^City;
        departureTime,
        arrivalTime: @TimeOfDay;
        flyingTime: @TimePeriod;

        Flight:
           (# Seats: [NoOfSeats] @Seat
              actualDepartureTime,
              actualArrivalTime: @TimeOfDay;
              actualFlyingTime: @TimePeriod;

              DepartureDelay:
                 (#
                 exit(actualDepartureTime - departureTime)
                 #)
           #);

        DisplayTimeTableEntry: (# ... #);
        ...
   #)
```

Figure 8.4 The `FlightType` pattern.

seems obvious to represent these entries as instances of a pattern representing the concept of a flight entry.

For our flight reservation system more objects are needed. The flight SK451 between Copenhagen and Los Angeles actually takes place most days of the year. A table for handling reservations must contain an entry for each day the flight takes place. Each such entry should include information about seat reservations for that day, etc. For a flight entry like SK451, we can include a concept that classifies all flights corresponding to SK451.

Patterns representing flight entries and actual flights are shown in Figure 8.4.

The `FlightType` pattern is supposed to be used for modeling entries in a flight timetable. For each entry in the timetable there is an instance of the `FlightType` pattern; such instances represent flight entries like `SK451` and `SK273`. A `FlightType` object includes information about source, destination, departure time, arrival time, flying time, etc.

```
TimeTable90: @
  (# ...
     SK451: @FlightType;
     SK273: @FlightType;
      ...
     Init:<
        (#  ...
        do  ...
            'Copenhagen' -> SK451.source;
            'Los Angeles' -> SK451.destination;
            ...
        #)
  #);
ReservationTable90: @
  (#
      SK451Flights: [365] ^TimeTable90.SK451.Flight
      SK273Flights: [365] ^TimeTable90.SK273.Flight
       ...
  #)
```

Figure 8.5 Patterns `TimeTable` and `ReservationTable`.

An attribute like `departureTime` is actually modeling the scheduled departure time, which may vary from day to day. A table for handling reservations must contain an entry for each day the flight takes place. Each such entry should have information about the reservation of seats for that day, and it might include information about the actual departure time, etc. in order to compute various kinds of statistics. Each `FlightType` object has a local class pattern `Flight`, which models the actual flights taking place. Instances of the `Flight` pattern have attributes characterizing a given flight, including a repetition of `Seat` objects, the actual departure time, the actual arrival time, and the actual flight time.

Objects representing the timetable and the reservation table for 1990 are shown in Figure 8.5. Note that `SK451Flights` is a repetition of references to instances of the class `Flight` pattern of the object denoted by `SK451`, whereas `SK273Flights` denotes instances of the `Flight` pattern attribute of `SK273`. The actual flight `SK451` taking place at day no. 111 of year 1990 is thus modeled by the object denoted:

```
ReservationTable90.SK451Flights[111]
```

Seat no. 48 for the flight of that day may then be reserved by executing:

```
ReservationTable90.SK451Flights[111].Seats[48].Reserve
```

assuming that `Seat` objects have a `Reserve` attribute. When the flight has taken place, the actual times for departure, arrival and the flight time can be entered into the flight object. The difference between the estimated flight time and the actual flight time can be computed by executing:

```
ReservationTable90.SK451Flights[111].DepartureDelay
```

which returns the difference between `actualDepartureTime` and `departureTime`. Note that `DepartureDelay` refers to the global reference `departureTime` in the enclosing `FlightType` object. This would not have been possible if `Flight` were not defined locally to `FlightType`. In the example above, `Flight` is a class pattern attribute of `FlightType`. In addition, `FlightType` instances have the reference attribute destination and the procedure pattern attribute `DisplayTimeTableEntry`. For the different instances `SK451` and `SK273` of the `FlightType` pattern, the attributes `SK451.destination` and `SK273.destination` are different attributes. Also, `SK451.DisplayTime-TableEntry` and `SK273.DisplayTimeTableEntry` are different procedure patterns, since they are attributes of different instances. In the same way, the class patterns `SK451.Flight` and `SK273.Flight` are different, since they are attributes of different `FlightType` objects.

8.4 Exercises

(1) Write a pattern `Document` with the following properties:

(a) A document is a sequence of characters numbered from 1.

(b) It is possible to define one or more selections in a document. A selection identifies an interval of the characters in the document including a position between two characters. A selection should be represented by a `Selection` object.

(c) A document has a current selection which is a reference to a `Selection` object.

(d) Text can be inserted by replacing the characters identified by the current position.

(e) The text identified by the current selection can be deleted.

(f) There is a distinguished document called `Clipboard`.

(g) A `Selection` object has the following operations:

- `Copy` which copies the selected text to the `Clipboard`.

- `Cut` which deletes the selected text and stores it on the `Clipboard`.
- `Paste` which replaces the selected text with the text on the `Clipboard`.

(h) A `Selection` object is created by giving an interval to a document.

(i) The current selection may be replaced by a reference to another `Selection` object.

Define the pattern `Selection` as a local pattern of `Document`.

(2) Write a `HyperText` pattern with the following properties:

(a) A hypertext consists of a set of links.

(b) A link consists of a source and a destination, each being a reference to an anchor of a document.

(c) A hypertext has an operation define link which takes a source- and destination anchor as parameters.

(d) It has an operation for scanning all links.

Use the `Document` pattern of the previous exercise and the `Selection` pattern for representing the anchor concept.

8.5 Notes

Block structure was first introduced in the Algol-60 programming language. An Algol block corresponds to an object descriptor in BETA. The purpose of this chapter has been to show that block structure as found in Simula and BETA, but abandoned in Smalltalk-80, is a natural and powerful mechanism. When modeling phenomena, it is useful to be able to characterize an object by means of a class. In addition, block structure is useful for a number of technical problems in programming.

Block structure is not the only way in which Simula and Smalltalk differ. Simula contains Algol-60 as a subset and supports block structure, static (lexical) name binding, and compile-time type checking, but Smalltalk has none of these features. Smalltalk is more in the style of Lisp, with a flat set of definitions (classes), dynamic name binding and run-time type checking.

The Scheme language is an example of a Lisp dialect with block structure and lexical name binding.

In Simula the use of nested classes is limited by a number of restrictions. BETA does not have these restrictions.

Block structure is a controversial subject that has given rise to much discussion in the literature. In what follows we comment on this discussion.

- *Locality.* The major advantage of block structure is locality. This makes it possible to restrict the existence of an object and its description to the environment (object) where it has meaning.
- *Scope rules.* There are (at least) the following aspects of scope rules for names declared within an object:
  - They only exist when the object exists. This is a consequence of locality.
  - Access to global names and redeclaration of names.

    Global names may or may not be seen within a block. In (Wulf and Shaw, 1973) it is argued that the use of global variables within nested blocks is a source of errors. It is considered a problem that a name can be redeclared within an internal block. There is, however, no reason to allow such redeclaration in a language if it is found to be a problem.

    Also, it has been argued that it may be difficult to see which global names are being used within an internal block. Again, this is not inherently tied to block structure and can be avoided. In languages like Euclid ((Lampson *et al.*, 1977)), a block must explicitly import from the enclosing block all names being used.
  - Access to names within a block from 'outside' the block may be restricted. The hidden/protected mechanism of Simula is an example of this.
- *Syntax.* In (Hanson, 1981) it is said that:

  > 'Block structure can make even moderately large programs difficult to read. The difficulty is due to the physical separation of procedure-headings from their bodies....'

  In (Tennent, 1982) it is demonstrated that this is merely a matter of syntax. By using the syntax from Landin's ISWIM it is possible to place internal procedure declarations after the body of the block.

In the design of BETA, the above-mentioned problems were considered minor. The reason is that in BETA block structure is not a mechanism intended for 'programming in the large'. Block structure should be used for 'programming in the small'. In languages such as Algol-60 and Pascal, where block structure is the only structuring mechanism, the above problems may be more serious.

The grammar example is inspired by (Liskov and Zilles, 1974), who make use of abstract data types in the CLU language. Since CLU does not have block structure, the `Symbol` class is declared outside the `Grammar` class, which gives problems with restricting the implementation details of the `Grammar` class. For a discussion of these problems see (Liskov and Zilles, 1974; Madsen, 1987).

The flight reservation example is often described as an instance of what is called the *Prototype Abstraction Relation Problem* as formulated by Brian Smith (Smith, 1984). The problem is that a flight entrance like SK471 (a prototype) may be viewed as an instance of the class of flight entries and also as a class whose instances are the actual SK471 flights. To model this it is necessary to be able to describe SK471 both as an object and as a class. This is not possible in languages like Smalltalk. The metaclass mechanism of Smalltalk can do some of this, but is not general enough. The BETA solution describes SK471 as an object with a class attribute.

Chapter 9

Virtual Class Patterns

Virtual patterns are used to describe the common structure of pattern attributes in a super-pattern. In Chapter 7 the notion of virtual patterns was introduced by means of virtual procedure patterns. In this chapter, the virtual concept is further explored by giving examples of virtual patterns used as classes.

In BETA there is no technical difference between procedure patterns and class patterns, it is simply a matter of how instances are generated. For procedure patterns, instances are generated in the action-part and immediately executed. The instance then becomes inaccessible since no reference to it is saved. For class patterns, 'named' instances are generated in the sense that a reference to the instance is saved.

9.1 Directly qualified virtual class patterns

As already mentioned, the specification of a virtual class pattern is identical to the specification of a virtual procedure pattern – the difference is in how instances are generated. Consider Figure 9.1: the class `Graph` has class attributes `Node` and `Link` which define the elements of a graph. `Node` and `Link` are specified as virtual classes. Subclasses of `Graph` may extend the definitions of `Node` and `Link` corresponding to specific different kinds of graphs. Instances of `Node` will therefore always have the attribute `Connected`, and instances of `Link` will have the attributes `Source` and `Dest`. As can be seen, the virtual procedure `Connect` makes use of these attributes.

Note that the `Node` classes in two different instances of `Graph` are different classes, as they are attributes of different objects. A `Node` object from one `Graph` object cannot become part of another `Graph`.

In the `DisplayableGraph` subclass, the definitions of `Node` and `Link`

```
Graph:
  (# Node:< (# Connected: @boolean #);
     Link:< (# Source, Dest: ^Node #);
     Root: ^Node;
     Connect:<
       (# S,D: ^Node; L: ^Link
       enter(S[],D[])
       do &Link[]->L[];
          S[]->L.source[]; D[]->L.Dest[];
          true->S.Connected->D.Connected;
          INNER
       #);
  #);
DisplayableGraph: Graph
  (# Node::< (# DispSymb: ^DisplaySymbol #);
     Link::< (# DispLine: ^DisplayLine #);
     Connect::<
       (# DL: ^DisplayLine
       enter DL[]
       do DL[]->L.DispLine[]; INNER
       #);
     Display:< (# .... #)
  #);
TravellingSalesmanGraph: Graph
  (# Node::< (# Name: ^Text #);
     Link::< (# Distance: @integer #);
     Connect::<
       (# D: @integer
       enter D
       do D->L.Distance; INNER
       #);
  #);
DG: ^DisplayableGraph;
TG: ^TravellingSalesmanGraph
```

Figure 9.1 Example of virtual class patterns.

have been extended. This is reflected in the extended definition of `Connect` which has an additional parameter `DL`. The execution of `Connect` implies the generation of a `Link` object (`&Link`). This `Link` object is an instance of the extended `Link` class, and the reference `L` denotes this instance. Thus `L.DispLine` is a valid expression. The reference `DG.Root` is known to denote an instance of the extended `Node` class, thus an expression like `DG.Root.DispSymb` is valid.

The definition of `TravellingSalesman` is similar, but with different extensions of `Node, Link` and `Connect`.

9.2 General parameterized class patterns

In the previous chapters there have been examples of patterns describing registers for inserting various elements. The `Register` in Chapter 3 may be used to store `integer` objects; the `ReservationRegister` pattern in Chapter 6 may be used to store `Reservation` objects. These patterns have a similar structure: the main difference is the type of elements that can be inserted in a register. From a modeling point of view, it is desirable to be able to describe a general generic `Register` pattern which can be used to insert arbitrary elements. Special registers restricted to reservations or records could then be defined as sub-patterns of this general `Register` pattern.

The `Register` pattern in Figure 9.2 is an example of such a general pattern. The only main difference from the previous register patterns is the virtual class attribute `Content`. `Content` is the type of the elements of the `Register`, and is qualified by the most general `Object` pattern. This means that a `Register` object may include instances of all patterns. Note that the qualification of `Content` is described using a pattern name – most examples so far have used the form of direct qualification of virtual patterns.

In sub-patterns of `Register` it is possible to restrict the type of elements to be stored in the register. Figure 9.3 shows an example of a register for storing `Record` objects. The `RecordRegister` pattern is defined as a sub-pattern of `Register`, where the qualification of the virtual class pattern is extended to the `Record` pattern. This means that the elements of the register must be instances of `Record` or sub-patterns of `Record`.

A `Display` attribute has been added to `RecordRegister`. The virtual pattern `Display` scans through all the elements of the set and invokes their `Display` pattern. This is possible as all elements in the register are known to be instances of `Record` or its sub-patterns. Such objects all have a `Display` attribute.

It is possible to make further sub-patterns of `RecordRegister`. A `Student` register can be declared, as in Figure 9.4, where all objects in this register are `Student` objects. Here we have made a final binding of `Content`, which means that it is not possible to make further restrictions of the qualification of `Content` in sub-patterns of `StudentRegister`.

```
Register:
  (# Content:< Object;
     Table: [100] ^Content; Top: @integer;
     Init:< (# ... #);
     Has: Find
       (# Result: @boolean;
          NotFound::(#do false->Result #)
       do true->Result
       exit Result
       #)
     Insert:
       (# New: ^Content
       enter New[]
       do (if (New[]->Has) // false then ... if)
       #);
     Remove: (# ... #);
     ForAll:
       (# Current: ^Content
       do (for inx: Top repeat
               Table[inx][]->Current[];
               INNER
       for)#);
     Find:
       (# Subject: ^Content; index: @integer;
          NotFound:< Object
       enter Subject[]
       do 1->index;
          Search:
            (if (index<=Top) // true then
                (if Subject[] // Table[index][] then
                    INNER;
                    leave Search
                if);
                index+1->index;
                restart Search
            else &NotFound
        if)#);
  #)
```

Figure 9.2 The Register pattern parameterized with virtual patterns.

```
RecordRegister: Register
   (# Content::< Record;
      Init::< (# ... #);
      Display:<
        (#
        do ForAll(#do Current.Display #); INNER
        #)
   #)
```

Figure 9.3 Sub-pattern of `Register`.

```
StudentRegister: RecordRegister
   (# Content:: Student;
      UpdateStatus: Find
        (# Status: @StatusType;
           NotFound:: (# ... #)
        enter Status
        do Status->Table[index].Status
        #)
   #)
```

Figure 9.4 Example of a specialization of the `Register` pattern.

9.3 Notes

Even though the most common use of redefinitions of virtuals (methods) is to reflect specialization, most object-oriented languages with virtuals do not require definitions of virtuals in sub-classes to be specializations of the virtual definitions in the super-class. A sub-class method in Smalltalk and Flavors need not have more than the identifier in common with the corresponding method in the super-class. A recent improvement of Simula has made it possible to specify the parameters that all procedure definitions in sub-classes must have, but apart from that, a definition of a virtual in a sub-class consists of a pure redefinition of the virtual definition in the super-class.

In the use of these languages it has, however, been recognized that a pure redefinition of the virtual is not always what is wanted. When (re)defining a virtual in a sub-class, the definition (or effect) of the virtual in the super-class is sometimes needed. In Smalltalk this is obtained by simply sending a message to the super-class (from within the method of the sub-class), so that the method of the super-class is performed, i.e. the opposite of `inner`. Flavors provides a more sophisticated scheme (e.g. before and after methods). In Simula the virtual definition in the super-class is simply not accessible as part of or after a binding of the virtual.

In the case where pattern attributes are used to generate and execute item objects, they correspond to local procedures in Simula and to methods in Smalltalk and Flavors. As BETA has a general sub-pattern concept, also covering item objects acting as local operations, we have in Smalltalk terms 'classes and sub-classes of methods.' It is not a new idea to use the class/sub-class mechanism for methods. In 1975 Vaucher proposed prefixed procedures as a structuring mechanism for operations (Vaucher, 1975). In BETA this is a consequence of a more general notion of pattern/sub-pattern. As Vaucher has demonstrated, a class/sub-class mechanism for methods is useful in itself.

The essence of specialization by sub-patterns is that objects of a sub-pattern of a pattern `P` should have all the properties of `P`-objects. There is, however, no way to guarantee this, since a sub-pattern may introduce properties that 'contradict' the intentions of the super-pattern.

Languages supporting classes/sub-classes do not prevent programmers from making such sub-classes, although, by default, objects of sub-classes behave like objects of the super-class. One example of this is that an object of a sub-class inherits the attributes (in terms of variables and procedures/methods) of the super-class. The term *inheritance* is very often used instead of sub-classing. This reflects the fact that inheritance of 'code' is often considered to be the major benefit of sub-classing. In BETA, sub-classing is primarily considered a mechanism for modeling conceptual hierarchies, although it may be used for code sharing as well. This is one of the major differences between the American and the Scandinavian schools of object-oriented programming (Cook, 1988).

Chapter 10

Part Objects and Reference Attributes

Classification and composition are fundamental means for apprehending the real world. Classification is the means by which we form and distinguish between different classes of phenomena and concepts. Composition is the means by which we understand phenomena and concepts as a composition of other phenomena and concepts.

In the previous chapters we have seen a number of examples of using patterns, sub-patterns and virtual patterns for supporting classification. In Chapter 8 we have seen how nested patterns (block structure) may be used to support localization, which is one form of composition. In this chapter we shall take a closer look at *part-objects* which supports another form of composition called *whole-part composition*. This form of composition is useful for structuring phenomena into wholes and parts. The modeling aspects of whole-part composition are mentioned in Chapter 2, and are further discussed in Chapter 18 (Section 18.5.2). In this chapter we shall give a number of examples of using part-objects in BETA to model whole-part composition.

We also give examples of how to use (dynamic) *reference attributes* for supporting *reference composition*, which is a third form of composition. Reference composition is also discused in Section 18.5.2.

10.1 Part objects

The construct for declaring a part object was introduced in Chapter 3. The stick figure from Figure 2.3 may be described in BETA, as shown in Figure 10.1. In addition to the parts of Figure 2.3, operations for graphical animation of a stick man have been added. It is possible to move, draw and clear a stick man on a screen, and it is possible to wave the hands and wriggle the toes. An instance of a stick man may be declared in the

```
StickMan:
  (# theHead: @Head;
     theBody: @Body;
     LeftArm,RightArm: @Arm;
     LeftLeg,RightLeg: @Leg;
     move: (# ... #);
     draw: (# ... #);
     clear: (# ... #);
     ...
  #);
Head: (# ... #);
Body: (# ... #);
Arm: (# theHand: @Hand; ... #);
Leg: (# theFoot: @Foot; ... #);
Hand: (# wave: (# #); ... #);
Foot: (# bigToe: @Toe; ... #);
Toe: (# wriggle: (# #); ... #)
```

Figure 10.1 Partial BETA description of a stick man

following way:

```
Joe: @StickMan
```

The stick man `Joe` may be manipulated in the following way:

```
Joe.move;
Joe.wave;
Joe.LeftLeg.theFoot.bigToe.wriggle
```

The `move` operation may be implemented by invoking a corresponding `move` operation on the parts:

```
move:
  (# pos: @point
  enter pos
  do pos->theHead.move; pos->theBody.move;
     pos->LeftArm.move; pos->RightArm.move;
     pos->LeftLeg.move; pos->RightArm.move;
  #)
```

`Clear` and `draw` may be implemented similarly.

Operations of a compound object are often composed from operations of its part objects. An example of this is the `move` operation, which is defined as a composition of move operations on the parts. The move operation illustrates that whole-part composition is also relevant for action-sequences.

A StickMan is also characterized as having an operation for wriggling the left big toe. In contrast to the move operation, no operation for this is defined as an attribute of StickMan. Instead, the wriggle operation of the bigToe part is used directly using the notation Joe.LeftLeg.theFoot.bigToe.wriggle.

A compound object may thus be characterized by having operations that invoke operations of its parts and by operations defined in its parts.

In some situations it may be more convenient to 'propagate' an operation of a part to the whole object. The wriggle operation may, for example, be propagated to the StickMan object by defining the following operation of StickMan:

```
LeftBigToeWriggle: (#do LeftLeg.theFoot.BigToe.wriggle #)
```

Note that if all the ten toes can wriggle, then ten such operations may have to be defined.

10.1.1 Independent and dependent parts

The above example shows that a compound object may directly use an operation of its parts or it may define operations which control its parts. The parts are independent of the whole object in the sense that they are instances of patterns defined without knowledge about being part of some other object. In some situations it may be desirable that the definition of a part has knowledge about the compound object. This is possible by placing the definitions of the patterns inside the whole object. By doing this it is possible to refer to attributes of the whole object from the parts.

In this section we shall show how it is possible to use virtual patterns to define part objects that refer to the whole object. Consider the following pattern defining an address:

```
Address:
  (# Street: @text;
     StreetNo: @integer
     Town,Country: @text;
     printLabel:<
        (#
        do INNER;
           {print Street, StreetNo, Town, Country};
        #)
   #)
```

In this definition of an `Address`, it is not decided whether or not it is the address of a person, company, organization, etc. For this reason, the `printLabel` operation has been made virtual. In the examples below it is shown how the `Address` pattern may be used to define addresses of persons and companies:

```
Person:
  (# name: @text;
     adr: @Address(# printLabel::<(#do {print name} #);
  #);
Company:
  (# name,director: @text;
     adr: @Address
       (# printLabel::<(#do {print name and director} #);
  #);
```

The address part of `Person` objects is defined as a singular instance of the pattern `Address`. The virtual procedure pattern `printLabel` refers to the `name` field of the enclosing `Person` object. The address part of a `Company` is handled in a similar way, but here the `printLabel` refers to the `name` and `director` fields of the enclosing `Company` object.

References to part objects

It is possible to obtain references to part objects, as already mentioned in Chapter 3.

```
P: ^Person; C: ^Customer; A1,A2: ^Address
```

Given the references defined above, it is possible to assign a reference to the address part of `P` and `C` to `A1` and `A2` as follows:

```
P.adr[]->A1[]; C.adr[]->A2[]
```

This may be useful in situations where there is a need to handle objects with similar parts. In the above example, it may be useful to handle objects that all have address parts. Consider the following declarations:

```
Areg: @Register(# content::< Address #);
```

The `Areg` is supposed to contain a list of `Address` objects. In this list it is possible to insert any object that has an `Address` part:

```
P.adr[]->Areg.insert; C.adr[]->Areg.insert
```

It is now possible to scan this register and print all the labels:

```
Areg.scan(#do thisElm.printLabel #)
```

As may be seen, the `Areg` object and the code that uses it are independent of the actual objects having the `Address` part. The only common thing for these objects is that each has an `Address` part.

Part objects *versus* sub-patterns

The reader may have noticed that the possibility of treating `Person` objects and `Company` objects as `Address` objects may technically be obtained by using sub-patterns. We might have described `Person` and `Company` as sub-patterns of `Address`:

```
Person: Address
  (# name: @text;
     printLabel::< (#do {print name} #);
  #);
Company: Address
   (# name,director: @text
      printLabel::<(#do {print name and directory} #);
   #)
```

Even though this will technically work in the same way, there is a major difference with respect to modeling. When using part objects we consider the address property to be an aspect of a person and company. When using sub-patterns, we consider persons and companies to be classified as 'addressable' objects. None of these views can be said to be the right one: it depends on the actual situation where the objects are to be used.

Multiple part objects

It is of course possible to have several part objects as, for example, shown in the stick man example. This means that the technique used for having `Address` objects as part objects can be generalized to having several part objects, each representing different aspects of the whole object.

10.2 Reference attributes

In the previous sections a number of examples of using static references/part objects for modeling whole-part hierarchies have been given. In this section the use of dynamic reference attributes for modeling reference composition will be given. Reference composition is used to describe compound objects with parts which are not 'physically' contained in the whole object, an example being the bank account defined in Chapter 3. A `bank` account has a `Customer` attribute, and it is of course not a good model to consider the `Customer` object to be a part of the `Account`. Instead, a *reference* to the `Customer` is considered a part of the `Account`:

```
Account:
  (# Customer: ^Person;
     ...
```

```
    #)
```

In general, reference composition may be used to represent arbitrary relations. The `Customer` attribute of an `Account` may be seen as representing a 'customer' relation between an account and a person. In this example the relation is *one way*, in the sense that the reference is from the account to the person, and not vice versa. It is, of course, possible to represent *two way* relations. Consider patterns representing books and authors:

```
book:
  (# theAuthor: ^Author;
     ...
  #);
Author:
  (# theBook: ^Book;
     ...
  #);
```

There are numerous examples of relationships of this kind. The relationship between a vehicle and its owner is another example, and it may be modeled in BETA as follows:

```
Vehicle: (# owner: ^Person; ... #)
```

As with the 'customer' relation, the 'owner' relation is simple in the sense that an attribute of a `Vehicle` object refers to the owner of the vehicle. The above representation of the 'owner' relation cannot be used to identify a vehicle owned by a person. As before, it is possible to introduce a reference attribute of a `Person` object to refer to a `Vehicle`:

```
Person: (# owns: ^Vehicle; ... #)
```

The above description assumes that a vehicle is owned by at most one person, and that a person owns at most one vehicle. Such a relation is called a *one-to-one* relation. A `Person` object representing a person that does not own a vehicle could be represented by letting the `owns` reference have the value `NONE`. If we assume that a vehicle always has an owner, then the `owner` attribute of `Vehicle` objects will never be `NONE`.

In practice, a given person may own several vehicles and we might want to represent this fact. In BETA this can be done using repetitions of references, as in the following example:

```
Person: (# owns: [...] ^Vehicle; ... #)
```

In practice, it may be inconvenient to use repetitions to represent such relationships. Instead we might have a `Set` pattern for representing sets of references to objects:[1]

[1]The Mjølner BETA System has such a `Set` pattern defined in its basic library.

```
Person: (# owns: @Set(# element::<Vehicle #); ... #)
```

This type of relation is called *one-to-many.*

The relation 'Author writer-of Book' is an example of a *many-to-many* relation. An author may write several books, and a book may have several authors.

Representing relations as patterns

Often it is useful to represent relationships as instances of patterns. This may be the case for relations that are not binary, or if additional attributes are needed to characterize the relation. In the following example a pattern `Quartet` defines a relation covering phenomena such as 'The Beatles.' Phenomena like 'The Mills Brothers' and 'Simon and Garfunkel' may be represented as objects that are instances of patterns modeling relations such as 'Trio' and 'Duo':

```
Quartet:
  (# p1,p2,p3,p4: ^Person;
     init:< (# do INNER #)
  #);
...
theBeatles: @Quartet
  (# init::<(#do JohnLennon[]->p1[]; ... #)
  #)
```

This an example of reference composition. Often more attributes than just references may be associated with a relation. For a quartet its salary, list of engagements, etc. may be represented. Consider the 'owner/owns' relation for vehicles. A `Registration` pattern may be used to represent the relation:

```
Vehicle: (# R: ^Registration ; ... #);
Registration:
  (# V: ^Vehicle;
     P: ^Person;
     RegistrationDate: @Date;
     ...
  #);
Person: (# owns: @Set(# element::Registration; ... #)
```

10.3 Exercises

(1) Complete the stick man example. Use a suitable graphics package from the Mjølner BETA System to implement the graphics for drawing a stick man.

(2) Describe the many-to-many relation 'Author writer-of Book' where an author may have written several books, and a book may have several authors. Discuss possible properties of the relation.

(3) Describe patterns modeling arbitrary binary relations.

10.4 Notes

For many years the field of object-orientation has been focusing primarily on classification/specialization, and has to some extent neglected composition. This may be due to the fact that support for composition has been available in programming and design languages from the very beginning, whereas support for classification was new with the introduction of sub-classing (inheritance). There has thus been a tendency to forget about composition and try to use inheritance for supporting composition also. Composition is just as important as classification for organizing and structuring knowledge. A general discussion of part objects may be found in (Faber and Krukow, 1990). Sub-classing versus inheritance is discussed in (Sakkinen, 1989). The importance of composition has mainly been recognized within the database field, and object-oriented analysis and design, (see, for example, (Kim *et al.*, 1987; Coad and Yourdon, 1990; Booch, 1991)).

The use of relations for data modeling has been central in the database area (see also the bibliography in Chapter 18).

The stick man example is from (Blake and Cook, 1987) where it is discussed how to support whole-part objects in Smalltalk-80, which does not have direct support for this. It is suggested to use instance variables for supporting parts, but since instance variables are not visible from outside an object, it is not possible to execute an operation corresponding to:

```
Joe.LeftLeg.theFoot.bigToe.wriggle
```

They extend Smalltalk to allow methods with names like:

```
LeftLeg.theFoot.bigToe.wriggle
```

The `StickMan` object may then define the meaning of the `wriggle` operation. If no method with the above name exists, then an instance variable `LeftLeg` is assumed to exist, and the message `theFoot.bigToe.wriggle` is send to `leftLeg`, which may have a method `theFoot.bigToe.wriggle` or it may propagate the message further.

As proposed in, for example, (Raj and Levy, 1989), code reuse does not have to be obtained solely by means of sub-classing (inheritance), but may also be obtained by part objects. A discussion of part objects in BETA, including inheritance from part objects, may be found in (Madsen and Møller-Pedersen, 1992). This includes a comparison of multiple inheritance using multiple super-classes and multiple inheritance using part objects. If only inheritance of code is a concern, then multiple inheritance from part objects is almost the same as multiple inheritance from multiple super-classes. It is similar to multiple inheritance in C++ without virtual base classes. Most languages with multiple inheritance include a renaming scheme to handle identical names inherited from different super-classes. With part objects, the inherited attributes will have to be accessed using a remote name, i.e. no name conflicts will exist. However, some people find the use of remote names to be to clumsy. (Madsen and Møller-Pedersen, 1992) propose a renaming scheme for part objects.

Additional language constructs for supporting part objects are also proposed by (Madsen and Møller-Pedersen, 1992). One of these language mechanisms is the *location of a part object.* Consider the `Address` example, and consider first the situation where `Person` and `Company` are sub-patterns of `Address`:

```
Person: Address
  (# name: @text;
     printLabel::< (#do {print name} #);
  #);
Company: Address
   (# name,director: @text
      printLabel::<(#do {print name and directory} #);
   #);
P: ^Person; C: ^Company; A: ^Address
```

Here the following types of assignments are possible:

```
P[]->A[]; C[]->A[]; A[]->P[]; A[]->C[]
```

The first two types of assignments are always legal, since `A` is 'less qualified' than `P` and `C`. The latter two assignments are only legal if `A` refers to a `Person` or `Company`, respectively. This is, in general, not known at compile-time, and a run-time check is needed to test the validity of the assignment. For a discussion of this, see (Madsen *et al.*, 1990). Consider now the situation where `Address` is represented as a part object:

```
Person:
  (# name: @text;
     adr: @Address(# printLabel::<(#do {print name} #);
  #);
```

```
Company:
  (# name,director: @text;
     adr: @Address
       (# printLabel::<(#do {print name and director} #);
  #);
P: ^Person; C: ^Company; A: ^Address
```

The assignments:

```
P.adr[]->A[]; C.adr[]->A[];
```

correspond to the assignments `P[]->A[]; C[]->A[]` in the case where `Person` and `Company` are sub-patterns of `Address`. In both cases, the `Person` and `Company` objects are assigned to a reference qualified by `Address`. In the sub-pattern case, the whole object is assigned; in the part object case, a part object is assigned. In both cases only the `Address` aspects of the `Person` and `Company` objects are considered.

In the sub-pattern case it is possible to assign `A` to `P` or `C` and consider the whole object as a `Person` and `Company`. This is not possible in the part object case. (Madsen and Møller-Pedersen, 1992) have suggested that an object has a predefined attribute `loc` which refers to a possible containing object. If `A` refers to an `Address` object which is part of a `Person` object, then `A.loc` refers to the whole `Person` object. If `A` instead is part of a `Company` object, then `A.loc` refers to the whole `Company` object. If `A` refers to an object which is not part of another object, then `A.loc` is `NONE`. Using `loc` we may now execute assignments:

```
A.loc->P[]; A.loc->C[]
```

These assignments corresponds to the assignments:

```
A[]->P[]; A[]->C[]
```

in the sense that a less qualified reference is assigned to a more qualified reference, and both forms of assignments require a run-time check.

Chapter 11

Pattern Variables

In this chapter a more dynamic concept of patterns than ordinary and virtual patterns will be introduced. In the following example:

```
T: (# A: (# ... #)   {1}
      V: < D;
   do &A;
      &V
   #)
```

the evaluation `&A` always creates an instance of the pattern `A` as described at `{1}`. The name `A` is *constant* in the sense that it always denotes the same pattern. The evaluation `&V` creates an instance of some sub-pattern of `D`. The actual instance created is determined by the sub-patterns of `T` where `V` may be extended. The name `V` may be thought of as a variable that may denote different sub-patterns of `D`. `V` may be given different values in different sub-patterns of `T` and a given value for a sub-pattern will apply for all instances of the sub-pattern. In this chapter we will introduce the notion of a *pattern variable*, which may be assigned different patterns during a program execution.

11.1 Declaration of pattern variables

A pattern variable is defined as follows:

```
F: ##T
```

where `F` is the name of the pattern variable and `T` is its qualification. `F` may be assigned any pattern which is `T` or sub-patterns of `T`.

Consider the following patterns:

```
T1: T(# ... #)
T2: T(# ... #)
```

Then:

```
T1##->F##
```

assigns T1 as a pattern to F. F may be used to create instances in evaluations of the form:

```
F    &F    &F[]
```

just as for ordinary patterns. F may be assigned a new pattern:

```
T2##->F##
```

or to another pattern variable:

```
F##->F1##
```

where F1 may be declared as follows:

```
F1: ##T
```

Consider the following example:

```
(# T: (# do 'Here is '->puttext; INNER #);
   T1: T(#do 'T1'->putText #);
   T2: T(#do 'T2'->puttext #);
   F1,F2: ##T;
do T1##->F1##; &F1;          {1}
   T2##->F1##; &F1;          {2}
   F1##->F2##; &F2;          {3}
#)
```

In line 1, the pattern T1 is assigned to the pattern variable F1. The subsequent invocation &F1 will then generate and execute an instance of T1. The text Here is T1 will be printed. In line 2 F1 is assigned a new pattern T2. The invocation &F1 will then generate and execute an instance of T2, and the text Here is T2 will be printed. Finally, in line 3 F1 is assigned to F2. Since F1 is referring to the pattern T2, the T2 pattern will also be assigned to F2. The invocation &F2 will thus generate and execute an instance of T2.

F is analogous to a reference R: ^T with respect to qualification. The reference R may refer to *instances* of T or sub-patterns of T. F may refer to the *pattern* T or to *sub-patterns* of T.

Structure reference of objects

For any object it is possible to obtain a reference to its structure. For an object reference R, R## returns the structure that was used to instantiate the object referred to by R. Consider references:

```
R1: @T1;
R2: ^T;
R3: @T2(# ... #)
```

The value of R1## is the pattern T1, since R1 is an instance of T1. The value of R2## is the structure of the object referred to by R2. Since R2 may refer to instances of T or sub-patterns of T, R2## may be any such pattern. The value of R3## is the structure T2(# ... #).

The following procedure pattern creates an object which is an instance of the same pattern/object-descriptor as its enter parameter:

```
MakeCopy:
  (# S,R: ^Object; F: ##Object
  enter S[]
  do S##->F##; &F[]->R[]
  exit R[]
  #)
```

The copy of the S-object will not have the same state as S. All simple objects (integer, etc.) will have their default values (0, etc.), and all references will be NONE. Some object-oriented languages provide a Clone operation which generates a copy with the same state. Such an operation is currently not available for BETA.

Relational operators

It is possible to compare pattern variables like:

```
F## = T1##        F## < T2##        R## <= Ti##
```

where = means the same pattern, < means that the left-side is a sub-pattern of the right-side, and <= means that the left-side is either equal to the right-side or a sub-pattern of the right-side.

It is also possible to test for equality of pattern variables using the if-imperative, as shown in Sections 6.1 and 7.6.

Block structure and relational operators

Consider the following declarations:

```
T: (# P: (# ... #); ... #);
X1,X2: @T
```

The two patterns `X1.P` and `X2.P` are different patterns, meaning that the expression `X1.P## = X2.P##` has the value `false`. This example is similar to the `Grammar` example discussed in Section 8.2, with `Pascal.Symbol` being different from `Simula.Symbol`.

If `X1` and `X2` are declared as dynamic references:

```
X1,X2; ^T1
```

then they may refer to the same object or to different objects. In the former case `X1.P## = X2.P##` will have the value `true`, whereas in the latter case it will have the value `False`.

'First class' values

Pattern variables make patterns 'first class' values in the sense that a pattern can be assigned to a variable, passed as a parameter to a procedure pattern, and returned as a result of a procedure pattern.

It is also possible to change the behavior at run-time of objects. Instead of using virtual procedure patterns it is possible to use variable procedure patterns. If variable procedure patterns are used, their value can be completely redefined in sub-patterns. Consider an extension of the example from the start of this chapter:

```
T: (# A: (# ...#);
      V:< D;
      F: ##P
   #)
```

For instances of `T` and instances of sub-patterns of `T`, the attribute `A` is constant, `V` may have different bindings in sub-patterns of `T`. The attribute `F` may have different bindings in different instances of the same sub-pattern of `T`, and the binding in a given instance may be changed dynamically:

```
T1: T(# ... #);
X1,X2: @T1
...
P1##->X1.F##; P2##->X2.F##; ...; P3##->X1.F##; ...
```

11.2 Example

The following is an example of the use of pattern variables.

Consider a drawing tool for drawing boxes and ellipses on a graphical screen using menus and a mouse. Whenever the user clicks a button on the mouse, one of two actions is performed: either a symbol is drawn on the screen or a symbol pointed at is moved. There is always a 'current action' to be performed. The current action is selected in the 'actions menu' where the user can select either 'draw' or 'move.' When 'draw' is selected, the current symbol is drawn on the screen. The current symbol is selected by the user via the 'symbol menu.'

The `DrawingTool` pattern in Figure 11.1 describes the drawing tool. It has attributes representing the two types of symbols and the two types of actions. It has a pattern variable for referring to the current selected symbol (`CurrentSymbol`) and one for referring to the current selected action (`CurrentAction`). The procedure pattern attribute `SelectAction` is executed when the user selects an entry in the action menu. `SelectSymbol` is executed when the user selects an entry in the symbol menu. `DoAction` is executed when the user clicks a button on the mouse.

When `DoAction` is executed, an instance of the pattern variable `CurrentAction` is executed. Since `CurrentAction` will refer to either the `DrawAction` or the `MoveAction`, one of these two actions will be executed.

When `DrawAction` is executed, an instance of `CurrentSymbol` is created. Since `CurrentSymbol` will refer to either `Box` or `Ellipse`, either a box or ellipse object is created.

11.3 Exercises

(1) In Section 7.6 the attribute `jobType` was introduced as an integer variable. For this to work properly, `jobType` must be initialized for each job object. Consider how `jobType` instead could be defined as a virtual pattern attribute thereby avoiding the initialization problem.

(2) The pattern `qua` may be used in the following way:

```
R: ^T;
..
(R[]->qua(# qual::T1 #)).x->a
```

The pattern `qua` checks if `R##<=T1##`. If this is true it returns a reference qualified by `T1`. It is thus possible to use `qua` for testing the qualification of a pattern and subsequently use it in a computed remote name.

Implement `qua` in BETA.

(3) Extend the drawing tool from Section 11.2 to include connectors between boxes and ellipses.

```
DrawingTool:
  (# Symbol: (# ... #);
     Box: Symbol(# ... #);
     Ellipse: Symbol(# ... #);

     Action: (# ... #);
     DrawAction: Action
       (# F : ^Symbol
       do ... &CurrentSymbol[]->F[]; ...
       #);
     MoveAction: Action(# ... #);

     CurrentSymbol: ##Symbol;
     CurrentAction: ##Action;

     SelectAction:
       (# item : @text
       enter item
       do (if item
           // 'draw' then DrawAction##->CurrentAction##
           // 'move' then MoveAction##->CurrentAction##
          if)
       #);
     SelectSymbol:
       (# item: @text
       enter item
       do (if item
           // 'box' then Box##->CurrentSymbol##
           // 'ellipse' then Ellipse##->CurrentSymbol##
       if)#);
     DoAction:
       (#
       do CurrentAction
       #)
  #)
```

Figure 11.1 The pattern `DrawingTool`.

11.4 Notes

Procedure variables are known in many languages. In Lisp-based languages and functional programming languages it is usually possible to pass functions around as arguments of functions and return functions as the result of other functions. In Algol-60 it is possible to pass a procedure/function as an argument to a procedure/function. It is not possible to return a procedure/function as a result or to declare procedure variables. In C it is, for instance, possible to have pointers to functions.

Most object-oriented languages do not have constructs similar to pattern variables. Pattern variables as described here were suggested by Ole Agesen, Svend Frølund and Michael H. Olsen in their Masters Thesis (Agesen *et al.*, 1990).

Pattern variables make the principal distinction between class-based languages such as BETA and classless languages such as *Self* more blurred. One of the advantages of classless languages is that since object references can be passed as parameters, etc., this gives the power of passing classes around as parameters. As has been seen, pattern variables provide the same power.

In BETA it is possible to write a 'classless' program by means of singular objects. 'Instances' of these singular objects may be created as shown above. It is, however, not possible to define sub-classes of such objects.

One may ask the question whether or not it is useful to have both patterns and objects. Languages like *Self* demonstrate that it is possible to have only objects. The reason for having both patterns and objects in BETA is that for modeling purposes it is important to distinguish between concepts, and phenomena and their representation in terms of patterns and objects. If objects are used for representing concepts, and instances are created by means of cloning, it may be very difficult to understand the structure of a program. In the Cecil language (Chambers, 1992), which is claimed to be classless, objects are divided into various categories including abstract and template. An abstract object can only be used for inheritance and a template object can only be used for instantiation. The motivation for this categorization of objects is to avoid certain run-time errors when manipulating such objects. It is very difficult to see the principal difference between a template object and a pattern.

Chapter 12

Procedural Programming

In this section we show how to support procedural programming, i.e. viewing a program as a collection of procedures that manipulate a set of data structures. The data structures are implemented as instances of classes used like Pascal records. In Chapter 3, various examples of procedural programming were given. The patterns `Factorial`, `Power` and `Reciproc` are all done in a procedural style. Modern procedural languages like Modula and Ada include a *module* (called a *package* in Ada) construct. In this chapter we describe the BETA alternatives to the module/package construct.

Two interesting issues in programming languages are the notions of *higher order procedures* and *types*. A higher order procedure is a procedure parameterized by procedures and/or types. Similarly, a higher order type is a type parameterized by procedures and/or types. A procedure or type specified as a parameter is called a *formal procedure* or *formal type*. The procedure or type passed as a parameter is called the *actual procedure* or *actual type*.

There has been a tendency to restrict support for formal procedures in procedural languages. Algol-60 has full support of formal procedures, whereas languages like Pascal and Ada have restricted forms. In Ada formal procedures and formal types are to a limited extent supported by so-called *generic* modules. It is outside the scope of this book to describe generic modules and other language constructs that support higher order procedures and types. In this chapter we present examples of virtual patterns used as formal procedures and types.

In the following, language constructs such as module, package, generic and higher order procedure and type will be mentioned to compare how such constructs may be expressed within the object-oriented framework presented here. It will be an advantage if the reader is familiar with such constructs. It is, however, possible to read the following sections without such knowledge. The main purpose of this chapter is to present various

```
Complex:
   (# I,R: @real;
       Plus:
          (# X,Y: @Complex
          enter X
          do X.I+I->Y.I; X.R+R->Y.R
          exit Y
          #);
       Mult: ...
   enter(I,J)
   exit(I,J)
   #);
C1,C2,C3: @Complex
...
C2->C1.Plus->C3
```

Figure 12.1 Complex class.

useful programming techniques.

12.1 Functional classes

In object-oriented programming languages there is often an asymmetry between operands of a function. Consider the class `Complex` in Figure 12.1. The function `+` is modeled by the attribute `Plus` of `Complex`. An ordinary expression `C1 + C2` then has the form `C2->C1.Plus`. As can be seen, the arguments `C1` and `C2` are treated differently.

This has often been criticized. The authors of CLU (Liskov and Zilles, 1974) decided to qualify the operations using class-name instead of instance-name. The above operation looks like the following in CLU:

```
C3:=Complex$Plus(C1,C2)
```

A consequence is that all operation-calls must be denoted in this way.

In Smalltalk the asymmetry has been kept. Numbers are viewed as instances of a class and respond to messages, although this may not be the most natural way of modeling numbers in a programming language. Below we show that the procedural/functional style can be expressed in BETA.

Consider the definition of a complex package in Figure 12.2. The `ComplexRing` class defines a set of attributes that implement complex

```
(#
   ComplexRing:
     (#
         Complex:
           (# I,R: @real
           enter(I,R)
           exit(I,R)
           #);
         Create:
           (# R,I: @real; C: @Complex
           enter(R,I)
           do R->C.R; I->C.I
           exit C
           #);
         Plus:
           (# A,B,C: @Complex
           enter(A,B)
           do A.I+B.I->C.I; A.R+B.R->C.R
           exit C
           #);
         Mult: ...
      #);

     CR: @ComplexRing; {package object}
     X,Y,Z: @CR.Complex;
do
   (1.1,2.2)->CR.create->X;
   (3.1,0.2)->CR.create->Y;
   (X,Y)->CR.plus->Z
#)
```

Figure 12.2 Complex package.

numbers. The object `CR` is an instance of `ComplexRing`. The attributes of `CR` may then be used as shown in the example. In CLU, the operations are qualified by a type name; here they are qualified by an object name. As can be seen, the definition of complex numbers is 'functional.' There is no asymmetry between the arguments of the operations. Objects like `CR` are called *package objects*.

```
T: (# T1: (# ... #);
      T2: (# ... #);
      ...
      Tn: (# ... #);

      F1: (# X: @T2; y: @T3; z: @T1
          enter(x,y)
          do ...
          exit z
          #);
      F2: (# ... #);
      ...
      Fm: (# ... #)
   #);

aT: @T;
a: @aT.T1; b: @aT.T2; c: @aT.T3;
...
(b,c)->aT.F1->a
```

Figure 12.3 Definition of a set of mutually dependent classes.

Mutually dependent classes

In CLU a class defines a single abstract data type. In Ada it is possible to define a package consisting of *mutually dependent types*, i.e. types that must know about one another's representation. It is straightforward to generalize the technique used for the `ComplexRing` class to define mutually dependent classes. Figure 12.3 illustrates a sketch of class that describes package objects with attributes consisting of n classes and m operations.

In Figures 12.4 and 12.5 an example of two mutually dependent classes is shown. The pattern `VectorMatrixPackage` defines two class patterns, `Vector` and `Matrix`, and a number of associated operations. The `Matrix` operations make use of the representation of a `Vector` object.

The notation used in the above examples has two immediate drawbacks:

- It may be awkward to always have to qualify attributes of a package object with the name of the package object. This can be avoided by a mechanism similar to the with-statement of Pascal or inspect-statement of Simula:

```
VectorMatrixPackage:
  (# Vector:
       (# S: [100] @Integer;
          Get: (# i: enter i exit S[i]#);
          Put: (# e,i: @integer enter(e,i) do e->S[i] #)
       #);
     Matrix:
       (# R: [100] ^ Vector;
          Init:<
            (#do (for i:R.range repeat &Vector[]->R[i][] for); INNER#
          Get: (# i,j: @integer enter(i,j) exit R[i].S[j] #);
          Put: (# e,i,j: @integer enter(e,i,j) do e->R[i].S[j] #)
       #)
     VectorBinOp:
       (# V1,V2: ^ Vector
       enter(V1[],V2[]) do &Vector[]->V3[]; INNER exit V3[]
       #);
     AddVector: VectorBinOp
       (#do (for i: V1.S.range repeat V1.S[i]+V2.S[i]->V3.S[i] for)#)
     ...
     MatrixBinOp:
       (# M1,M2,M3: ^ Matrix
       enter(M1[],M2[]) do &Matrix[]->M3[]; M3.init; INNER exit M3[]
       #);
     AddMatrix: MatrixBinOp
       (#do (for i: M1.R.range repeat
                 (for j: M1.R[i].S.range repeat
                      M1.R[i].S[j] + M2.R[i].S[j]->M3.R[i].S[j]
       for)for)#);
     ...
     MultMatrixByVector: ...
   #);
```

Figure 12.4 Vector and matrix package.

```
with aT do
(# a: @T1; b: @T2; c: @T3;
do (b,c)->F1->a
#)
```

Of course, this only works if there is just one instance of the class T. Ada also has a variant of the `with` statement. BETA does not have a with-statement.

```
MultMatrixByVector:
  (# V: ^ Vector; M1,M2: ^ Matrix
  enter(M1[],V[])
  do &Matrix[]->M2[];
     (for i: V.S.range repeat
          (for j: M1.R[i].S.range repeat
               V.S[i] * M1.R[i].S[j]->M2.R[i].S[j]
     for)for)
  exit M2[]
  #)
```

Figure 12.5 Vector and matrix package.

- If only one instance of the class is needed, it may also be desirable to avoid declaring the class. This can be accomplished by defining the package object as a singular object:

```
aT: @(# T1: ...; T2: ...; ... Tn: ...;
        F1: ...; F2: ...; ... Fm: ...;
     #)
```

- An alternative to the `with` statement and singular objects is to use a singular inserted object prefixed by `T`, as in

```
(# ...
do T(# {All declarations in T are visible here} #)
#)
```

This technique is often used in practice.

The examples in this section involve package objects that have only class- and procedure attributes. There is thus no state associated with these package objects. Since an <object-description> may contain variable declarations, it is possible to describe package objects with state. A singular package object like `aT` is then quite similar to an Ada package. A class, like `T` or `ComplexRing`, describing package objects corresponds to an Ada generic package without generic parameters. An instance of such a class corresponds to an instantiation of an Ada generic package. Later in this chapter we discuss how patterns can be used to model generic packages with generic parameters.

12.2 Higher order procedure patterns

It is possible to define higher order procedure patterns using virtual procedure patterns and/or pattern variables as formal procedures. By *higher order procedure pattern* we understand a procedure pattern that is parameterized by a pattern or returns a pattern as a value.

Consider the following patterns:

```
IntFunc: (# X,Y: @integer enter X do INNER exit Y #);

PlotFunc:
   (# F:< IntFunc;
      first,last: @Integer;
      Device: ^ Image
   enter(first,last,Device[])
   do (first,last)->forTo
        (# inx: @Index
        do (inx,(inx->F))->Device.PutDot
   #)#)
```

The pattern PlotFunc is supposed to plot the values of the function F in the interval [first,last]. Assume that we have functions:

```
Square: IntFunc(#do X*X->Y #);
Double: IntFunc(#do X+X->Y #)
```

The following 'function calls' will then plot the values of these functions:

```
(15,30,somePlotter[])->PlotFunc(# F::Square #);
(20,40,somePlotter[])->PlotFunc(# F::Double #);
```

Assume that we want to plot the value of the factorial function as described in Chapter 3. Factorial has not been specified as a sub-pattern of IntFunc. We may 'pass' Factorial in the following way:

```
(1,6,somePlotter[])->PlotFunc(# F::(#do X->Factorial->Y#)#)
```

In the above example, virtual patterns are used for parameterizing a procedure. The following example shows how this can be done using pattern variables. This style is similar to a traditional style of higher order procedure patterns:

```
PlotFunc:
   (# F: ##IntFunc;
      first,last: @Integer;
      Device: ^ Image
```

```
    enter(F##,first,last,Device[])
    do (first,last)->forTo
         (# inx: @Index
         do (inx,(inx->F))->Device.PutDot
    #)#);
...
(Square##,15,30,somePlotter[])->PlotFunc;
(Double##,20,40,somePlotter[])->PlotFunc;
```

In the above example, a pattern variable was used as an enter-parameter. The next example shows a procedure pattern that returns a pattern variable via the exit-list. The example shows how to define a function comp for composing two integer functions:

```
comp:
  (# f,g: ##IntFunc; h: IntFunc(#do x->f->g->y #)
  enter(f##,g##)
  exit h##
  #);
C: ##IntFunc;
...
(Double##,Square##)->comp->C##;
5->C->x {x=100}
```

12.3 Virtual classes and genericity

(Meyer, 1987a) presents an interesting comparison between genericity and inheritance, showing that, in general, inheritance cannot be simulated by genericity while genericity can be simulated by inheritance. However, the techniques for simulating so-called *unconstrained genericity* become rather heavy. For this reason, unconstrained genericity was included in Eiffel.

In this section we show to what extent virtual classes can replace genericity using the example of a general class `Ring` (Meyer, 1988) with the attributes `Zero, Unity, Plus` and `Mult`. We use `Ring` to define subclasses `Complex`, and a general class `Vector` parameterized by `Ring`. The `Vector` class is in turn used to define a `ComplexVector` class.

The first version of class `Ring` is defined in a *pure object-oriented style*, i.e. operations like `+` are asymmetrical; `a+b` is performed as `a->b.plus`. In the next section another version of class `Ring` is defined using a *functional style*. Here the `+` is defined as a function of two arguments.

12.3.1 Pure object-oriented definition of class Ring

The pure object-oriented version of class Ring is shown in Figure 12.6. The general class Ring defines the virtual procedure attributes Zero, Unity, Plus and Mult. In addition, a virtual class attribute ThisClass (explained below) is included. The class Complex is one example of a sub-class of Ring.

A more interesting sub-class of Ring is the class Vector, which includes a virtual class attribute ElementType qualified by Ring. ElementType defines the class of the elements of the vector, i.e. the elements of the vector have all the properties of a ring. Class ComplexVector is a sub-class of Vector where the virtual class ElementType is extended to be class Complex. (In this example a vector consists of 100 elements. By using a virtual procedure, yielding an integer value, it is straightforward to parameterize the size of the vector.)

The virtual class ThisClass is used to ensure that the argument of, say Plus, is always of the same type as the current class. In Complex it is therefore extended to be a Complex, and in Vector it is extended to Vector. If the reference A in the definition of Plus in class Ring was defined as A: ^ Ring, then in the extension of Plus in Complex the reference A might refer to any Ring object. An explicit check would be needed to ensure that A refers to a Complex object. In addition, an operation like V1[]->C2.Plus would be valid. Instead of explicitly defining a virtual class like ThisClass, it would be more convenient to have a predefined name for this. For BETA this was suggested in (Kristensen *et al.*, 1983b). In (Borning and Ingalls, 1981) a proposal for Smalltalk was made. In Eiffel the expression **like** current corresponds to ThisClass.

12.3.2 Functional definition of class Ring

In this section a functional version of class Ring is given. In languages with a package concept one can define packages that contain the definition of a type and the operations on this type. A package is not a class, but rather a definition of a single object. A generic package, on the other, hand resembles a class, but this is very limited. In object-oriented terminology, a generic package can only be used for creating a single instance (a package). It is actually just templates that are elaborated at compile time; it is not possible to add properties like in sub-classes.

It is possible to model a generic package by a class with virtual class and virtual procedure attributes representing the formal types and formal operations of the package.

In Figure 12.7 a functional definition of the class Ring is given, together with a sub-class ComplexRing that defines the type complex and operations on complex objects. The virtual class attribute plays the role

```
Ring:
  (#  ThisClass:< Ring;
      Plus:< (# A: ^ThisClass enter A[] do INNER #);
      Mult:< (# A: ^ThisClass enter A[] do INNER #);
      Zero:< (# do INNER #);
      Unity:< (# do INNER #)
  #);
Complex: Ring
  (# ThisClass::< Complex;
     I,R: @real;
     Plus::<(# do A.I->I.Plus; A.R->R.Plus #);
     Mult::< (# ... #);
     Zero::< (# do 0->I->R #);
     Unity::< (# ... #)
  #);
Vector: Ring
  (# ThisClass::< Vector;
     ElementType:< Ring;
     R: [100] ^ ElementType;
     Plus::<
       (#
       do (for i: 100 repeat
                A.R[i]->R[i].Plus
       for)#);
     Mult: ...  Zero: ...  Unity: ...
  #);
ComplexVector: Vector
  (# ThisClass::< ComplexVector;
     ElementType::< Complex
  #)
C1,C2: @Complex;
V1,V2: @ComplexVector
...
C1.Unity; C2.Zero; C1[]->C2.Plus;
V1.Unity; V2.Unity; V1[]->V2.Plus;
```

Figure 12.6 Object-oriented definition of class `Ring`.

of the type. The operations on the type are defined in a functional (symmetrical) way on instances of class `Type`. The `Type` class is extended in sub-classes of the `Ring` class. To use a `ComplexRing` it is necessary to create an instance of it (in the example, `CR` is such an instance). All complex

```
Ring:
  (# Type:< Object;
     Plus:<
       (# X, Y, Z: ^Type
       enter(X[],Y[])
       do &Type[]->Z[];
          INNER
       exit Z[]
       #);
     Mult: ... Zero: ... Unity: ...
  #)
ComplexRing: Ring
  (# Type::< (# I,R: @real #);
     Plus::< (#do X.I + Y.I->Z.I; X.R + Y.R->Z.R #);
     Mult: ... Zero: ... Unity: ...
  #);
CR: @ComplexRing;
C1,C2,C3: ^ CR.Type
...
CR.Unity->C1[]; CR.Zero->C2[];
(C1[],C2[])->CR.Plus->C3[]
```

Figure 12.7 Functional definition of `Ring`.

references and operation calls are referred to as attributes of `CR`. The `Ring` and `ComplexRing` classes can be compared to generic packages in Ada and `CR` to a generic instantiation. The next example further illustrates this.

In Figure 12.8 a vector is defined using a functional class. The important thing to notice is that the element type of a vector ring is not a virtual class, instead, it is described by the reference `actualRingElement`. The reason is that a `VectorRing` instance must be parameterized by a specific ring, i.e. an instance of `RingElement`, otherwise the elements of a vector include, say, complex numbers from different complex rings, which seems inappropriate in this case. (However, it is possible to model this if desired.) In the example, the reference `actualRingElement` is given a value when `init` is executed. (`CR` is the `ComplexRing` from Figure 12.7.) This is, however, not satisfactory, since `actualRingElement` should not change value after the initialization, but it should denote the same `ComplexRing` during the life time of the `VectorRing`. This can be accomplished by making `actualRingElement` a 'call-by-const'[1] parameter

[1]'Call-by-const' was used in the first version of Pascal.

```
VectorRing:Ring
  (# RingElement:< Ring;
     actualRingElement: ^RingElement;
     Type::< (# V: [100] ^actualRingElement.Type #);
     Init:<
       (# aRing: ^RingElement
       enter aRing[]
       do aRing[]->actualRingElement[]
       #);
     Plus::<
       (#
       do (for i: 100 repeat
               (X.V[i][],Y.V[i][])
               ->actualRingElement.Plus
               ->Z.V[i]
          for)
       #);
     Mult: ... Zero: ... Unity: ...
  #);
ComplexVectorRing: VectorRing
  (# RingElement::< ComplexRing #);
CVR: @ComplexVectorRing;
A,B,C: @CVR.Type
...
CR[]->CVR.Init
```

Figure 12.8 Functional definition of the class `Vector`.

of the class `VectorRing`. It may then be bound when instantiating a `VectorRing` (or one of its sub-classes) and not modified afterwards. Since such parameter mechanisms are well known it will not be further elaborated.

12.3.3 Class attributes *versus* type attributes

It could be argued that the definition of `ComplexRing` does not demonstrate the need for or usefulness of class attributes. The attribute `Type` could also be defined using a pure (record) type, as in Pascal. Such record objects could, for instance, only be assignable and comparable, but not have procedure and class attributes as do classes.

However, by using a class attribute it is possible to combine the object-oriented and functional styles. The `Type` class of `ComplexRing` may have

The Mjølner BETA System

Try the BETA language using a professional programming environment

The Mjølner BETA System is an implementation of the BETA language with a large set of libraries, user application frameworks, etc.

Free demo version is available for evaluation

☑ **Yes, I want to get more info about the Mjølner BETA System**

Name ____________________

Company ____________________

Address ____________________

____

____

____

Phone ____________________

Fax ____________________

E-mail ____________________

BETA Book A-W 1993-1

The Mjølner BETA System

Try the BETA language using a professional programming environment

The Mjølner BETA System is an implementation of the BETA language with a large set of libraries, user application frameworks, etc.

Free demo version is available for evaluation

☑ **Yes, I want to get more info about the Mjølner BETA System**

(For US and Canada)

Name ____________________

Company ____________________

Address ____________________

____

____

____

Phone ____________________

Fax ____________________

E-mail ____________________

BETA Book A-W 1993-2

Place
stamp
here

Mjølner Informatics ApS
Science Park Aarhus
Gustav Wieds Vej 10
DK–8000 Aarhus C.
DENMARK

Place
stamp
here

For US and Canada

MADA
10062 Miller Avenue, Suite 202B
Cupertino, CA 95014
USA

```
ComplexRing:Ring
  (# Type::<
       (# I,R:@real;
          Incr: (# do I+1->I; R+1->R #)
       #);
       ...
  #);
```

Figure 12.9 Complex with local `Incr` operation.

a procedure attribute `Incr` that increments a complex number by 1 (see Figure 12.9). It seems more natural to express such an operation in an object-oriented style than in a functional style.

With the addition of the `Incr` it is possible, in addition to functional expressions, to specify evaluations like:

```
...; C1.Incr; ...
```

12.3.4 More on extending virtual classes

In this section, the `Vector` class of Figure 12.6 will be further elaborated. As shown in Figure 12.10, a `VectorOfVector` class parameterized by `Vector` is defined. A new virtual class `Elm` has been introduced to stand for the parameter of the class `VectorOfVector`. The use of `::` instead of `::<` specifies that this is the final extension of `ElementType`, i.e. it is no longer virtual. In general, it is useful to be able to specify that a virtual attribute can no longer be extended.

A note on syntax may seem appropriate here. The syntax for defining and extending virtuals in examples like the `Ring` may be too heavy. Instead, a usual positional notation for definition and extension of virtuals is being considered.

12.4 Notes

The examples in this chapter show that even the procedural style of programming can be supported within a language primarily intended for the object-oriented style of programming. As pointed out by others (Cox, 1984; Nygaard and Sørgaard, 1987), a programming language should support more than one style. Object-oriented programming, procedural programming and, to a limited extent, functional programming are supported by languages like Simula, BETA and C++.

```
VectorOfVector: Vector
  (# ElementType:: Vector(# ElementType:: Elm #)
     Elm:< Ring;
     ThisClass::< VectorOfVector
  #);
VectorOfVectorOfComplex: VectorOfVector
  (# ThisClass::< VectorOfVectorOfComplex;
     Elm::< Complex
  #)
```

Figure 12.10 Class `VectorOfVector`.

A property common to most object-oriented programming languages is that everything has to be regarded as an object with methods, and that every action performed is message passing. The implication of this is that even a typical functional expression such as:

```
6+7
```

gets the unnatural interpretation:

```
6.plus(7)
```

In Smalltalk the expression `6+7` is interpreted as the message `+` with argument `7` is sent to the object `6`. The result of this message is that the object `13` is returned. Even though `6` and `7` are objects, there is no reason why `+` may not be regarded as an object that adds two integer objects:

```
plus(6,7)
```

Thinking object-oriented does not have to exclude functional expressions when this is more natural. Functions, types and values are in fact needed to describe measurable properties of objects.

Chapter 13

Deterministic Alternation

In our computerized models we must be able to represent actions taking place in the application domain being modeled. Examples of such actions are deposit of money in a bank account, reservation of a seat on a flight, pushing a button, etc. For certain actions the ordering in time is important, for instance, in the case with the sequence of deposits and withdrawals on a specific bank account. In the previous chapters we have seen how to describe a *sequential ordering* of actions.

Just as it is important to be able to describe that two actions are ordered in time, it is important to be able to describe that there is no ordering in time between two actions. The deposit of money in one bank account and the withdrawal of money from another may take place independently in the sense that it is not important to describe an ordering in time between the two actions. In our computerized models we must be able to model several action sequences taking place *in concurrency*. From time to time the action sequences may have to be *synchronized*. This is, for instance, the case when two or more agents try to book the same seat. A computerized model must be able to represent the synchronization of action sequences.

A number of activities may be viewed as compound systems consisting of several concurrent action sequences. Examples of this are machines consisting of several parts, each executing an independent action sequence. In other cases an activity may be characterized by performing several action sequences, but at most one at a time. The activity will then shift between the various action sequences. An example of this is a cook making dishes. This involves several ongoing activities by the cook who constantly shifts between those requiring his attention. Another example is the agents of a travel agency. They often perform complex tasks consisting of several more or less independent activities. An agent may be involved in 'tour planning,' 'customer service' and 'invoicing.' The agent will alternate between these activities. When an agent shifts to a new activity, the current activity is temporarily suspended. Later when the agent returns to this activity it is resumed at the point of suspension. This form of sequencing is called *alternation.*

A processor handling several devices may naturally be described by alternation. The handling of each device generates an action sequence. The processor then alternates between these action sequences dependent on when the devices need to be served.

Alternation should not be confused with true concurrency, where a number of tasks take place at the same time. In alternation, at most one of the tasks takes place at a given time.

Deterministic alternation is the situation where the object decides by itself how to alternate between the different tasks. *Nondeterministic alternation* is the situation where external events cause the object to shift to another task.

In the travel agency example, each agent serves a number of customers and has a file for each customer. A task for an agent is to process a customer file. During a working day the agent alternates between the tasks processing the customer files. Most of the time the agent will decide the order of the tasks. However, external events such as telephone calls may force the agent to change task.

Action sequencing appears in several ways in programming languages. The simplest mechanism is *sequential execution*, where procedures are executed sequentially and the dynamic structure of active procedure activations is organized as a stack.

To model concurrency and alternation, a program execution may be organized as several sequential processes. This mode of execution is called *multi-sequential execution.* Several language constructs that support *multiple action sequences* have been proposed.

One example of a multi-sequential execution is *coroutine sequencing.* A coroutine is an object that has its own stack of procedure activations. A program execution will then consist of a number of coroutines. The processor will then alternate between executing these coroutines. A coroutine may temporarily suspend execution and another coroutine may be executed. A suspended coroutine may later be resumed at the point where it was suspended. The sequencing between coroutines is *deterministic* and *explicit*, since the programmer specifies as part of the coroutine when it shall suspend its actions and which coroutine is to take over.

In a number of situations a program execution has to deal with multiple action sequences that go on concurrently. Coroutines are not suitable to support such concurrent action sequences. In the coroutine situation, each coroutine has exclusive access to common data and there is no need for synchronization. However, to handle explicitly the sequencing between a large number of symmetric coroutines requires strict discipline of the programmer. In the concurrent situation, it is often necessary to be able to deal with *nondeterminism*: for example, a system with multiple processors.

In BETA, action sequences are associated with objects; objects may execute their actions as part of the execution of other objects. Such objects are of kind *item* and have been covered in previous chapters. Objects may also execute their actions concurrently with other objects, or they may execute their actions *alternating* with other objects. Such objects are of kind *component*.

The alternation between two or more action sequences may be *deterministic* or *nondeterministic*. In this chapter, deterministic alternation in BETA will be described. Concurrency is covered in Chapter 14 and nondeterministic alternation in Chapter 15.

In BETA, deterministic alternation is supported by component objects used as coroutines.[1] Coroutines makes it possible to alternate between 'stacks of executions.' Objects are 'state machines' in the sense that the result of a remote procedure call may depend on the state of the variables of the object. For objects that are coroutines, the state may include a point of execution. In general, such an execution state involves a stack of procedure activations currently called. The possibility of saving the state of execution makes coroutines useful for a large number of applications. These applications may be grouped as follows:

- With respect to the modeling of real-life phenomena, the main motivation for coroutines is to model objects that perform alternating activities. The alternation between coroutines may be deterministic in the sense that the sequencing is decided by the object itself. The shifts between coroutines may be triggered by events performed by other concurrent objects, leading to nondeterministic alternation. One main reason for introducing coroutines in BETA is for modeling objects that alternate between a number of sequential processes (tasks).
- Coroutines may be used to create an *illusion of concurrency*. The basic scheduling of coroutines is usually explicit, since a coroutine relinquishing control names the coroutine that is to take over. It is possible to eliminate the explicit scheduling by construction of a coroutine scheduler (an example of this is shown in Section 13.4.2).
- A certain class of algorithms is best understood as a set of interlocked sequential execution stacks. This includes backtracking and pattern matching. In Section 13.3 an example of such an algorithm is given.
- A *generator* is a coroutine capable of producing a sequence of values. A new value is produced for each invocation of the coroutine. The

[1] In the following, the term 'coroutine' will often be used as a synonym for objects of the kind component.

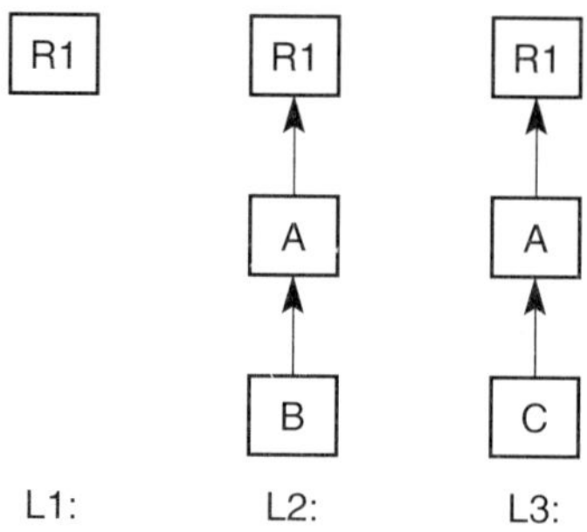

Figure 13.1 Snapshots of the execution stack.

next value depends on the sequence of previously generated values. In Section 13.2 an example of a generator of factorial numbers is given.

13.1 Execution stacks

In this section we will take a closer look at execution stacks, and introduce the basic elements of coroutines. Consider the following object:

```
R1: @
  (# A: (# do ...; B; ...; C; ... #);
     B: (# do ...; L2: ... #);
     C: (# do ...; L3: ... #);
  do ...; L1: A; ...
  #)
```

The execution of `R1` is organized in terms of a stack of active objects, illustrated in Figure 13.1. At the label `L1` the stack only consists of the object `R1`, and at `L2` the stack consists of `R1`, `A` and `B`. At `L3`, `B` has terminated and `C` has been called. Each object on the stack has a structural attribute called the *return link*. The return link consists of a *dynamic reference* to the calling object and a *code point* in the calling object from where the call was made. The arrows in the diagrams represent these dynamic references.

The organization of action sequences in terms of stacks is useful for modeling sequential executions. To model multi-sequential executions, it is necessary to be able to organize a program execution in terms of several stacks. Consider the following object:

```
R2: @
  (# X: (# do ...; Y; ... #);
```

```
      Y: (# do ...; K1: Z; ... #);
      Z: (# do ...; K2: ... #)
   do ...; X; ... K3:
   #);
```

The execution of R2 may also be illustrated by means of a stack in the same way as for R1. In this chapter we will introduce language mechanisms that make it possible to describe an object that alternates between executing R1 and R2. First, part of R1 may be executed, then part of R2, then part of R1, etc. Such a scenario is described below, and illustrated in Figure 13.2:

(13.2.a) The initial state of execution consists of three objects: R1, R2 and P*. The object P* represents some active object. P* is the object that alternates between executing R1 and R2. The objects R1 and R2 are passive. The dynamic reference of these objects refer to the top element of the stack, which initially is the object itself.

(13.2.b) Assume that P* starts by executing R1. This is done by attaching R1 to the stack of P*. This figure illustrates the state of execution when R1 is at the label L1.

(13.2.c) This figure illustrates the situation when R1 is at the label L2.

(13.2.d) At this point we assume that the execution of R1 is temporarily suspended, and that P* starts executing R2 by attaching R2 to its stack. The situation when R2 is at the label K2 is shown in this figure. Note that the execution stack of R1 is shown with the dynamic reference of R1 referring to the top element of its stack.

(13.2.e) At this point the execution of R2 may be suspended and the execution of R1 may be resumed. This figure shows the situation with R1 at the label L3.

(13.2.f) R1 may continue execution until it terminates. In this case, P* may resume execution of R2. This figure shows the situation where R1 is terminated and R2 is at the label K3, i.e. immediately before it terminates.

The above scenario may be described by the following object:

```
(# R1: @ |
     (# A: (# do ...; B; C; ... #);
        B: (# do ...; L2:suspend; ... #);
        C: (# do ...; L3: ... #);
     do ...; L1: A; ...
```

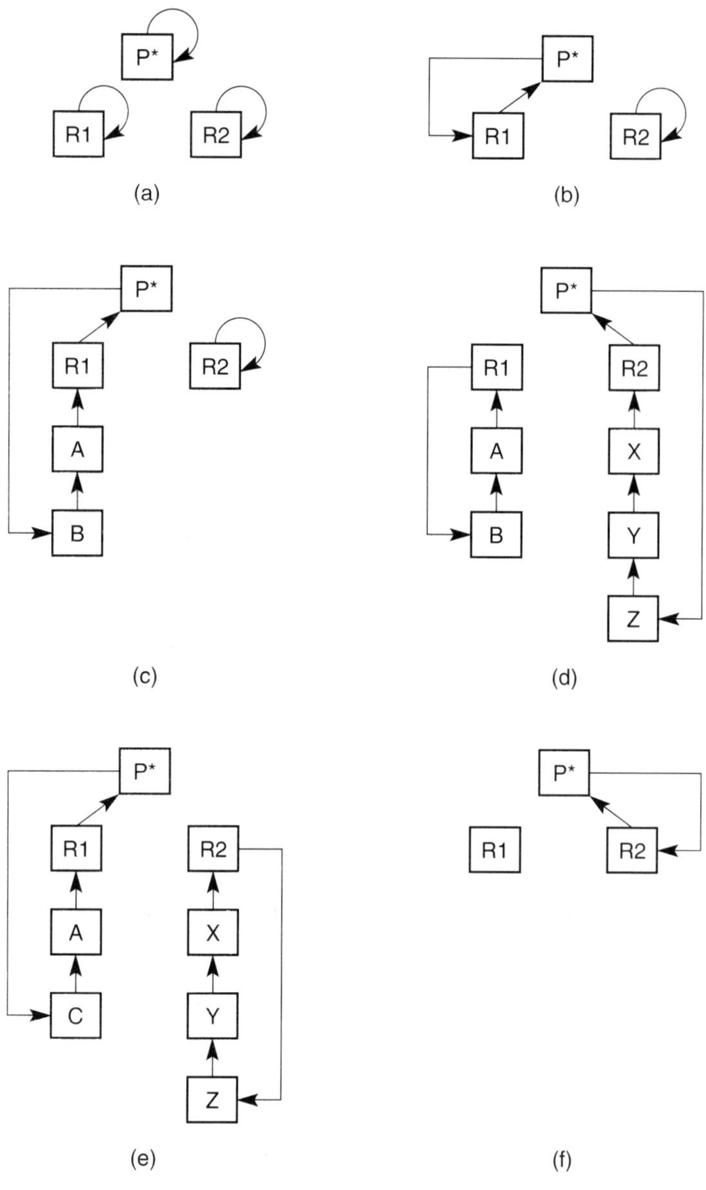

Figure 13.2 Snapshots of alternating execution stacks.

```
      #);
    R2: @ |
      (# X: (# do ...; Y; ... #);
         Y: (# do ...; K1: Z; ... #);

         Z: (# do ...; K2: suspend;... #)
      do ...; X; ...; K3:
      #);
  do M0: R1; R2; R1; R2
  #)
```

The symbol | describes that the objects `R1` and `R2` may be executed alternately. The imperative **`suspend`** used within `R1` and `R2` describes that the execution of `R1`/`R2` is temporarily suspended. The object containing `R1` and `R2` plays the role of `P*`. The situation at label `M0` then corresponds to the situation in Figure 13.2.a. The situations corresponding to Figures 13.2.b-e illustrate the execution of the above object. In the following section, the language mechanisms for coroutine sequencing are described in detail.

13.1.1 Language constructs for basic coroutine sequencing

In the above example, the terms attach, suspend and resume have been used for describing the alternation between execution of `R1` and `R2`. The precise meaning of these terms will be given below.

In addition, BETA constructs for creating and executing objects of the kind component are described. The construction modes for the generation of components are completely analogous to those for items. The term 'object' will be used whenever we describe something that is true for all three kinds of objects. When a kind, like a component, is explicitly mentioned, the explanation is only valid for that kind of object:

Component. An object that can be the basis for an execution stack is called a *component*. In Section 5.10.1 it was said that there are two different kinds of objects: items and components. The objects that can be elements of the stack of a component are usually of kind item corresponding to instances of procedure patterns. However, as we shall see later, they may also be of kind component.

The declarations

```
R1: @ | P;
R2: @ | P (# ... #)
```

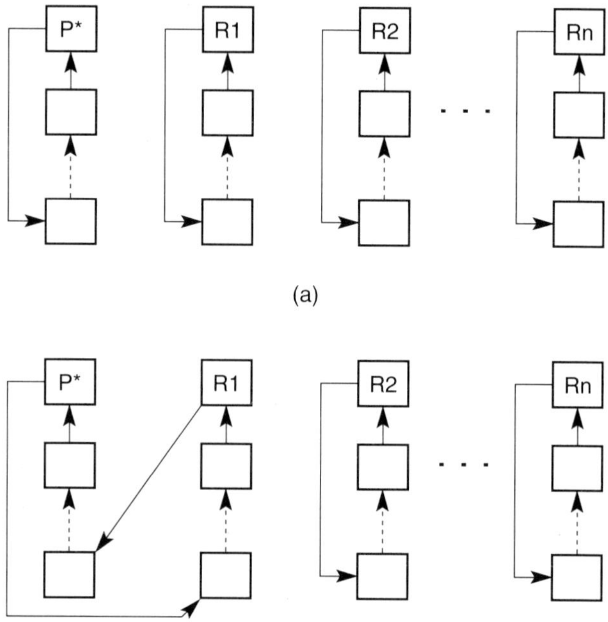

(a)

(b)

Figure 13.3 General execution state.

describe that component instances are created. R1 is an instance of P, whereas R2 is a singular component. R1 and R2 are *static component references* that will constantly denote the newly created components. These components are called *static components* or *part components.* R1 and R2 will each have their own stack of active objects. Initially, the stack consists of R1 and R2, respectively.

The declaration

```
S: ^ | P
```

describes a *dynamic component reference.* The reference S may denote component instances of the pattern P. S may be assigned a reference to R1 by:

```
R1[] -> S[]
```

A component instance may be dynamically generated by:

```
&|P[] -> S[]
```

Active stack. A program execution consists of a number of component stacks, as shown in Figure 13.3.a. It consists of the stack of P*, called the *active stack*, and the stacks R1, R2 ,..., Rn, which are said to be *suspended.* The object on top of the active stack is called the *active object*; the top-most component on the active stack is called the *active component.* The active object may execute the actions ATTACH and SUSPEND.

Attachment. An action ATTACH(R), where R is not a member of the active stack, implies that the stack R is *attached* to the active stack. Technically this happens by interchanging the return link of P* and R. Figure 13.3.b illustrates the situation after ATTACH(R1). The execution of R is said to be *resumed.*

An imperative like:

```
R
```

where R is a component implies that R is attached to the active stack of the component executing R.

The component executing R is said to attach R.

Suspension. An action SUSPEND(R), where R is a member of the active stack, implies that the stack of R is removed from the active stack. Technically this happens by interchanging the return link of P* and R. (Note that this interchange is the same as for attach. The difference in effect depends on whether or not R is part of the active stack.) R is said to be *suspended.*

Assume that R is the currently operating component. The imperative:

```
suspend
```

implies that R is detached from the active stack. R is now said to be *suspended.*

Termination. If the currently operating stack finishes execution of the imperative in its do-part, termination of the component will take place. This implies execution of an implicit suspend. A subsequent attachment will result in an **abort** event.[2]

Program object. A BETA program to be executed by a BETA processor always has the form:

[2]This implies that the program terminates with a run-time error.

```
(# ...
do ...
#)
```

that is, a BETA program is a singular object descriptor. This singular object is actually of the kind component, which means that it is the basis for an execution stack. When a BETA program is executed, this program object is always active. The object `P*` used in the above examples may be thought of as the program object. Intuitively, it may be useful to think of the program object as associated with a processor of the underlying hardware.

Attachment of `R` implies that the component denoted by `R` will be executed. This means that the actions described by the imperatives in the do-part of `R` are executed. The execution of the component continues until the component executes a suspend imperative. This will return the control to the point of the attachment. A subsequent execution (attachment) of the component will resume the component after the suspend imperative. This pattern may be continued until the component has completed execution of its do-part.

The example in Figure 13.4 `TrafficLight` describes components that when executed alternate between two states, `red` and `green`. The `Controller` component initializes the state of `North` to `red` and the state of `South` to `green`. It repeatedly waits for some time, and then switches the lights. The 'variable' `state` is a static reference denoting an instance of the pattern `Color`. The `Color` instance is an object of the kind item whereas all the other objects are components. An item is not a coroutine. In this example the `Color` instance is used as an ordinary variable.

13.2 Generators

Components may have enter/exit parts. Prior to the attachment of a component, a value may be assigned `to` the enter part of the component. When a component suspends execution or terminates, a value may be assigned *from* its exit part. If `R` is a component having enter/exit parts, then attachment of `R` with parameter transfer has the form:

```
X -> R -> Y
```

where `X` and `Y` are evaluations. The value of `X` is assigned to the enter-part of `R`, then the component `R` is attached, i.e. execution of `R` is resumed. Finally, when `R` suspends execution the exit part of `R` is assigned to `Y`.

```
(# TrafficLight:
     (# state: @ Color
     do Cycle(#
        do red->state;
           SUSPEND;
           green->state;
           SUSPEND
     #)#)
   North,South: @ | TrafficLight;
     {Declaration of two component instances of TrafficLight}
   Controller: @ | {Declaration of a singular component}
     (#
     do North; {attachment of North}
          {North.state=red}
        South; South; {two attachments of South}
          {South.state=green}
        Cycle(#
        do {wait some time}
           South; North; {switch the states}
     #)#)
do Controller {attachment of Controller}
#)
```

Figure 13.4 Example of components.

In Figure 13.5 an example of a component having enter/exit parts is given. The component `Factorial` computes `N!`. A call of the form `E -> Factorial -> F` returns `E!` in `F`. A subsequent call `Factorial -> F` returns `(E+1)!`. At any time a new enter parameter may be given. Factorial values computed previously are saved in a table, i.e. each factorial value is only computed once. `Factorial` is an example of a generator that computes a sequence of values.

13.3 Components and recursive procedure patterns

The examples so far have shown coroutines that only have a fixed number of procedure objects (items) as part of their actions. Such simple coroutines may be simulated using simple variables, since there is only a finite set of suspension points. If coroutines are combined with (recur-

```
(# Factorial: @ | {a singular component}
     (# T: [100] @ Integer; N,Top: @ Integer;
     enter N
     do 1->Top->T[1];
        Cycle(#
        do (if (Top<N) // True then
               {Compute and save (Top+1)!...N!}
               (Top+1,N)->ForTo
                 (#do {T[inx-1]=(inx-1)!}
                      T[inx-1]*i->T[inx]
                      {T[inx]=inx!}
                 #);
               N->Top
           if);
           N+1->N;
           {suspend and exit T[N-1]: }
             SUSPEND;
           {When execution is resumed after SUSPEND,}
           {a new value may have been assigned}
           {to N through enter}
        #)
     exit T[N-1]
     #);
  F: @ Integer
do 4->Factorial->F; {F=4!}
      {This execution of Factorial will result in
       computation of 1!, 2!, 3! and 4!}
   Factorial->F; {F=5!}
      {Here 5! was computed}
   3->Factorial->F; {F=3!}
      {No new factorials were computed by this call}
#)
```

Figure 13.5 A generator for factorial numbers.

sive) procedure calls, it is much more complicated to simulate the state of execution at suspension points. In this section, examples of combining coroutines and recursive procedure patterns will be presented.

The example in Figure 13.6 shows a component that generates the factorial numbers. For each activation of `Factorial`, the next factorial number is generated. This is done by means of a recursive procedure

```
(# Factorial: @ |
     (# Next:
          (# n: @integer
          enter n
          do n*F -> F;
             SUSPEND;
             n+1-> &Next
          #);
        F: @ Integer
     do 1->F-> &Next
     exit F
     #);
   v: @Integer
do Factorial->v; { v=1 }
   Factorial->v; { v=2 }
   Factorial->v; { v=6 }
   L:
   Factorial->v; { v=24 }
#)
```

Figure 13.6 Recursive generator for factorial numbers.

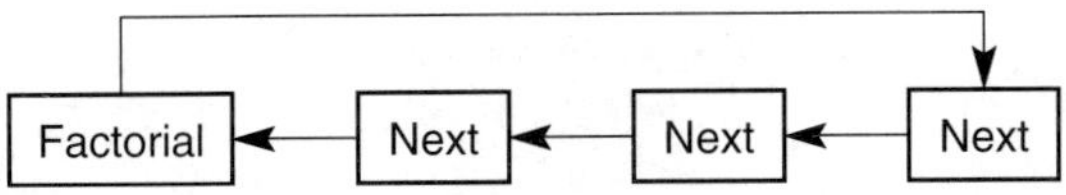

Figure 13.7 Recursive component for computing factorial

pattern, `next`.[3] When `Factorial` has computed the next number, it suspends its execution and exits the number. For each activation, the component stack will grow with a new instance of `next`. In Figure 13.7, the execution stack of `factorial` is shown when execution is at the label `L`.

The example in Figure 13.8 shows the power of combining components with execution of recursive procedure patterns. It is a classic example of using coroutines. The program describes a merge of two binary search trees. The attribute `Traverse` performs an in-order traversal of the tree:

[3]This is not the most clever way of computing factorial, but it illustrates the principle.

```
(# BinTree:
     (# Node: {The nodes of the binary tree}
          (# elem: @ Integer;
             left,right: ^ Node
          #);
        root: ^ Node;

        Traverse: @ |
          (# next: @ Integer;
             Scan:
               (# current: ^ Node
               enter current[]
               do (if (Current[]=NONE) // False then
                      current.left[]->&Scan;
                      current.elem->next;
                      SUSPEND;
                      current.right[]->&Scan
               if)#);
          do root[]->&Scan;
             MaxInt->next; Cycle(#do SUSPEND #);
             {Exit maxInt hereafter}
          exit next
          #); {Traverse}
     #); {BinTree}
   b1,b2: @ Bintree; e1,e2: @ Integer
do ...
   b1.Traverse->e1; b2.Traverse->e2;
   Merge:
     Cycle(# ...
     do (if (e1=MaxInt) and (e2=MaxInt)//True then leave Merge if);
            (if (e1<e2) // True then e1->print; b1.Traverse->e1
             else e2->print; b2.Traverse->e2
     if)#)
     ...
#)
```

Figure 13.8 Merge components.

`Traverse` is a component that will suspend and exit the elements in the nodes visited during the traversal. The main program starts by executing `Traverse` for each of the trees `b1` and `b2`. The smallest element of `b1` will then be delivered in `e1`, and the smallest element of `b2` will be delivered

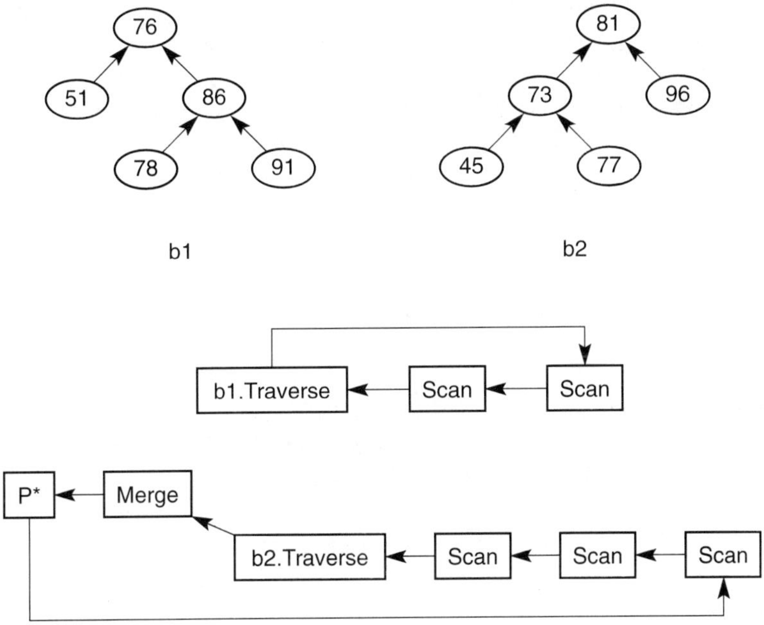

Figure 13.9 Illustration of merge components.

in `e2`. The `merge` loop will then print the smallest of the two elements; for example, if `e1` is the smallest, then `e1` is printed and `b1.Traverse` will exit the next element of `b1`. This continues until there are no more elements in the two trees. Figure 13.9 shows an example of two binary search trees and a snapshot of the execution state, taken immediately after the attach of `b2.Traverse`. `b1.Traverse` is detached at the leftmost node (`51`) and `b2.Traverse` is resumed at the node labeled `45`.

13.4 Abstract super-patterns

A major design goal for BETA has been to design a language with a small number of basic but general primitives. In addition, much emphasis has been put into the design of powerful abstraction mechanisms, as in this way it is possible to define more specialized constructs. Object-oriented languages provide powerful constructs for defining patterns that describe the general properties of a class of (partial) program executions. Often, such patterns are intended to be used as super-patterns of more specialized patterns, and it is not meaningful to create instances of these patterns. Patterns that should only be used as super-patterns are called *abstract super-patterns.*

In this section, examples of defining abstract super-patterns in BETA will be given, including modeling of symmetric coroutines in the style of Simula and the illusion of concurrent programming.

13.4.1 Symmetric coroutines

The components described in the previous section behave like so-called *semi-coroutines.* They are so called because there is an asymmetry between the calling coroutine and the coroutine being called. The caller explicitly names the coroutine to be called, whereas the called coroutine returns to the caller by executing **suspend**, which does not name the caller explicitly. There is another kind of coroutine, called a *symmetric coroutine*, which explicitly calls the coroutine to take over. It does not return to the caller by means of **suspend**, giving a symmetric relation between the coroutines. In this section it will be shown how to model symmetric coroutines.

The `SymmetricCoroutineSystem` pattern of Figure 13.10 is an abstract super-pattern that describes the general properties of a symmetric coroutine system. The attribute `SymmetricCoroutine` of `SymmetricCoroutineSystem` is an abstract super-pattern describing the properties of a symmetric coroutine. It must be used as a super-pattern for all components that are to take part in the symmetric coroutine scheduling. The `Run` attribute is intended for initiating the first `SymmetricCoroutine`. `Run` may be viewed as a primitive scheduler.

A `SymmetricCoroutine` is active until it makes an explicit transfer of control to another `SymmetricCoroutine`, done by means of the `Resume` attribute. Note that `Resume` is a virtual pattern, which means that it is possible to extend the definition of `Resume` in sub-patterns of `SymmetricCoroutine`.

The `Resume` pattern makes use of the pseudo-reference `this(SymmetricCoroutine)`, which refers to the enclosing `SymmetricCoroutine` object. Assume that `A` and `B` are different instances of `SymmetricCoroutine` or one of its sub-patterns. In `A.Resume`, `this(SymmetricCoroutine)` refers to `A`; in `B.Resume`, `this(SymmetricCoroutine)` refers to `B`. For any enclosing pattern `P` there is a pseudo-variable `this(P)`.

A `SymmetricCoroutineSystem` terminates when the active `SymmetricCoroutine` terminates execution without using `resume`. This may

```
SymmetricCoroutineSystem:
  (# SymmetricCoroutine:
       (# Resume:<
            (#
            do this(SymmetricCoroutine)[]->next[];
               SUSPEND {suspend caller}
            #)
       do INNER
       #)
     Run: {start of initial SymmetricCoroutine}
       (#
       enter next[] {global reference declared below}
       do ScheduleLoop:
            Cycle
            (# active: ^ | SymmetricCoroutine
                 {currently operating component}
            do (if (next[]->active[])
                 // NONE then leave ScheduleLoop
               if);
               NONE->next[];
               active; {attach next SymmetricCoroutine}
               {Active terminates when it executes either}
               {resume, or suspend or it terminates}
       #)#);
     next: ^ | SymmetricCoroutine;
      {Next SymmetricCoroutine to be resumed}
do INNER
#)
```

Figure 13.10 A general symmetric coroutine system.

happen either by executing a suspend or by terminating its action part.

In Figure 13.11, an example of a program using the pattern `SymmetricCoroutineSystem` is given. The problem to be solved (Grune, 1977) is to copy characters from input to output. Any occurrence of a string `'aa'` must be converted to `'b'`, and a string `'bb'` must be converted to `'c'` (the latter includes `'a'`s converted to `'b'`s). A string `'abcaadbbeaabf'` will thus be converted into `'abcbdcecf'`. The `Converter` terminates by means of **suspend** when a newline character (`nl`) is recognized at the outermost level of `DoubleBtoC`. Notice that the description of the `Resume` attribute has been extended to include an enter parameter in `DoubleBtoC`.

```
Converter: @ | SymmetricCoroutineSystem
  (# DoubleAtoB: @ | SymmetricCoroutine
       (# ch: @ Char
       do Cycle(#
          do Keyboard.GetNonBlank->ch;
             (if ch // 'a' then
                 Keyboard.GetNonBlank->ch;
                 (if ch // 'a' then 'b'->DoubleBtoC.Resume
                  else
                     'a'->DoubleBtoC.Resume;
                     ch->DoubleBtoC.Resume
                 if)
             else ch->DoubleBtoC.Resume
       if)#)#);
     DoubleBtoC: @ | SymmetricCoroutine
       (# ch: @ Char;
          Resume::< (# enter ch #);
       do Cycle(#
          do (if ch
              // 'b' then
                 DoubleAtoB.Resume;
                 (if ch // 'b' then 'c'->Screen.put
                  else
                     'b'->Screen.put;
                     ch->Screen.put
                 if)
             // nl then SUSPEND
             else ch->Screen.put
            if);
            DoubleAtoB.Resume
       #)#)
do DoubleAtoB[]->Run
#)
```

Figure 13.11 A `SymmetricCoroutineSystem`.

13.4.2 Quasi-parallel systems

In this section it is shown how to simulate concurrency by means of coroutines. The example is inspired by the *Process* module in (Wirth, 1982). In Figure 13.12, an abstract super-pattern for defining quasi-parallel sequencing is presented. A `QuasiParallelSystem` defines an abstract super-pattern `Process` defining coroutines that may take part in the

```
QuasiParallelSystem:
  (# ProcessQueue:
       (# Insert: {Insert a process; insert of NONE has no effect}
              ...;
          Next:
            {Exit and remove some process;
             If the queue is empty, then NONE is returned} ...;
          Remove: {Remove a specific process} ...;
       #);
     Active: @ ProcessQueue; {The active processes}
     Process: {General quasi-parallel processes}
       (# Wait: {Make this(Process) wait for a send to S}
            (# S: ^ ProcessQueue
            enter S[]
            do this(Process)[]->S.Insert;
               this(Process)[]->Active.Remove;
               SUSPEND
            #);
          Send: {Activate a process from S}
            (# S : ^ ProcessQueue
            enter S[]
            do S.Next->Active.Insert;
               SUSPEND
            #)
       do INNER;
          this(Process)[]->Active.Remove
       #); {Process}
     Run: {The scheduler}
       (# Ap: ^ | Process {Currently active Process}
       do ScheduleLoop:
            Cycle(#
            do (if (Active.Next->Ap[])
                 // NONE then leave ScheduleLoop
               if);
               Ap[]->Active.Insert; {Ap is still active}
               Ap; {Attach Ap}
       #)#)
  do INNER
  #)
```

Figure 13.12 A general quasi-parallel system.

```
ProducerConsumer: @ | QuasiParallelSystem
  (# B: @ Buffer;
     notFull,notEmpty: @ ProcessQueue; {Signals}
     Producer: Process
       (# Deposit:
            (# E: @ BufferElement
            enter E
            do (if B.Full // True then notFull[]->Wait if);
               E->B.put;
               notEmpty[]->Send
            #)
       do INNER
       #);
     Consumer: Process
       (# Fetch:
            (# E: @ BufferElement
            do (if B.Empty // True then notEmpty[]->Wait if);
               B.Get->E;
               notFull[]->Send
            exit E
            #);
       do INNER
       #);
     P1: @ | Producer(# ... E1->Deposit; ... #);
     C1: @ | Consumer(# ... Fetch->E1; ... #);
  do P1[]->Active.Insert; C1[]->Active.Insert;
     &Run
  #)
```

Figure 13.13 A producer/consumer system.

quasi-parallel sequencing. A coroutine that is to take part in the scheduling must be a specialization (sub-pattern) of the `Process` pattern. Instances of sub-patterns of `Process` are hereafter called *processes*.

The `ProcessQueue` pattern defines a queue of processes. All active processes are placed in an instance of `ProcessQueue` called `Active`. Each time a process suspends execution, a new process is selected from this queue.

Communication among processes is synchronized by means of *signals* (c.f. (Wirth, 1982)). A process may send and wait for (some other process sending) a signal. In the example a signal is implemented as a `ProcessQueue`.

In Figure 13.13, the classic producer/consumer system is implemented as a quasi-parallel system. Patterns describing the behavior of producers and consumers are defined. Producers and consumers communicate by means of the buffer `B` and the signals `notFull` and `notEmpty`. A producer component `P1` and a consumer component `C1` are declared.

13.5 Exercises

(1) The `Register` pattern in Chapter 6 has a `ForAll` pattern that scans through all elements of the register. Make a version of `Register` where the `ForAll` attribute is implemented as a component, and where each call `R.ForAll` returns the next element of register `R`.

(2) Write a program that generates fibonacci numbers. The program should use a component (coroutine) that works as a generator.

Fibonacci numbers are defined as follows:

```
Fib(1) = 1
Fib(2) = 1
Fib(n) = Fib(n-1) + Fib(n-2)
```

(3) Define a quasi-parallel system where the processes communicate by means of synchronous message passing using procedure patterns `SendMessage` and `ReceiveMessage`.

Let `S` and `R` be references to processes, and let `M1` and `M2` be references to messages. Process `S` can execute:

```
(R[],M1[])->SendMessage
```

meaning that `S` wants to send the message `M1` to `R`. `S` cannot continue until `R` has accepted the message. This happens when `R` executes:

```
S[]->ReceiveMessage->M2[]
```

meaning that `R` wants to receive the message from `M2`. `R` cannot continue before a message is ready from `S`.

(4) Modify the above quasi-parallel system such that the message passing is asynchronous. This means that a process executing a `SendMessage` can continue immediately, i.e. it does not have to wait for the receiver to execute `ReceiveMessage`.

13.6 Notes

The notion of coroutine sequencing was proposed by (Conway, 1963). Simula was one of the first languages to include coroutines for supporting *quasi-parallel sequencing*. A major application area of Simula is discrete event simulation. The `Simulation` class of Simula includes abstractions for creating an illusion of concurrency to be used when modeling concurrent actions.

It is only recently that mechanisms for supporting multiple action sequences have been introduced in languages supporting object-oriented programming. In Smalltalk it is, to a limited extent, possible to model multiple action sequences by means of the classes `Process, Semaphore` and `ProcessScheduler`.

In (Marlin, 1980) a distinction is made between two types of coroutine sequencing. The first, the *implicit sequencing* kind, only communicates via first-in-first-out queues, and there is no explicit transfer of control between the coroutines. *Call-by-need* parameters, *lazy evaluation*, *streams* (as in (Rees and Clinger, 1986)) and the system described in (Kahn and MacQueen, 1977) are examples of this kind of coroutine.

For the second kind of coroutine, the *explicit sequencing* kind, it is possible to transfer control explicitly from one coroutine to another.

Only a few programming languages have support for explicit coroutine sequencing. Simula is one of the few languages that offers an advanced design. It introduced the distinction between semi-coroutines and symmetric coroutines, a semi-coroutine being executed by means of the new- or call-imperative; a subsequent detach returns control to the caller. Symmetric coroutines are always explicitly scheduled by means of the resume-imperative.

Unfortunately, the details of coroutine sequencing in Simula are very complicated. The problem is to understand how semi-coroutines, symmetric coroutines and prefixed blocks are integrated. This means that even experienced Simula programmers may have difficulties in figuring out what is going on in a program using coroutines. The details of Simula's coroutines sequencing are described in (Dahl *et al.*, 1968).

A simplified version of Simula's coroutine mechanism has been presented by (Dahl and Hoare, 1972). A formal description of part of the coroutine mechanism has been presented by (Wang and Dahl, 1971). This formalization has been further elaborated in (Lindstrom and Soffa, 1981). In (Wang, 1982), it was shown that the semantics of Simula's coroutine mechanism was inconsistent. The problem was that deallocation of block instances could not be performed as stated by the original language definition. It is argued that the simple model of (Wang and Dahl, 1971) cannot cope with full Simula. Wang presents a detailed analysis of Simula's coroutine mechanism, and gives certain proposals for changes. These proposals have since led to a change in the semantics of Simula (Swedish Standard, 1987).

The diagrams used for illustrating the BETA coroutine mechanism may be viewed as an informal variant of the Wang and Dahl model. The model is operational, and may be viewed as an abstract implementation (in fact, the current implementation in BETA follows this model very closely). It may be argued that a more abstract and less operational model should be used for explaining the semantics. However, from an object-oriented perspective, where coroutines are viewed as models of alternating sequential processes from the real world, this model appears quite natural.

Explicit coroutine sequencing in the form of symmetric coroutines is also present in Modula-2. According to (Henry, 1987), there are several problems with the definition of the coroutine mechanism in Modula-2.

For a further discussion of the history and motivation for coroutines see (Marlin, 1980) and (Horowitz, 1983).

Coroutines in BETA are similar to semi-coroutines in Simula. The BETA constructs are simpler and more general than those of Simula. In addition, BETA offers the possibility of including parameters when calling coroutines. It has been shown that the BETA constructs for semi-coroutines may be used to define a set of attributes that model Simula's symmetric coroutines.

The construct `Cycle(# do Imp' #)` is similar to a prefixed block in Simula, where prefixed blocks play a major role in quasi-parallel sequencing. This is not the case in BETA.

The `Simulation` class of Simula is a classical example of an abstract super-class. It introduces the notions of processes and event notices along with a scheduling mechanism. Simulation programs may then be expressed as specializations of the `Simulation` class. The term 'abstract super-pattern' (super-class) originates from Smalltalk. In Eiffel, abstract super-class is called 'deferred class.'

More than 20 years of experience with Simula has demonstrated that the coroutine mechanism is extremely useful, and since Simula is an object-oriented language, coroutines are certainly useful within an object-oriented framework. A major difference between Simula and Smalltalk is that Smalltalk classes do not have a do-part. It should, however, be straightforward to reinvent the do-part of Smalltalk classes, thereby allowing Smalltalk objects to be active coroutines.

The experience with Simula's coroutine mechanism has been the starting point for BETA design. As mentioned above, the details of Simula's coroutine mechanism are very hard to understand, and inconsistencies in the semantics have recently been detected. However, in most Simula programs these problems do not show up. Another problem with Simula's coroutine mechanism was the inability to transfer parameters when calling a coroutine. The lack of parameters makes it clumsy to implement generators in Simula, since parameters must be transferred by means of global variables.

In the design of BETA, an attempt has been made to include a simple and general coroutine mechanism that keeps the advantages of Simula. The simple mechanism, together with a powerful abstraction mechanism, makes it possible to implement a wide variety of sequencing schemes. The symmetric coroutines and quasi-parallel systems in Section 13.4.1 are examples of this. BETA adds nothing to the basic principles of coroutine sequencing used in Simula. However, the technical details of coroutine sequencing in BETA are much simpler than those of Simula. In addition, coroutines in BETA may have parameters. This makes it easier to use BETA coroutines as generators. Coroutine (component) calls appear like procedure calls (items) whereby a high degree of uniformity between procedures and coroutines is obtained.

The arrival of Modula-2 has resulted in a renaissance for coroutines. However, coroutines in Modula-2 are considered low-level facilities for implementing concurrent processes. According to (Henry, 1987) this has implied that the status of coroutines in Modula-2 is unclear. In BETA the coroutine mechanism is a well integrated part of the language.

Icon (Griswold *et al.*, 1981) is an example of a language that supports generators.

Chapter 14

Concurrency

The subject of this chapter is the concurrent execution of objects. In the previous chapter, we have described how to use objects of the component kind for describing programs consisting of several execution stacks. It was shown how to describe a deterministic alternation between components.

Components may also be executed concurrently, i.e. two or more components may execute their actions at the same time. A basic mechanism for starting the concurrent execution of a component will be introduced.

Concurrent components may interact in different ways: they may access the same objects by, for example, executing procedure pattern attributes of these objects; or they may communicate directly by accessing attributes of each other.

It is well known that the concurrent execution of objects requires a mechanism for synchronizing the access to shared objects, just as direct communication between objects may require synchronization. The basic mechanism in BETA for synchronization is called a *semaphore*. Semaphores are, however, only useful for very simple synchronization problems. We therefore introduce high-level abstractions for handling more complicated synchronization problems, including *monitor* for guaranteeing exclusive access to an object, and a so-called *rendezvous* mechanism for handling direct communication between objects.[1] All the concurrency abstractions being introduced can be defined by means of semaphores. For some of the abstractions, the complete definition will be given; for others, their semantics will just be defined in English.

By means of textual nesting (block structure) it is possible to specify *compound systems*. A system may specify concurrent or alternating execution of one or more internal objects, and such a compound system will then have several ongoing action sequences. External systems may communicate directly with the internal systems without synchronizing with the enclosing system.

[1]The Mjølner BETA System includes a library of such abstractions.

14.1 Concurrent execution of components

Concurrent execution of a component may be described by means of the *fork-imperative*:

```
S.fork
```

where S is a reference to a component. The meaning of S.fork is that execution of S will take place concurrently with the execution of the component executing S.fork. Execution of S will continue until S executes a suspend or has finished execution of its do-part. If S suspends its execution by means of an explicit suspend, it may be resumed by means of a new S.fork. The fork action is in many ways similar to attachment, as described in the previous chapter. The difference is that execution takes place concurrently.

The following example includes a bank account of a person (Joe) and two components, one corresponding to a bank agent depositing money in Joe's account, and one representing Joe. Joe will only be withdrawing money from the account:

```
(# Account: (# ... #);
   JoesAccount: @Account;
   bankAgent: @ |
     (#
     do cycle(#do ...; 500->JoesAccount.deposit; ... #)
     #);
   Joe: @ |
     (# myPocket: @integer
     do cycle
          (#do ...;
               100->JoesAccount.Withdraw->myPocket; ...
          #)
     #)
do ...
  bankAgent.fork;{start concurrent execution of bankAgent}
  Joe.fork;      {start concurrent execution of Joe}
#)
```

From time to time, the bankAgent will deposit DKK 500 in JoesAccount. Joe will similarly withdraw DKK 100 from his account. The fork imperatives describe that the bankAgent and Joe are executed concurrently.

14.1.1 Simple synchronization

The above example works well as long as the bankAgent and Joe do not access JoesAccount at the same time. There is, however, no guarantee that this will not happen. Assume that:

```
500->JoesAccount.deposit
```

and:

```
100->JoesAccount.Withdraw->myPocket
```

are executed at the same time. Assume that the balance on the account is DKK 800 before the actions are executed. The following sequence of actions may then take place:

```
{deposit:}  compute balance + amount giving the value 1300
{withdraw:} compute balance - amount giving the value 700
{deposit:}  store 1300 in balance
{withdraw:} store 700 in balance
```

The final effect of the two actions will be that balance ends up having the value 700. This is, of course, wrong, since 500 has been deposited and 100 has been withdrawn. The final value of balance should thus have been 1200.

This is a standard example of two concurrent objects accessing a *shared object* or more generally a *shared resource.* In general, it is not possible to predict anything about the order of execution of actions made by concurrent objects. The above example of a possible sequence is just one example of many possibilities. The actual scenario depends on the underlying hardware used for implementing the BETA processor. The value of balance may be completely undefined depending on how the underlying hardware handles simultaneous access to a memory location. It is therefore necessary to make sure that at most one component accesses the account object at a given time.

Semaphores

To handle synchronization, we introduce the notion of a *semaphore*,[2] which may be thought of as a kind of signaling device similar to a traffic light. If the light is green you may proceed, but if the light is red you must wait. Consider an intersection between two roads: the intersection may be considered a shared resource of the vehicles. To avoid two or more vehicles in the intersection at the same time, access to the shared resource (intersection) is controlled by a traffic light.

A semaphore works in the following way: it may be in two states, red and green. When an object wants to access a shared resource controlled by a semaphore, it checks its state:

[2] Webster: *Semaphore: Any apparatus for signaling, as by lights, flags, etc.*

- **Check-in:** If the state is green, the state is changed to red and the object accesses the resource. When the object has finished accessing the resource, the state is changed to green.
- **Check-out:** If the state is red, the object waits until the state becomes green. The waiting takes place in a queue together with other possible objects waiting for access to the resource. When the state becomes green, the first object in the queue may execute check-in, as described above.

BETA has a predefined pattern representing a semaphore. An instance of `semaphore` has two operations `P` and `V`,[3] corresponding to check-in and check-out, respectively. Consider the following example, describing two concurrent components `A` and `B`:

```
(# S: @semaphore;
   A: @ | (# do imp1; S.P; imp2; S.V; imp3 #);
   B: @ | (# do imp4; S.P; imp5; S.V; imp6 #);
do S.V; A.fork; B.fork
#)
```

- The component `A` may execute `imp1` and `imp3` concurrently with any action executed by `B`.
- Similarly, `B` may execute `imp4` and `imp6` concurrently with any action executed by `A`.
- `A` and `B` cannot concurrently execute `imp2` and `imp5`. This is ensured by the semaphore `S`. If, for instance, `A` has executed `S.P`, then `B` will be delayed when executing `S.P` and it can only continue when `A` has executed `S.V`. The semantics of a semaphore is that two components cannot at the same time execute an operation on the same semaphore object. This means that `A` and `B` cannot execute `S.P` at the same time.

The semaphore described above has two states, red and green, and is therefore called a 'binary semaphore.' The `Semaphore` pattern in BETA is actually a so-called *generalized semaphore*. Such a semaphore has an integer value:

- The `P` operation decrements the value and as long as it is positive, the calling component is not blocked. When the value becomes negative, the calling component is delayed.
- The `V` operation increments the value. As long as the value is less than one, a waiting component is reactivated.

[3]Semaphores were introduced by Dijkstra, who named the `P` operation after the Dutch word *passeren*, meaning to 'pass', and the `V` operation after *vrygeven*, the Dutch word for 'to release'.

- If a semaphore is initialized to a positive value n, then n components may check-in with the semaphore before subsequent components are delayed. Initially, a semaphore has the value zero, meaning that it is closed. A semaphore is usually initialized to the value 1 using the `V` operation.

The `semaphore` pattern may be described as follows:

```
Semaphore:
  (# P: (#
        do (if (cnt-1->cnt)<0 // true then
               {delay calling component in Q} if)
        #);
     V: (#
        do (if (cnt+1->cnt)<1 // true then
               {reactivate a waiting component from Q} if)
        #);
     Count:
     {returns no.of. processes waiting on this(Semaphore)}
       (# V: @integer
       do (if cnt<0 then -cnt->V if)
       exit V #);
     cnt: @integer;
     Q: @Queue
  #);
```

The state of a `semaphore` is represented by an integer `cnt` and a queue `Q` for keeping track of delayed processes. Since `cnt` and `Q` are accessed from both the `P` and `V` operation, at most one of these operations may be executed at a time, in other words, the execution of `P` and `V` must be *indivisible*. The `Semaphore` is a pre-defined pattern of the BETA language, and is defined to have the property that execution of an operation `P` or `V` is indivisible. The above description of `Semaphore` is thus not how it is implemented in the Mjølner BETA System, since the above description does not handle indivisibility of the `P` and `V` operations.

We may use a semaphore to guarantee exclusive access to each bank account, as shown in the following revised version of the `Account` pattern:

```
Account:
  (# mutex: @Semaphore; {semaphore controlling access}
     balance: @integer;
     Deposit:
       (# amount,bal: @integer
       enter amount
       do mutex.P;
```

```
            balance+amount->balance->bal;
            mutex.V
         exit bal
         #);
      Withdraw:
         (# amount,bal: @integer
         enter amount
         do mutex.P;
            balance-amount->balance->bal
            mutex.V
         exit bal
         #);
      Init:< (#do mutex.V; {Initially open} INNER #)
   #)
```

Execution of the `Deposit` and `Withdraw` operations will no longer be able to make simultaneous access to `balance`. It is, of course, possible to access `balance` directly, but this is breaking the rules of the game. In Chapter 17 it is shown how to protect attributes like `balance` such that it is not possible to break the 'rules'.

Semaphore is a simple and primitive mechanism for obtaining synchronization. In the above example it is relatively easy to be convinced that the synchronization works correctly. In a system with several concurrent objects and several shared objects, it may be difficult to describe synchronization by means of semaphores. Programs that make heavy use of semaphores may be difficult to read and write. Instead, we shall introduce a number of abstract patterns for handling more complicated forms of synchronization and communication.

14.2 Monitors

The use of semaphores, as in `Account`, is a common way of defining objects shared by two or more concurrent components. We shall therefore introduce an abstraction that makes it easier to define such objects. The following pattern describes a so-called *monitor* pattern:

```
Monitor:
  (# mutex: @Semaphore;
     Entry: (# do mutex.P; INNER; mutex.V #);
     Init:< (#do mutex.V; INNER #)
  #)
```

A `Monitor` object has a semaphore attribute and a local procedure pattern, `Entry`, used to define operations. The `Account` may be described using `Monitor` in the following way:

```
Account: Monitor
  (# balance: @integer;
     Deposit: Entry
       (# amount,bal: @integer
       enter amount
       do balance+amount->balance->bal
       exit bal
       #);
     Withdraw: Entry
       (# amount,bal: @integer
       enter amount
       do balance-amount->balance->bal
       exit bal
       #);
  #)
```

In the following, a monitor means some sub-pattern of `Monitor`. An *entry pattern* (or `entry operation`) means a sub-pattern of `Entry` defined within some monitor. Monitor is one example of a high-level concurrency abstraction that can be defined by means of semaphores.

14.2.1 Monitor conditions

It may happen that a component executing an entry operation of a monitor is unable to continue execution due to some condition not being fulfilled. Consider, for instance, a bounded buffer of characters. Such a buffer may be implemented as a monitor with two operations `Put` and `Get`: the `Put` operation cannot be executed if the buffer is full, and the `Get` operation cannot be executed if the buffer is empty. A sketch of such a buffer monitor may look as follows:

```
buffer: Monitor
  (# R: [100] @char; in,out: @integer;
     Put: Entry
       (# ch: @char
       enter ch
       do {wait if buffer is full};
          ch->R[in]; (in mod R.range)+1 ->in;
       #);
     Get: Entry
       (# ch: @char
       do {wait if buffer is empty}
          R[(out mod R.range)+1->out]->ch;
       exit ch
```

```
        #);
    #)
```

The meaning of a wait is that the calling component is delayed until the condition becomes true. The `Monitor` pattern is extended with an attribute `wait` for this purpose:

```
Monitor:
  (# mutex: @Semaphore;
     Entry: (# do mutex.P; INNER; mutex.V #);
     Wait:<
       (# cond: @boolean
       do ...; INNER;
          (if cond//false then {wait} if)
       #);
     Init:< (#do mutex.V; INNER #)
  #)
```

The `Wait` operation must be executed in the following way:

```
wait(#do <some condition>->cond #)
```

where `<some condition>` is a boolean expression. If a `wait` is executed within a monitor entry, the calling component will be delayed until the condition becomes true. While the component is delayed, monitor operations can be executed by other components. A delayed component will be resumed provided that the condition is true and that no other component is executing a monitor operation, i.e. exclusive access to the monitor is still guaranteed.

We may now give the complete version of the `buffer` pattern. The content of the buffer is:

```
R[out+1], R[out+2], ... R[in-1]
```

where all the indexes are modulo `R.range`. The buffer is full if `in=out` and it is empty if `in=(out+1)`, again modulo `R.range`.

```
(# buffer: @Monitor
     (# R: [100] @char; in,out: @integer;
        full: (# exit in=out #);
        empty: (#exit (in = (out mod R.range)+1) #);
        Put: Entry
          (# ch: @char
          enter ch
          do wait(#do (not full)->cond #);
             ch->R[in]; (in mod R.range)+1 ->in;
```

```
           #);
         get: Entry
           (# ch: @char
           do wait(#do (not empty)->cond #);
              R[(out mod R.range)+1->out]->ch;
           exit ch
           #);
         init::< (# do 1->in; R.range->out #)
       #);

    prod: @ | (#do cycle(#do ...; ch->buffer.put; ... #)#);
    cons: @ | (#do cycle(#do ...; buffer.get->ch; ... #)#)
 do buffer.init;
    prod.fork; cons.fork
 #)
```

Monitors and conditions are useful for describing simple cases of shared objects (by simple we mean a limited use of conditions). If the conditions for delaying a calling component become complicated, the monitor may similarly become difficult to program and read.

14.3 Direct communication between components

In the previous section we have described a mechanism for concurrent components to communicate through shared objects. In many cases it appears more natural for concurrent components to communicate directly instead of using shared objects. Consider the following example:

```
(# S: @ | (# P: (# ... #) do ...; R.Q; ... #);
   R: @ | (# Q: (# ... #) do ...; S.P; ... #)
do S.fork; R.fork
#)
```

Here the concurrent components S and R call operations on each other. The state of S may, however, not be meaningful when R executes P, and vice versa. In the following sections we will introduce abstractions for making it possible to synchronize such communication.

14.3.1 Synchronized communication between components

In this section we will introduce the notion of *synchronized execution of objects*. A component S may request execution of an object attribute of a component R. The component R must accept that that the request can be fulfilled.

Synchronized communication is described in an abstract pattern System. A System defines the notion of a Port for controlling the communication. A Port has an Entry pattern for defining procedure patterns controlled by the port; it also has an Accept operation for signaling that an operation associated with the port can be executed. The System has the following structure:

```
System:
  (# Port:
       (# mutex,m: @semaphore;
          Entry: (#do m.P; INNER; mutex.V #);
          accept: (#do m.V; mutex.P #)
       #)
  do ... INNER; ...
  #)
```

The following object illustrates two communicating systems:

```
S: @ | System
   (# ...
   do ... E1->R.M->E2 ...
   #);
R: @ | System
   (# P: @Port;
      M: P.Entry(# ... enter ... do ... exit ... #);
      ...
   do ...; P.accept; ...
   #)
```

The system S may execute a *request*, which is a normal remote procedure call:

```
E1->R.M->E2
```

Since M is a sub-pattern of a port entry, the execution of M has to be accepted by R before it is executed.

For M to be accepted, R must execute an *accept*, which has the following form:

```
P.accept
```

The *communication* is carried out when S is executing R.M and R is executing P.accept. Both S and R are blocked until the communication takes place. A communication has the effect that S and R together execute the evaluation:

```
E1->M->E2
```

This takes place as follows:

(1) When S executes E1->R.M->E2, an instance of M is created and E1 is transferred to the enter part of this instance (since E1-> is optional there need not be an assignment to the enter-part). S is now ready to execute the do-part of the M-instance.

(2) When R executes P.accept, R has signaled that the do-part of a instance of a sub-pattern of P.Entry may be executed. R will wait until such an execution has taken place.

(3) When both R and S are ready, the do-part of M can be executed.

(4) When the do-part of M has been executed, R will continue execution. In addition, a possible exit-part of M is transferred to E2.

The object S executing R.M is called the *sender*, and the object R having M as an attribute is called the *receiver*.

In the following example, two systems Prod and Cons communicate via a single element buffer represented by a SingleBuf system. The SingleBuf system alternates between accepting a Put and a Get:

```
(# SingleBuf: @ | System
     (# PutPort,GetPort: @Port;
        bufCh: @char;
        Put: PutPort.entry
          (# ch: @char enter ch do ch->bufCh #);
        Get: GetPort.entry
          (# ch: @char do bufCh->ch exit ch #);
     do cycle(#do PutPort.accept; GetPort.accept #)
     #);
   Prod: @ | System
     (#
     do cycle(#do ...; c->SingleBuf.put; ... #)
     #);
   Cons: @ | System
     (#
     do cycle(#do ...; SingleBuf.get->c; ... #)
     #)
do Prod.fork; SingleBuf.fork; Cons.fork;
#)
```

14.3.2 Ports controlling several operations

It is possible to associate more than one operation with a port, as illustrated in Figure 14.1. The `Master`-system transmits a sequence of values to the two `Slave`-systems, and each `Slave`-system computes the sum of the values being received. Each value is received and accumulated by a synchronous execution of `Add`. A `Slave` object can be used according to the following protocol:

(1) The `Clear` operation must be used to initiate a new sequence of summations. A `Clear` thus terminates any ongoing summation.

(2) The `Add` operation accumulates a new value.

(3) The `Result` operation returns the current sum.

In the example, positive numbers are transmitted to `Slave1` and negative numbers are transmitted to `Slave2`.

14.3.3 Restricted acceptance

An accept operation on a port signals that any object is allowed to execute an operation associated with the port. Sometimes it is desirable to restrict the possible objects that are allowed to execute a port operation. The restriction may specify that one specific object is allowed to execute a port operation, or it may specify that instances of a specific pattern are allowed to execute a port operation. These two types of restrictions are described in the following two sections.

Object restriction

It is possible to restrict the sender of an operation by declaring the port as an instance of the `ObjectPort` pattern. The `Accept` operation of an `ObjectPort` has an enter parameter which is a reference to the object that is allowed to execute a port operation. The syntax for this is:

```
S: ^ | T; {some component reference}
P: @ObjectPort;
F: P.Entry(# do ... #);
...
S[]->P.accept;
```

The example in Figure 14.2 describes an abstract pattern for handling reservations of some kind. The reservations are supposed to be stored in some register. The actual way this is done is supposed to be described in sub-patterns of `ReservationHandler`. At most, one person at a time is allowed to make reservations. An agent making a reservation must perform the following steps:

```
(# Slave: System
     (# receive: @Port;
        Clear: receive.entry(# do 0->sum #);
        Add: receive.entry
          (# V: @integer enter V do sum+V->sum #);
        Result: receive.entry(# S: @integer do sum->S exit S #);
        sum: @integer;
     do 0->Sum;
        Cycle(# do receive.accept #);
     #);
   Slave1: @ | Slave;
   Slave2: @ | Slave;
   Master: @ | System
     (# Pos,Neg: @integer; V: [100] @integer;
     do {Read values to V}
        Slave1.Clear; Slave2.Clear;
        (for inx: V.Range repeat
              (if True
               // V[inx] > 0 then V[inx]->Slave1.Add
               // V[inx] < 0 then V[inx]->Slave2.Add
        if)for);
        Slave1.Result->Pos;
        Slave2.Result->Neg;
     #)
do Master.fork; Slave1.fork; Slave2.fork
#)
```

Figure 14.1 Example of concurrent systems.

(1) The register must be locked by executing the `Lock` operation.

(2) The agent may then perform one or more reservations using `Reserve`.

(3) The agent terminates the reservation session by executing `Close`.

The example includes a sketch of a handler for hotel reservations. The system `P` describes a scenario of an agent making two hotel reservations.

Qualified restriction

The `ObjectPort` described above makes it possible to ensure that only one specific system may execute a port operation. It is often desirable to specify that a port operation may be executed by a restricted set of systems. By using a port instantiated from `QualifiedPort`, it is possible

```
ReservationHandler: System
  (# start: @Port;
     Lock: start.entry
       (# S: ^ | System
       enter S
       do S[]->sender[]; false->closed; INNER
       #);
     sender: ^ | System;
     request: @ObjectPort;
     Reserve:< request.Entry;
     Close:< request.Entry(# do true->closed; INNER #);
     closed: @boolean
  do cycle
     (#
     do start.accept;
        loop: cycle
         (#
         do sender[]->request.accept;
            (if closed//true then leave loop if)
     #)#)
  #);
HotelResHandler: @ | ReservationHandler
  (# Reserve::<
       (# guestName: @text; noOfPersons,roomNo: @integer
       enter(GuestName,noOfPersons)
       do ...
       exit roomNo
       #);
      {Representation of register of hotel reservations}
  #);
P: @ | System
  (# rno1,rno2: @integer
  do P[]->HotelResHandler.Lock;
     ('Peter Olsen',4)->HotelResHandler.Reserve->rno1;
     ('Anne Nielsen',1)->HotelResHandler.Reserve->rno2
     HotelResHandler.Close
  #)
```

Figure 14.2 Example using a restricted port.

to define port operations that may be executed by objects qualified by a specific pattern. The syntax for this is:

```
(# Producer: (# ... #);
   Consumer: (# ... #);
   SingleBuf: @ | System
     (# PutPort,GetPort: @QualifiedPort;
        bufCh: @char;
        Put: PutPort.entry(# ch: @char enter ch do ch->bufCh #);
        Get: GetPort.entry(# ch: @char do bufCh->ch exit ch #);
     do cycle
        (#do Producer##->PutPort.accept;
             Consumer##->GetPort.accept
        #)
     #);
   Prod: @ | Producer
     (#
     do cycle(#do ...; c->SingleBuf.put; ... #)
     #);
   Cons: @ | Consumer
     (#
     do cycle(#do ...; SingleBuf.get->c; ... #)
     #)
do Prod.fork; SingleBuf.fork; Cons.fork
#)
```

Figure 14.3 Single buffer using a qualified port.

```
T: (# ... #);  {some pattern}
P: @QualifiedPort;
F: P.Entry(# do ... #);
...
T##->P.accept;
```

Port operations associated with `P` may now be executed by an object which is an instance of `T` or a sub-pattern of `T`.

The example in Figure 14.3 illustrates the use of a qualified port. The single buffer example is modified such that `Put` can only be executed by `Producer` objects and `Get` can only be executed by `Consumer` objects.

14.4 Compound systems

Composition is a fundamental means for organizing objects. We have several examples of defining an object as compositions of other objects using part objects, references and block structure. We have also seen how the do-part of an object may be composed of other objects. In this section we shall show how to construct *compound systems* that are system objects consisting of several internal multiple action sequences.

In BETA the actions to be performed by a system may be distributed among several internal systems. The internal systems may be more or less independent, and they may access common data (items in an enclosing system), communicate with each other, communicate with external systems or control communication between external systems, and the enclosing system. In the following, examples of such compound systems are described.

For compound systems consisting of several internal concurrent systems, we are often interested in describing that execution of the outermost system cannot terminate before execution of all inner systems has terminated. The outermost system may have to do some initialization before executing the inner systems, and it may have to do some finalization (clean-up) when they have finished execution. The `System` pattern has an attribute `conc` which can be used for this purpose. `Conc` can be used in the following way:

```
S: @ | system
   (# S1: @ | system(# ... do ... #);
      S2: @ | system(# ... do ... #);
      S3: @ | system(# ... do ... #);
      ...
   do ...;
      conc(#do S1.start; S2.start; S3.start #);
      ...
   #)
```

When `S` is executed, it will eventually execute the `conc` object, where the do-part describes that concurrent execution of `S1`, `S2` and `S3` is initiated. The do-part of `conc` will then wait for termination of `S1`, `S2` and `S3`. When they have terminated, execution continues after `conc`.

14.4.1 Indirect communication between internal systems

The internal systems of a compound system may communicate indirectly via global objects in the enclosing system. Such shared objects should be defined as monitor objects.

The example in Figure 14.4 describes a histogram, represented by the `Histogram` system, which is an example of a compound system. The `Histogram` system consists of two internal systems and a monitor, the monitor representing the data in the histogram. The `Display` system

```
(# Histogram: @ | system
     (# histogramData: @monitor
          {representation of the histogram}
          (# R: [100] @integer;
             Add: entry (# i: @integer enter i do R[i]+1->R[i] #);
             Sub: entry
               (# i: @integer enter i do (R[i]-1,0)->Min->R[i] #);
             Get: entry(# i,V: @integer enter i do R[i]->V exit V #)
            #);
        Display: @ | system
          (# i: @integer
          do cycle(#
             do (i+1) mod 100->i;
                (i,i->histogramData.Get)->Screen.show
          #)#);
        Update: @ | system(#do cycle(#do request.accept #) #);
        request: @Port;
        newValue: request.entry
          (# V: @integer
          enter V
          do (if V>0 then  V->histogramData.Add
              else -V->histogramData.Sub
             if)
          #)
     do conc(#do Display.start; Update.start #)
     #);
   S: | system(#do cycle(#do ...; someValue->Histogram.newValue #)
do conc(#do Histogram.start; S.start #)
#)
```

Figure 14.4 Example of compound system.

constantly displays the histogram on a screen. The histogram may be changed by means of external requests. The `Update` system handles possible external requests and updates the histogram data.

The `Display` and `Update` systems need not synchronize as the `Display` system always displays the latest version of the histogram. Since `histogramData` is represented as a monitor, the operations on the histogram data are indivisible.

The `Display` system reads the histogram by requesting execution of the global item `Get`. Similarly, the `Update` system updates the histogram data by execution of `Add` and `Sub`. Note that `newValue` is an attribute of

`Histogram`, but controlled by the internal `Update` system. `S` is some system using `Histogram`, and it communicates with the `Histogram` system independently of its internal concurrent behavior.

14.4.2 Communication with internal systems

From outside a system it is possible to communicate directly with its internal systems without synchronizing with the enclosing system. The `Pipe` system in Figure 14.5 consists of three internal concurrent systems, `DisAsm`, `Squash` and `Asm`. A `Pipe` object receives a sequence of text lines, transforming substrings `**` into `^`. Then the input lines are formatted into lines consisting of 80 characters. A blank is inserted between the original input lines. This job is divided between the internal systems:

- The `DisAsm` system receives an input line and transmits each character in the line to the `Squash` system. Note that the `DisAsm` system controls a `Port` in an enclosing system object.
- The `Squash` system replaces substrings `**` by `^` and transmits the output to `Asm`.
- The `Asm` system formats the character sequence into lines consisting of 80 characters.

The `Prod` system transmits input lines to the `Pipe`, and the `Cons` system receives lines from the `Pipe`. From these clients the internal concurrent behavior does not affect the use of the `Pipe`.

14.5 Readers and writers problem

A classical synchronization problem is the so-called *readers and writers* problem, which may be formulated in the following way: an object is shared by a number of concurrent components. The components may be divided into two classes, depending on how they use the shared object:

Readers: A reader component will only observe the state of the object. Several readers may access the object at the same time.

Writers: A writer component will modify the state of the object. A writer must have exclusive access to the object.

As an example of a shared object, consider a document. Several readers are allowed to extract parts of the document or print it. Several writers are allowed to modify the document by inserting new text or by deleting text. However, each such operation must be indivisible. The following pattern defines a document in the form of a monitor. The operations

```
(# Prod: @ | System(#do cycle(#do getLine->Pipe.Put #)#);
   Pipe: @ | System
     (# In: @Port;
        Put: In.Entry(# L: @text enter L do L->inLine #);
        inLine: @text;
        DisAsm: @ | System
          (#
          do cycle(#
             do In.accept;
                inLine.scan(#do ch->Squash.put #);
                ' '->Squash.put
          #)#);
        Squash: @ | System
          (# P: @Port; ch: @char;
             Put: P.Entry(# c: @char enter c do c->ch #);
          do cycle(#
             do P.accept;
                (if ch // '*' then
                    P.accept;
                    (if ch // '*' then '^'->Asm.put
                     else '*'->asm.put; ch->asm.put if)
                 else ch->Asm.put
          if)#)#);
        Asm: @ | System
          (# P: @Port; ch: @char
             Put: P.entry(# c: @char enter c do c->ch #);
          do cycle(#
             do OutLine.clear;
                (for i: 80 repeat P.accept; ch->OutLine.put for);
                Out.accept
          #)#);
        Out: @port;
        Get: Out.Entry(# L: @text do OutLine->L exit L #)
        OutLine: @text
     do conc(#do DisAsm.start; Squash.start; Asm.start #)
     #);
   Cons: @ | System(#do cycle(#do Pipe.Get->putLine #)#)
do conc(#do Prod.start; Pipe.start; Cons.start #)
#)
```

Figure 14.5 Compound system with internal communicating systems.

Insert and Delete are usual entry operations, i.e. they have exclusive access to the monitor. The operations `GetSub` and `Print` are defined as sub-patterns of `readerEntry`, which is defined in `monitor`. `ReaderEntry` is a control pattern for defining operations that can be executed at the same time. A `readerEntry` cannot, however, be executed at the same time as an entry operation:

```
Document: monitor
  (# doc: @text
     Insert: entry
       (# i,j: @integer; T: @text
       enter(i,j,T)
       do {insert T between pos. i and j in doc}
       #);
     Delete: entry
       (# i,j: @integer
       enter(i,j)
       do {delete characters from pos. i to j in doc}
       #);
     GetSub: readerEntry
       (# i,j: @integer; T: @text
       enter(i,j)
       do {get from doc substring i-j to T}
       exit T
       #);
     Print: readerEntry
      (# P: ^ printer
      enter P[]
      do {send document to printer P}
      #)
  #)
```

The `readerEntry` may be defined as follows:

```
Monitor:
  (# mutex,countMutex: @Semaphore;
     rCount: @integer;
     entry: (# do mutex.P; INNER; mutex.V #);
     readerEntry:
       (#
       do countMutex.P;
          (if rCount+1->rCount // 1 then mutex.P if);
          countMutex.V;
          INNER;
          countMutex.P;
```

```
            (if rCount-1->rCount // 0 then mutex.V if);
            countMutex.V
         #);
       ...
   #)
```

The variable `rCount` keeps track of the number of concurrent read operations taking place at the same time. When the first read operation is started, the monitor is entered by executing `mutex.P`. Subsequent read operations can now enter without being blocked by `mutex`. An attempt to enter via `entry` cannot take place as long as a reader is executing. When the last reader leaves the monitor, it is opened by execution of `mutex.V`. The semaphore `countMutex` is used for guaranteeing exclusive access to `rCount`.

The above definition of the `monitor` has the property that no reader will wait unless the shared object is accessed by a writer, meaning that a reader will not have to wait just because a writer is waiting for other readers to release the object. An alternative would be to define the `monitor` in such a way that when a writer wants access, it will get it as fast as possible, i.e. possible new readers will have to wait. This is left as an exercise.

14.6 Exercises

(1) Consider the master/slave example. A `Slave` object computes a summation of the values received. Define a `Slave` pattern that accumulates the computation of a binary function F. This should be done by defining an abstract pattern `Slave` that is parameterized with a function `F`, and a null element `null`. If the `Slave` receives the values `v1,v2, ..., vn`, it should compute:

```
null->ac; (ac,v1)->F->ac; (ac,v2)->F->ac; ...;
(ac,vn)->F->ac
```

(2) Make a complete definition of the `wait` attribute of the `Monitor` pattern using semaphores.

(3) Make a complete definition of the patterns `Port`, `Entry` and `accept` using semaphores.

(4) Consider the histogram example in Figure 14.4. What consequences may it have to define the `Get` attribute in the following way?

```
Get: Entry(# i: @integer enter i exit R[i] #)
```

Discuss the problems of referring to objects in an enclosing monitor or system from the enter or exit parts of an entry operation.

(5) Define a monitor pattern that handles the readers and writers problem in such a way that a writer will get access to the shared object as quickly as possible. Possible new readers should then wait until the writer has finished.

(6) Describe in BETA a machine that can make coffee and soup. The machine has the following characteristics:

1. The customer can push either `makeCoffee` or `makeSoup`.
2. If `makeCoffee` has been pushed, he/she can take out the coffee. Similarly, if `makeSoup` has been pushed.
3. `makeCoffee` and `makeSoup` cannot be pushed again until the coffee/soup has been taken out.

Next, extend the machine to be able to make tea also. The extended machine should be described as a sub-pattern of the coffee and soup machine.

(7) Consider a system with nested internal concurrent systems, where the internal systems manipulate the ports in the enclosing system:

```
S: @ | system
  (# p1: @port; p2: @port; p3:@port;
     m1: p1.entry(# ... #); ...
     m2: p2.entry(# ... #); ...
     m3: p3.entry(# ... #); ...

     S1: | system(# ... do ... p1.accept; ... #);
     S2: | system
       (# ... do ... p2.accept; ...; p3.accept; ... #)
  do conc(#do S1.start; S2.start #)
  #)
```

Discuss which operations a sender can apply to `S` depending on the `accept` operations executed by the inner systems. Will the operations that can be applied to `S` be mutually disjoint or concurrent? Discuss the advantages and disadvantages of this.

(8) The `system/port` patterns described in this chapter are static in the sense that a `system` can only open one port at a given time unless there are internal `systems`.

Design and implement a new `system/port` where a `system` can open more than one `port` at the same time.

Compare this style of communication with that using nested concurrent systems from the previous exercise.

(9) Consider a system `A` that can be in one of three states, `state1`, `state2` or `state3`. In each state one or more ports may be open. When communication takes place, `A` changes to a new state depending on some conditions. If `cond1` is true, the next state is `state1`, if `cond2` is true, the next state is `state2`, and if `cond3` is true, the next state is `state3`. Describe `A` in BETA.

Consider a system `B`, which is like `A` except that `state1` consists of two substates `state11` and `state12`. System `B` changes to `state11` if `cond1 and cond11` is true and to state `state12` if `cond1 and cond12` is true. Describe `B` in BETA as a sub-pattern of `A`.

14.7 Notes

It is outside the scope of this book to give a complete bibliography of concurrent programming. Important contributions to this work have been made by Dijkstra (Dijkstra, 1968), Concurrent Pascal (Brinch-Hansen, 1975) (and other work by Brinch-Hansen), CSP (Hoare, 1978), and Ada (US Department of Defense, 1980).

The semaphore concept was introduced by Dijkstra in (Dijkstra, 1968). The monitor concepts were introduced in (Hoare, 1978; Brinch-Hansen, 1975). The BETA `conc` pattern is similar to Dijkstra's parbegin, parend, but the constituent parts of a `conc` object are systems (as in CSP) and not arbitrary imperatives.

Synchronization between system objects is similar to the handshake in CSP or rendezvous in Ada. In CSP, both the sender part and the receiver part in a communication must be named. In Ada, only the sender must name the receiver, whereas the receiver accepts all systems. The BETA approach includes these two extremes as special cases.

Few programming languages support compound systems in a general sense. In Ada, for example, it is possible to specify compound systems in the form of nested tasks. However, the communication with internal tasks is limited. It is not possible in Ada to call entry procedures of internal tasks of a task.

The idea of using semaphores and abstract classes and procedures to define higher level concurrency abstractions was first proposed by Jean Vaucher in (Vaucher, 1975), where it was shown how to define a monitor abstraction.

Most concurrent programming languages have built-in mechanisms for concurrency, communication and synchronization. The actual mechanisms differ from language to language. Monitors and rendezvous are typical examples. BETA has currently no built-in mechanisms except for semaphore and fork, because it is possible to define abstract patterns for many of the commonly used high-level constructs. Experience with this strategy may, however, imply that some built-in mechanisms should be introduced.

Chapter 15

Nondeterministic Alternation

In Chapter 13 the notion of *alternation* was introduced. Alternation is a sequencing form used to describe a system that executes several activities, but at most one at a time. As mentioned in the introduction to Chapter 13, alternation is a useful mechanism for modeling agents that alternates between a number of more or less independent activities. Alternation may also be used to structure a program using components without explicitly having to synchronize access to common objects. This is in contrast to concurrency, which is a sequencing form used for describing a system that executes several activities at the same time. In the concurrent situation, access to shared objects may have to be synchronized.

Alternating execution of components may be used to handle the *nondeterminism* of communication in a system of concurrent components. A component involved in communications with more than one component may then wait for one or more acts of communication at the same time.

In many situations the different acts of communication are more or less independent. Assume that the system `A` communicates with systems `B`, `C`, `D` and `E`. Then it may be that the acts of communication with `B` and `C` are performed in one sequence and the acts of communication with `D` and `E` are performed in another sequence, but there is no sequencing between the two groups of communication. In such a situation it may be more natural to describe the communication sequences by means of alternating components. In the above example, system `A` can be described as a compound system consisting of two alternating components, one for communication with `B` and `C` and another for communication with `D` and `E`. In the next section we show how to describe this situation in BETA.

In Chapter 13, deterministic alternation (coroutine sequencing) has been described. In this chapter the nondeterministic form of alternation will be presented. Nondeterministic alternation is only meaningful together with concurrency. A system object executing concurrently with other systems may be involved in a number of ongoing dialogs with some of the other systems. Such a system will typically start an internal component (coroutine) for each such ongoing dialog. These components will then be executed alternately, and the scheduling will be nondeterministic depending on when the other systems are ready to communicate.

The mechanism for specifying alternation is not a primitive language mechanism, but is defined as an attribute of the `System` pattern.

15.1 Alternating execution of components

The following example shows a BETA program containing three components `C1, C2` and `C3`:

```
System
(# C1: @ | System(# ... SUSPEND ... #);
   C2: @ | System(# ... SUSPEND ... #);
   C3: @ | System(# ... SUSPEND ... #)
do alt(# do C1.start; C2.start; C3.start #)
#)
```

`C1`, `C2` and `C3` are objects of the *component* kind. Components may be executed alternately as specified by the imperative:

```
alt(#do C1.start; C2.start; C3.start #)
```

The `alt` pattern is an attribute of `System`. Alternating execution means that at most one of the components is executing its action part at a time. The components not executing actions are delayed at well defined points in their action sequence. These points are the same at which interleaving (i.e. shift of execution to another component) may take place. Interleaving may take place (1) at the beginning of the action-part of the component, (2) when the component is attempting to communicate (see below), and (3) when the component has suspended its action-sequence.

As mentioned, interleaving may, for instance, take place when the active components attempt to communicate with another component. *Communicate* here means that the component attempts to execute either an entry operation or an accept.

The situation mentioned at the beginning of this chapter with a system `A` performing one communication sequence with `B` and `C` and another sequence with `D` and `E` may take place as follows:

(1) The sequence involving `B` and `C` may, for example, be as follows: (a) `B` attempts to execute an entry operation `A.putB`, which will have to match a corresponding operation `PB.accept` executed by `A`; (b) `A` will then execute some actions `I1`; (c) `A` will then attempt to execute

```
(# A: @ | system
     (# PB: @port; putB: PB.entry(#...#);
        X1: @ | system
          (#
          do cycle(#do PB.accept; I1; C.putC; I2
          #);
        PD: @port; putD: PD.entry(#...#);
        X2: @ | system
          (#
          do cycle(#do PD.accept; J1; E.putE; J2
          #)
     do alt(#do X1.start; X2.start #)
     #);
   B: @ | system(#do ...; A.putB; ... #);
   C: @ | system
     (# PC: @port; putC: PC.entry(#...#)
     do ...; PC.accept; ...
     #);
   D: @ | system(#do ...; A.putD; ... #);
   E: @ | system
     (# PE: @port; putD: PE.entry(#...#)
     do ...; PE.accept; ...
     #);
do conc(#do A.start; B.start; C.start; D.start; E.start #)
#)
```

Figure 15.1 A skecth of an alternating system A.

an entry operation C.putC; (d) A will then execute some actions I2; (e) This sequence may be repeated.

(2) A similar sequence may be performed involving D and E.

This scenario is described in Figure 15.1. Note that A has two internal components, X1 and X2, each executing one of the sequences mentioned above. The alt control-pattern performs an alternating execution of X1 and X2, in which case at most one of X1 and X2 is executing at the same time.

Execution may alternate between X1 and X2 at the communication points PB.accept;, C.getC, PD.accept and E.putE. For example, if X1 is executing and it attempts to execute PB.accept, but B is not ready to execute A.putB, then X1 may be temporarily suspended and X2 may be resumed.

At some point, both `X1` and `X2` may be delayed while waiting for communication to take place: `X1` may be waiting at `PB.accept` and `X2` may be waiting at `E.putE`. The `X1` system may resume when `B` is ready to communicate, and `X2` may resume when `E` is ready to communicate. In this situation, `A` may be seen as waiting for a communication with either `B` or `C`, and it communicates with the first one which is ready.

The system `A` may be characterized as executing the following interleaved sequences of imperatives:

S1: `PB.accept; I1; C.putC; I2; PB.accept; I1; C.getC; I2;` ...

S2: `PD.accept; J1; E.putE; J2; PD.accept; J1; E.putE; J2;` ...

The S1 sequence is generated by `X1` and the S2 sequence is generated by `X2`. The two sequences are interleaved at the communication points `PB.accept`, `C.putC`, `PD.accept` and `E.putE`. The following sequence is one example of a possible interleaving of S1 and S2

```
PB.accept; I1; PD.accept; J1; E.putE; J2; C.putC; I2;
PD.accept; J1; PB.accept; I1; C.putC; I2; E.putE; J2; ...
```

15.2 A distributed calendar

Consider a distributed calendar system. Each person in an organization has a calendar object which keeps track of days where the person is engaged in meetings. For simplicity, a meeting is always one day.

A person who wants to arrange a meeting for a group of people can attempt to reserve a meeting date for this group. The calendar system then checks if the requested date is free, and checks with the calendars of those people involved if the date requested is free. If the date is free for all those involved, the date will be reserved.

While a calendar system is checking with the people involved in the requested meeting, it must be able to answer requests for meetings from other calendar systems.

In Figures 15.2 and 15.3 a `Calendar` pattern is described. For simplicity, only `Calendar` objects are assumed, i.e. no objects representing persons are included. This means that instead of reserving a meeting date for a group of people, a meeting is reserved for a group of `Calendar` objects.

The `ownerHandler` takes care of an initial reservation from the owner of the calendar. The `start`-port represents a state where the `ownerHandler` is ready to accept the `reserve` operation for reserving a meeting. The `end`-port represents a state where the `ownerHandler` is

```
Calendar: system
  (# days: [365] @integer; {representation of the calendar dates}
     ownerHandler: @ | system
       (# day: @integer; {date for initiated meeting}
          group: ^Calendars; {involved Calendars}
          start: @port;
          reserve: @start.entry
            (# D: @day; G: ^Calendars
            enter(D,G[]) do D->day; G[]->Group[]
            #);
          Ok: @boolean;
          checkGroup:
            (#
            do (if days[day]//free then
                   tmpBooked->days[day]; true->Ok;
                   group.scan
                   (#
                   do (day->theCalendar.othersHandler.reserve)
                       and Ok->Ok
                   #);
                   group.scan
                   (#
                   do Ok->theCalendar.othersHandler.confirm
                   #)
                   (if Ok//true then booked->days[day]
                    else free->days[day]
            if)if)#);
          end: @port;
          confirm: end.entry
            (# ok: @boolean do Ok->ok exit ok #);
       do cycle(#do start.accept; checkGroup; end.accept#)
       #);
     othersHandler: @ I system (# ... #)
  do alt(#do ownerHandler.start; othersHandler.start #)
  #)
```

Figure 15.2 A distributed calendar.

ready to accept the `confirm` operation, which informs the owner about whether or not the meeting could be reserved.

When a `reserve`-operation has been executed, the procedure pattern `checkDate` checks whether it is possible to reserve a meeting for that day.

```
othersHandler: @ | system
  (# start: @port;
     day: @integer;
     reserve: @start,entry
       (# d: @integer;
       enter d
       do (if (days[d->day]=free)->ok
           //true then tmpBooked->days[d]
          if)
       exit ok
       #);
     end: @port;
     confirm: end.port
       (# ok: @boolean
       enter ok
       do (if ok//true then booked->days[day]
           else free->days[day]
       if)#);
  do cycle(# start.accept; end.accept #)
  #)
```

Figure 15.3 The `othersHandler` of the distributed calendar.

First, the day must be free for the owner of the calendar. If this is the case, then the day is checked with all members of the group. Each group member is temporarily asked to reserve the day, returning true or false depending on whether or not they can. Finally, all members of the group are informed about whether or not the day is actually reserved.

The `othersHandler` takes care of the requests from other calendar systems. The `reserve` operation handles an initial reservation request from another calendar. It may immediately return false if the day is not free, otherwise it will make a temporary reservation. The `confirm` operation either books the day or frees the temporary reservation, depending on the enter parameter.

The `Calendars` pattern will not be given in detail. It represents a set of `Calendar` objects. It has a scan operation with the index variable `theCalendar` that iterates over all members of the set.

The elements of the repetition `days` may have the values `free`, `tmpBooked` or `booked`. These values may be implemented as integer values.

```
(# Buffer: System
     (# S: [S.range] @char; in,out: @integer;
        InPort,OutPort: @Port;
        Put: InPort.entry
          (# ch: @char
          enter ch
          do ch->S[in]; (in mod S.range)+1->in
          #);
        Get: OutPort.entry
          (# ch: @char
          do S[(out mod S.range)+1->out]->ch
          exit ch
          #);
        PutHandler: @ | System
          (#
          do Cycle(#
             do (if in // out then Pause {Buffer is full}
                    else InPort.accept; {accept Put}
          if)#)#);
        GetHandler: @ | System
          (#
          do Cycle(#
             do (if in // (out mod S.range +1))
                    then {Buffer is empty}
                    else OutPort.accept; {accept Put}
            if)#)#)
     do 1->in; S.range->out;
        alt(#do PutHandler.start; Gethandler.start #)
     #);
  Prod: @ | System(# ... ch -> Buf.Put; ... #);
  Buf: @ | Buffer;
  Cons: @ | System(# ... Buf.Get->ch; ... #)
do conc(#do Prod.start; Buf.start; Cons.start #)
#)
```

Figure 15.4 Bounded buffer with alternating components.

15.3 Bounded buffer

The example in Figure 15.4 describes a bounded buffer implemented using alternation. The internal components `PutHandler` and `GetHandler` control communication with the `Buffer`-system; `PutHandler` takes care

```
ExtendedBuffer: Buffer
  (# GetRear: OutPort.entry
       (# ch: @char
       do S[(in+S.range-1) mod S.range -> in] -> ch
       exit ch
       #);
  #)
```

Figure 15.5 Extended buffer.

of a sequence of Put-communications, and GetHandler takes care of a sequence of Get-communications.

The imperative Pause specifies that this is a point where interleaving may take place. Pause is not specified here, but may be implemented as a communication with some system in the environment, such as a timer-system.

Since the execution of the PutHandler and GetHandler components is alternating, each component has exclusive access to the buffer representation. Interleaving may only take place at InPort.accept, OutPort.accept and Pause.

In Figure 15.5 a sub-pattern of Buffer is defined. A new operation, GetRear, for also taking elements out from the rear of the buffer is added, showing that it is possible to add operations to a port, and thereby specialize the protocol of Buffer.

15.4 A simple game

Consider a very simple game between a player and a 'game process.' The game process is either in an even or an odd state. If the player probes the game process when it is in an even state, the player loses and the score is decreased by some value. If the game process is in the odd state, the player wins and his/her score is increased by some value. At random, the game process may change state, from even to odd or from odd to even. Also, the game process may change the value by which the score of the player is increased or decreased. The change of state and increment value is initiated by a demon process. The game process is thus constantly involved in a communication sequence with the player and the demon process.

A concurrent system representing a game-system, demon-system and a Player-system is described in Figures 15.6 and 15.7. Figure 15.6 shows

```
system
(# game: @ | system
     (# odd: (#exit 1 #); even: (#exit 0 #);
        state,score,inc: @integer;
        playerHandler: @ | system(# ... #);
        demonHandler: @ | system(# ... #);
     do alt(#do playerHandler.start; demonHandler.start #)
     #);
   demon: @ | system
     (#
     do cycle
        (# score: @integer
        do game.demonHandler.bump; random->pause;
           (if random mod 2 // 1 then
               game.demonHandler.changeInc->score;
               (if score<100//true then
                   1->game.demonHandler.setInc
                else 10->game.demonHandler.setInc
     if)if)#)#);
   player: @ | system
     (#
     do game.playerHandler.startGame; ...
        game.playerHandler.probe;...
        game.PlayerHandler.endGame
     #)
do conc(#do game.start; demon.start; player.start #)
#)
```

Figure 15.6 Overall structure of simple game system.

the overall structure of the concurrent system, including details of the demon-system and the player-system. The game system consists of two internal alternating systems, playerHandler and demonHandler. The details of these two systems are shown in Figure 15.7.

The playerHandler handles communication with the player and may be in one of three states: start, playing and final. Each state is represented by a port. In a start state, the startGame operation will be accepted; in a playing state, the probe and endGame operations will be accepted; in a final state, score will be accepted.

The demonHandler may be in two states, P1 and P2, also represented by ports. In state P1, the bump and changeInc operations are accepted; in state P2, the setInc operation will be accepted.

```
playerHandler: @ | system
  (# start: @port; {initial state: accepting StartGame}
     startGame: start.entry
       (#
       do 0->score; false->stopped; even->state; 1->inc
       #);
     playing: @port; {playing state: accepting Result, EndGame}
     probe: playing.entry
       (#
       do (if state
           // even then score-inc->score
           // odd then score+inc->score
          if)
       #);
     endGame: playing.entry(#do true->stop #);
     final: @port; {final state: accepting score}
     score: playing.entry(#do {display final value of score} #);
     stop: @boolean
  do start.accept;
     play:
       (#
       do playing.accept; (if stop//false then restart play if)
       #);
     final.accept
  #);
demonHandler: @ | system
  (# P1: @port;
     bump: P1.entry(#do (state+1) mod 2 -> state #);
     changeInc: P1.entry
       (# v: @integer do score->v; true->newInc exit v #);
     P2: @port;
     setInc: P2.entry(# v: @integer enter v do v->inc #);
     newInc: @boolean
  do cycle
     (#do P1.accept;
          (if newInc//true then P2.accept; false->newInc if)
     #)
  #);
```

Figure 15.7 Details of playerHandler and demonHandler.

The `demon` is represented by a concurrent system that performs a `bump` operation on the game at irregular intervals (controlled by a random number generator, not shown here). Sometimes the `demon` informs the game that it wants to change the value (`inc`) used to increment/decrement the score. The actual change of this value is dependent on the current score (`score`) of the player.

The player is also represented by a concurrent system that performs various operations on `game.playerHandler`.

15.5 Notes

A program describing a number of concurrent processes will usually involve nondeterminism. This is the case since the speed of independent processes cannot be predicted. Several different language mechanisms have been proposed to deal with nondeterminism, including the guarded I/O commands of CSP, which also appear in Ada. Guarded I/O commands introduce nondeterminism into a single sequential process. Alternating execution may be seen as an alternative to guarded commands. Instead of having nondeterminism in each system object, the nondeterminism is described as alternating the execution of component objects.

By using alternation and compound objects instead of guarded commands, logically independent action sequences are mixed into one action sequence. This may make the structure of the resulting program more clear. In addition, it simplifies implementation. A CSP-process and an Ada-task may have several open channels of communication waiting at one time. When a communication takes place it is possible that other open channels of communication of the objects involved must be closed. In BETA, each object may wait for at most *one* communication. No open channel of communication needs to be closed when a communication takes place. Finally, in CSP and Ada the use of input and output as guards is not symmetric: it is only possible to have input-commands (accept-statements) in a guarded command. The possibility of allowing output-commands as guards in CSP is mentioned in (Hoare, 1978). However, symmetric use of input-/output-guards greatly complicates the implementation.

Technically, most programs using alternation could be simulated by programs using concurrency, but concurrency implies that each system executes actions with a positive speed. On a single processor this implies time sharing using a clock. Some implementations of concurrency avoid this by shifting to another process only at a point of communication. If this is the case, the program actually consists of alternating components and not of concurrent systems. In a concurrent program no looping system can monopolize the processor, whereas this *is* the case with an alternating program.

Alternation is not an alternative to concurrency, but a supplement. A number of activities are, by their nature, alternating and nondeterministic, and such activities should not be modeled by concurrent systems, coroutines or guarded commands.

Chapter 16

Exception Handling

A large part of any software design is the handling of error situations or rare situations that are unlikely to happen. Consider the `Register` example in Figure 5.2. A register can hold up to 100 integers. If an attempt is made to insert more than 100 integers using the `Insert` pattern there is a problem. At the point of the comment {`Overflow`}, some code for dealing with this situation must be inserted. For 'small' programs it is common to print an error message and terminate the program execution. The user must then increase the constant 100, recompile the program and execute it again.

For most non-trivial programs it is not satisfactory just to terminate the program with an error message. Consider the situation where the register is part of a word processor program. An error message saying that some internal register has overflowed is in general not meaningful to a user of such a word processor. Furthermore, the user will not be able to increase constants of possible tables. Another example is a flight reservation system. Such a system runs over a very long period of time, and it would not be acceptable if a table overflow simply resulted in an error message and a subsequent termination of the program.

The program fragment using the `Register` pattern may of course keep track of how many elements are stored in a given `Register` object and then take some special action if more than 100 elements are to be inserted. This may, however, imply that the program is greatly complicated with code that tests for such rare situations. The code for the 'normal' situations may then be difficult to read. It would be desirable if the code for handling the 'rare' situations could be separated from the code handling the 'normal' situations.

There are many types of errors or exceptional situations which a program may have to deal with. An *exception* is a class of computational states that requires an extraordinary computation. It is not possible to give a precise definition of when a computational state should be classified as an *exception occurrence*; this is a decision for the programmer. In practice, most people have a good feeling of what is the 'main' computation and what are exceptional situations. The exceptional situations are all those situations which imply that the 'main' computation fails. The following is a list of examples of situations that are often considered exceptional:

Overflow of tables The example described above with table overflow in a `Register` object is typical for a large number of situations. Most software has objects with finite tables that may overflow.

Undefined results A procedure or function may not have a well defined result for all possible input parameters. One example of this is division by zero, and another is a procedure for inverting a matrix. If the matrix is singular, then the inverse is not well defined.

Incorrect usage by the user A user using a program or application in an erroneous way is one example of getting undefined results. Giving wrong input to a program is a common mistake made by users. In some situations this could be treated as an exception, but in many situations a program taking complex input is equipped with an input checker. A compiler is an example of this. In other situations it should be an explicit part of the user interface design.

Inconsistent data Programs often communicate by means of files: one program writes a file to be read by another program. The information on the file may then be written in a format agreed upon by the authors of the two programs. The data file could be inconsistent for a number of reasons: there could be errors in the first program, some other program could have manipulated the file, by mistake some other file could be used as input to the second program, etc.

A document saved by a word processor often has special information used by the word processor. It should be able to handle possible inconsistencies in this file.

Operating system errors Consider a word processor. When a document is saved, it may be that there is no more disk space. The user may try to open a document which cannot be interpreted by the word processor. The user may attempt to modify a document owned by another user. If the word processor does not handle such situations, the operating system will usually terminate the word processor with an error message which may not be meaningful to the user.

Language defined errors Run-time errors such as index errors and attempts to use NONE references may appear in even well tested programs. Since such situations appear because of errors in the program, it is in general difficult to recover from such errors. However, the program should at least terminate with an informative message.

Numeric errors Computers only support numbers with a finite amount of values. This means that the result of an arithmetic operation may result in a number which cannot be represented by the hardware. This kind of *arithmetic overflow* is an example of an exception.

A program must be able to deal with exceptions. A good design rule is to list explicitly the situations that may cause a program to *break down.* Many programming languages have special constructs for describing *exception handling.* In BETA, exception handling is usually described by means of virtual patterns. The purpose of this chapter is to show how to use virtual patterns for exception handling.

From the above discussion an exception handling mechanism should provide the following support:

Meaningful error messages As a minimum it should be possible to provide meaningful error messages when an exception occurs.

Recovery The program using an object should be provided with the possibility to recover from an exception raised by the object. Sometimes the recovery will be transparent in the sense that the 'normal' control flow may continue. In other situations the recovery may imply a termination or restart of part of the computation.

Separation of control flow The code for dealing with an exception should be isolated from the code handling the 'normal' case so as not to disturb the readability. Also an explicit indication of possible exceptions may be a useful property of a program.

In the following sections, a technique for using virtual patterns for exception handling will be presented. We start by introducing a simple version of exception patterns and show how these may be used for overriding error messages and for doing recovery from the exceptions (Sections 16.1–16.3). In Section 16.4 the difference between associating exceptions with class patterns and procedure patterns is described. System exceptions and language-defined exceptions are described in Sections 16.5 and 16.6, respectively. Finally, a more advanced design of exception patterns is described in Section 16.7.

16.1 Simple exceptions

In this section a simple use of exception patterns is shown. Consider the Register pattern in Figure 16.1 (it is a slightly revised version of the Register pattern from Chapter 5, Figure 5.2). The Register pattern is extended with two exception patterns. Overflow is invoked when the register overflows, and NotFound is invoked when an attempt is made to delete a key which is not in the register. These two exceptions represent two different classes of exceptions: the Overflow exception is fatal in the sense that it is probably not meaningful to continue the program; the NotFound exception may perhaps be an error. For many applications of Register it may not be an error to attempt to remove an element that is not in the register. Both exception patterns are sub-patterns of the Exception pattern, which describes the general properties of exceptions. Exception will be defined below.

Consider an application that has a register of registration numbers of some kind. The object Registrations represents this register. The Overflow exception is handled and the application terminates, but it overrides the default error message with one that is more meaningful for the user. The NotFound exception is not considered fatal, but a message describing the event is displayed to the user. The execution of an Exception instance will by default result in termination of the program unless a Continue has been executed. As can be seen, an explicit Continue is executed by NotFound:

```
Registrations: @Register
  (# Overflow::<
       (#
       do 'Too many registration numbers.'->msg.append;
          'Program terminates.'->msg.append
       #);
     NotFound::<
       (#
       do 'Attempt to delete:' ->PutText;
          key->screen.putInt;
          'which is not in the register'->PutText;
          Continue
       #)
  #)
```

```
Register:
  (# Table: [100] @integer; Top:  @integer;
     Init: (#do 0->Top #);
     Has: {Test if Key in Table[1:Top]}
       (# Key: @integer; Result: @boolean;
       enter Key
       do ...
       exit Result
       #);
     Insert: {Insert New in Table}
       (# New: @integer
       enter New
       do (if (New->&Has) // False then {New is not in Table}
              Top+1->Top;
              (if (Top<=Table.Range)
               // True then New->Table[Top]
               else
                 Overflow {An Overflow exception is raised}
       if)if)#);
      Remove: {Remove Key from Table}
        (# Key: @integer
        enter key
        do (Search:
              (for inx: Top repeat
                   (if Table[inx] // Key then
                       {remove key}
                       leave Search
              if)for);
              key->NotFound; {A NotFound exception is raised}
        :Search)#);
     Overflow:< Exception
       (#do 'Register overflow'->msg.Append; INNER #);
     NotFound:< Exception
       (# key: @integer
       enter key
       do key->msg.putInt;
          ' is not in register'->msg.Append;
          INNER
       #);
  #)
```

Figure 16.1 Pattern Register with exception patterns.

The Exception pattern may be defined as follows:

```
Exception:
  (# msg: @text;
     cont: @boolean;
     Continue: (# do true->cont #);
     Terminate: (#do false->cont #)
  do 'Program execution terminated due to exception'
       ->msg;
     INNER;
     (if cont//false then
         msg->PutText;
         {Terminate program execution}
     if)
  #);
```

The text object msg is supposed to hold a text to be displayed to the user in case the exception leads to termination of the program. The msg text is given a default value in the exception pattern. In sub-patterns of Exception, it is possible either to append more text to the message or override the message. In the Register pattern more text is appended. In the instance Registrations, the message is overridden in the Overflow pattern, whereas it is not used in NotFound as this exception continues execution.

The default action of an exception is to terminate execution, but this termination may be avoided by specifying an explicit Continue. The rationale behind this is that an exception is an error that must explicitly be dealt with by the programmer.

In the above example, NotFound is not considered to be an error for Registrations. This will probably be the case for most instances of Register. Also, it may not even be necessary to display a message, i.e. NotFound will be ignored. Each such instance of Register must, however, explicitly call Continue for NotFound. It would be more convenient if the programmer did not have to specify a handler in these cases. To do this, it must be specified within Register that the default for NotFound will be to continue execution. This can be done by inserting a call to Continue within the description of NotFound in Register. The call to Continue should be inserted before inner, since the sub-patterns of NotFound are able to override the continue by execution of Terminate.

A virtual pattern dealing with an exception is called an *exception pattern*, or just an *exception*. The invocation of an exception pattern is called an *exception occurrence*. An exception is said to be *raised* when an exception pattern is invoked. The object-descriptor associated with an exception pattern is called a *handler* or an *exception handler.*

An exception pattern defined in a pattern will be the *default handler* for the exception in the case where no further binding of it is made. A sub-pattern may extend the default handler by a further binding. A specific *instance handler* may be associated with each instance by instantiating a singular object with a further binding of the exception pattern.

16.2 Recovery

The handler associated with `Overflow` in `Registrations` provides a new error message, whereafter the program execution is terminated. The handler could instead execute a `Continue`, implying that the corresponding element would not be inserted in the table. Often the handler may be able to recover from the exception and continue the execution as if the exception had not appeared. In the register example it might be possible for the handler to remove some of the elements from the table, move some elements to another table or extend the size of the table. Whether or not this is possible will of course depend on the actual usage of the `Register`.

In BETA it is actually possible to extend the size of a repetition. An evaluation of the form:

```
25->Table.extend
```

will extend `Table` by 25 elements. An overflow handler for `Register` could then be defined as follows:

```
Register:
  (# Overflow:< Exception
       (#
       do Continue;
          INNER;
          (Table.range div 4)->Table.extend
       #);
     Insert:
       (# New: @integer
       enter New
       do (if (New->&Has) // false then
             {New is not in Table}
             Top+1->Top
             (if (Top<=Table.Range)
              //false then Overflow
             if);
             New->Table[Top]
```

```
            if)#);
            ...
    #)
```

The default handler for `Register` will execute a `Continue` and extend the size of `Table` by 25%. A further binding of `Overflow` may override the effect of continue. Also note the change in `Insert`: if control is returned to `Insert` after the execution of `Overflow`, it is assumed that the exceptional situation has been repaired by the handler, i.e. `Insert` may continue.

16.3 Partial recovery

Often it is not possible to do the simple kind of recovery mentioned in the preceding section. It may be necessary to interrupt the control flow and escape to an outer level in order to do the recovery. To do this there must be a well defined control point that can be used to break the current computation. Such a control point can be defined as a label, and the handler may then exit to this label by means of `leave` or `restart`, as illustrated in the next example:

```
do ...
   L: (# R: @Register(# Overflow::<(#do ... leave L #)#)
      do ... I->R.Insert; ...
      #);
   ...
```

In the case of an `Overflow` being raised by `Insert`, the execution of the object containing the declaration of `R` is terminated. This is a drastic way of handling the exception, since the `R` register including all its elements is abandoned. However, in many situations it is a better alternative than terminating the entire program execution.

In some situations the handler may be able to make a partial recovery and restart the computation from some point. This would correspond to replacing `leave` with `restart` in the above example. An example of this kind of partial recovery is given below.

16.4 Handlers for procedure patterns

The above examples have shown examples of associating handlers with class patterns. Such handlers will be the same for all activations of procedure patterns associated with the object, i.e. the code may have several invocations of, for example, `Insert`, and exceptions raised by all these

Inserts will have the same handler. In many situations it would be desirable to associate different handlers with the different invocations. This is possible by defining an exception pattern as an attribute of Insert. Consider the following description of Register:

```
Register:
  (# ...
     Insert: {Insert New in Table}
       (# Overflow:< {Procedure level exception}
            Exception(# ... #);
          New: @integer
       enter New
       do (if (New->&Has)
           // false then {New is not in Table}
              Top+1->Top
              (if (Top<=Table.Range)
               // false then Overflow if);
              New->Table[Top]
       if)#);
     Overflow:<
       Exception(# ... #); {Class level exception}
  #)
```

Handlers for different invocations of Insert may now be defined as follows:

```
(# R: @Register
     (# Overflow::<(# ... #); {Class handler for R} #)
do ...
   I->R.Insert
        (# Overflow::<(# ... #); {Procedure handler} #)
   ...
   J->R.Insert
        (# Overflow::<(# ... #); {Procedure handler} #)
   ...
#)
```

It may appear that there is no use for the class handler since only the procedure handlers associated with Insert will be called. However, the local procedure handlers may invoke the class handler if they are unable to deal with the situation:

```
I->R.Insert(# Overflow::<(#do ... R.Overflow #) #)
```

The situation where an exception handler invokes an enclosing handler is called *exception propagation.*

Sometimes it is desirable to automatically propagate an exception. In the above example there may be a mixture of invocations of `Insert` where some have a local procedure handler and others do not. For those which do not have a procedure handler it would be desirable for the exception to be automatically propagated to the class handler. This could be specified in the declaration of the exception in `Insert`:

```
Register:
(# Overflow:<(# ... #);
   Insert:
     (# Overflow:< Exception
          (#
          do INNER;
             (if {no binding of Overflow} then
                 this(Register).Overflow
             if)
          #)
        ...
     #)
   ...
#)
```

The idea is that if no binding has been made of `Overflow` in a possible sub-pattern of `Insert`, then the `Overflow` exception of the enclosing `Register` pattern is invoked. In Section 16.7 it is shown how to implement '`no binding of Overflow`'.

16.5 System exceptions

Any implementation of BETA, including the Mjølner BETA System, will provide libraries of patterns and objects for interfacing to the underlying operating system. A good example of this is a `File` pattern for interfacing to the file system of the computer. A large number of error conditions may appear when manipulating files. Below a simple version of a file[1] pattern is given, together with possible exceptions that may be raised.

```
File:
  (# name: @text; {The logical name of the file}
```

[1]This is a simplified version of the `File` pattern implemented by the Mjølner BETA System.

```
Open:
  {General super-pattern for OpenRead and OpenWrite}
  (# OpenError: FileException
       (#
       do 'Error during open.'->msg.append; INNER
       #);
     NoSuchFile:< OpenError
       (#
       do 'No such file.'->msg.append; INNER
       #)
  enter name
  do INNER
  #);
OpenRead: Open
  (# NoReadAcess:< OpenError
       (#
       do 'No permission to read.'->msg.append;
          INNER
       #)
  do {open the file for read}
     {May raise NoSuchFile or NoReadAccess}
  #);
OpenWrite: Open
  (# NoReadAccess:< OpenError
      (#
      do 'No permission to write.'->msg.append;
         INNER
      #)
  do {Open this(File) for write}
     {May raise NoSuchFile or NoReadAccess}
  #);
Get:
  (# ch: @char
  do {Get next char to ch}
     {May raise EOFerror}
  exit ch
  #);
Put:
  (# ch: @char
  enter ch
  do {Write ch to file}
     {May raise DiskFull}
  #);
```

```
      Close: (# do {close the file} #);
      Remove: (# do {Remove the file from the disk} #);
      FileException: Exception
        (#do 'Error in file:'->PutText; name->PutText;
             INNER
        #);
      DiskFull:< FileException
        (#do 'No more space on disk'->msg.append;
             INNER
         #);
      EOFerror:< FileException
        (#do 'Attempt to read past end-of-file'
               ->msg.append;
             INNER
        #)
    #)
```

The normal use of a File may be as follows:

```
   (# F: @File
   do {Prompt user for file name}
      N->F.openWrite;
      ...
      ch->F.put;
      ...
      F.close
   #)
```

In the following example, handlers are defined for some of the exceptions. When DiskFull is raised, the file is closed and removed, and the program terminates execution. If the file cannot be opened, or the user has no write permission to the file, the user is asked to try again:

```
   (# F: @File
        (# DiskFull::<
             (#
             do 'Please remove some files from the disk'
                  ->PutText;
                close; Remove; {Close and remove the file}
             #)
        #)
   do GetFileName:
       (#
       do {Prompt user for file name}
          N->F.openWrite
```

```
          (# NoSuchFile::<
               (#
               do 'File does not exist. Try again'
                    ->PutText;
                  Restart GetFileName
               #);
             NoWritePermission::<
               (#
               do 'You do not have write permission'
                    ->PutText;
                  'Try again'->PutText;
                  restart getFileName
               #)
    #)#);
   ...
   ch->F.put;
   ...
   F.close
#)
```

16.6 Language-defined exceptions

Language-defined exceptions have to be dealt with by providing pre-defined patterns in the environment. An implementation of BETA could provide a pre-defined pattern, Program, that has virtual patterns corresponding to all pre-defined language exceptions. The Program pattern could be described as follows:

```
Program:
  (# IndexError:< Exception
       (#
       do 'Index out of range'->msg.append;
           INNER
       #);
     RefIsNone:<  ...
     ArithmeticOverflow:< ...
     DivisionByZero:< ...
  do INNER
  #)
```

A BETA program may then provide handlers for the language-defined exceptions as shown in the following example:

```
Program
(# IndexError::< (# ... #);
   RefIsNone::< (# ... #);
   ArithmeticOverflow::< (# ... #);
   DivisionByZero::< (# ... #);
   ...
do ...
#)
```

The above `Program` provides handlers for all four kinds of exceptions.

It is possible to provide several levels of `Program` objects in order to have different handlers, for example, for `IndexError` in different parts of the program. This is illustrated in the following example:

```
Program
(# IndexError::< (# ... #);
   RefIsNone::< (# ... #);
   ArithmeticOverflow::< (# ... #);
   DivisionByZero::< (# ... #);
   ...
do ...
   Program
   (# IndexError::< {alternative handler for index error}
        (# .. #)
   do ...
   #)
#)
```

In the do-part of the outermost descriptor a new handler for index error is provided. This handler will then handle possible index errors in the innermost `Program` object.

The problem with this approach is that a handler must be supplied for all the language-defined exceptions, since the handlers in the outermost `Program` object are not automatically invoked for exceptions other than `IndexError`. In the next section, a more advanced exception mechanism is provided, which makes it easier to propagate exceptions from an inner `Program` object to an outer `Program` object.

16.7 Advanced design of exception patterns

In this section, a possible design for a more advanced exception mechanism is presented. The goal is to define an exception handling mechanism with the following properties:

- Better support for the propagation of language-defined exceptions that have no handler to a possible outer `Program` object.
- It should be possible to specify another termination level as a default. The simple `Exception` pattern (from the previous sections) terminates the entire program execution as a default action.
- When an object level is terminated, it should be possible to specify some 'clean-up' actions to be executed before termination to ensure *smooth termination.*

This is achieved by combining the `Exception` pattern with the `Program` pattern in the following way:

```
Program:
  (# Exception:
        (#msg: @text;
          cont: @boolean;
          Continue: (# do true->cont #);
          Terminate: (# do false->cont #)
        do 'Program execution terminated due to exception'
              ->msg;
           INNER;
           (if cont//false then
               (if outerMostProgram then msg->PutText if);
               CleanUp;
               leave Program
           if)
        #);
      CleanUp:<(#do INNER #);
      IndexError:< Exception
        (#
        do  (if {No binding} then
                 (if Outer[]<>NONE // True then
                     Outer.IndexError if)if)
            'Index out of range'->msg.append;
            INNER
        #);
     RefIsNone:<  ...
     ArithmeticOverflow:< ...
     DivisionByZero:< ...
     Outer: ^Program;
     DefineOuter:<(#do INNER #)
  do DefineOuter;
     INNER
  #);
```

The exception patterns may be used as follows:

```
(# Main: Program
     (# IndexError::< (# ... #);
        RefIsNone::< (# ... #);
     do ...
        L0:
         Program
         (# IndexError::< (# ... #)
              {New handler for index error}
            DefineOuter::<(#do Main[]->Outer[] #)
              {Propagate other exceptions}
              {to handlers in Main}
            CleanUp::<
              (#do {executed before termination}
                   {of this(Program)}
              #)
         do ...
            L1:
             (# Register: (# ... #)
             do L2:
                 (# Registrations: @Register
                       (# Overflow::< (# do ... #);
                          NotFound::< (# do ... #)
                       #)
                  do ...
                  #);
                 ...
             #);
        ...
        #)
     #)
do Main
#)
```

The options for the handlers of `Overflow` and `NotFound` in `Registrations` are:

(1) Do nothing: in this case the exception will imply a termination of the enclosing `Program` object of the `Register` definition, i.e. `L0` will terminate.

(2) Explicit `leave`: the exception handler may explicitly specify a leave of an arbitrary enclosing level (e.g. `L2, L1, L0` or `Main`).

(3) Explicit `Restart`: the handler may specify a restart of an enclosing level (e.g. `L2, L1, L0` or `Main`).

(4) Explicit `Continue`: the handler may execute `Continue` and thereby resume execution.

The `Program` pattern has attributes for supporting propagation from inner to outer `Program` objects. The `Outer` and `DefineOuter` attributes are used for specifying a `Program` object for propagation of exceptions that have no handlers. Sub-patterns of `Program` can have a further binding of `DefineOuter` for specifying an outer `Program` object. This mechanism assures that all language-defined exceptions except `IndexError` are propagated to the outermost `Program` object.

In some of the above examples, there is a need to test whether or not a virtual pattern has actually been bound in sub-patterns. This is possible using pattern variables. Consider the following example:

```
T: (# V:<  D;
      D:
        (#
        do ...
           INNER;
           (if V## // D## then {No further binding} if)
        #)
   #)
```

This is only possible using the above form of virtual specification. For the shorthand form:

```
V:< (# do ... INNER ... #)
```

it is not possible, since `V##` will refer to the actual binding of `V`. This means that we have to modify some of the `Exception` patterns in the above examples. It is possible to imagine a more explicit support in BETA for testing whether or not a virtual pattern has a further binding. This may be included in future versions of BETA.

16.8 Exercises

(1) Redo Exercise 1 in Chapter 11 such that an exception is raised when `R` is not `qualified` by `T`.

(2) Modify the `Register` in Figure 16.1 such that an exception is raised if an attempt is made to insert an element already in the register. What should the default behavior of this exception be?

16.9 Notes

The foundation of exception handling is the pioneering work by J.B. Goodenough (Goodenough, 1975). Most procedural languages with special language facilities for exception handling are more or less directly based on this work (e.g. languages like Clu and Ada). Several object-oriented languages have included special language facilities for exception handling (e.g. Smalltalk, Eiffel and C++).

All these facilities employ a dynamic approach to finding the handlers of a particular exception. This implies (with variations) that the handler for an exception is found by traversing the call chain of procedure invocations and enclosed blocks backwards, until a block or a procedure invocation is found in which a handler for the exception is defined. This dynamic approach implies the separate definition of the exception and the handler, and association of the exception with the handler based on the dynamic behavior of the program. This implies that it is very difficult to trace the exceptional computation (this works somewhat like a series of computed GOTOs), and it is very difficult to ensure that all exception occurrences will eventually be handled (i.e. it is very difficult to verify that a program will respond sensibly to all perceived exceptional conditions).[2]

This dynamic behavior (dynamic binding of handlers to exceptions) is often in contrast to the host language (e.g. Ada and Clu) that uses static name binding (e.g. when binding procedure invocations to procedure declarations). This has resulted in criticisms from several sources, e.g. C.A.R. Hoare (Hoare, 1981) states that '... *the objectives of languages including reliability, readability, formality and even simplicity ... have been sacrificed ... by a plethora of features ... many of them unnecessary and some of them, like exception handling, even dangerous.*'

As an alternative to the dynamic approach to exception handling, a proposal has been made for a static approach to exception handling by Jørgen Lindskov Knudsen (Knudsen, 1984; Knudsen, 1987) that is based on the sequel concept proposed by (Tennent, 1977). A sequel is a unification of continuations and procedures in the sense that it is like a procedure, except that it does not return to the point of its invocation, but instead terminates the block in which it is defined. When used for exception handling, this implies that a sequel in one definition defines an exception, its handler and the termination level of the exception (i.e. the enclosing block). The advantage of this approach is that the sequel concept follows the static binding rule of the host language and at the same time allows for efficient exception handling. The static approach

[2]It is important to note that exception handling in any programming language is only capable of handling exceptional conditions that have been perceived during program design.

has been further developed to incorporate support for smooth termination (i.e. allowing for clean-up, etc., of blocks being terminated during an exceptional 'backtrack') (Knudsen, 1987).

The BETA approach to exception handling is inspired by this static approach to exception handling. The rationale for the concrete design has been to introduce static exception handling into BETA without introducing any new language constructs, but instead utilizing the powerful abstraction mechanisms of the language to construct an exception handling concept. Exception handling as described in this chapter is merely a technique for using virtual patterns.

Chapter 17

Modularization

In previous chapters we have introduced language mechanisms for describing objects and patterns of a BETA program execution. In this chapter, language mechanisms for describing the physical organization of BETA programs will be introduced. A non-trivial BETA program will usually consist of several pages, so it is desirable to be able to split such a description into smaller, more manageable units. Such units are in general called *modules*. A module is a convenient part of a program typically kept in a file (or in a database), manipulated by an editor, and translated by a compiler.

Modularization is of the utmost importance when writing programs that are more than small examples. Since the examples must be fairly small in a book like this, it is difficult to adequately illustrate and motivate modularization. The language constructs will be introduced using very small examples to illustrate the principles. The modularization techniques described below are absolutely necessary for large programs and highly recommended even for moderately sized programs. The reasons for this may be summarized as follows:

- Most reasonably sized programs can be conveniently split into modules of logically related elements, since it is cumbersome to handle large programs. Large programs are easier to understand if split into a number of smaller units.
- When editing it is easier to manage a number of small modules instead of one large program.
- When several people are working on a project, each person can work on his own set of modules.
- Modules can be saved in a library and shared by several programs. Good modularization mechanisms will thus improve *reusability* of code as well as designs.

- It is good practice to split a module into *interface modules* (often referred to as *specification modules*) and *implementation modules.* An interface module defines how a module can be used, and an implementation module describes how a module is implemented. This makes it possible to prevent users of a module from seeing details about data representation and implementation of algorithms.
- Certain modules may exist in several *variants.* One example of this is different implementations of the same (interface) module. Another example is variants of a module corresponding to different computers. If a module has several variants it is important that the common part of two or more variants exists in only one copy. It should only be necessary to separate out the code that differs between variants, otherwise maintenance becomes more complicated, since the same change may have to be made for several variants.
- A module may be used as a unit to be *separately compiled.* When changing parts of a large program, it is not acceptable to be forced to recompile the whole program, since this may take several hours. With separate compilation of modules, only the modules that have been changed and those that are affected by these changes have to be recompiled. Below we explain how one module may be affected by changes in another.

In the following section, language constructs for describing modularization are introduced. Thereafter, we discuss how to apply these language constructs and why they are useful and necessary.

17.1 Fragments

The language constructs for describing program modularization are **not** considered part of the BETA language. The reason is that BETA is a language for describing objects and patterns of a BETA *program execution,* while the modularization language is for describing the physical organization of just the *program.* The structuring of the program execution in terms of objects and patterns will of course also be reflected in the program, but in addition the program itself may be organized in modules that do have to follow the structuring in terms of objects and patterns. The two languages are thus intended for quite different purposes. The modularization language is called the *fragment language,* since it describes the organization of BETA programs in terms of *fragments.* (The notion of a fragment will be introduced below.) The fragment language is used for communicating with *The Fragment System,* which is the component of the Mjølner BETA System that handles storing and manipulation of fragments. The terms *fragment language* and *fragment system* are used interchangeably when this causes no confusion.

The fragment language is independent of BETA. The principles behind the fragment language can in fact be used to describe modularization of most programming languages. The fragment language is *grammar-based.* The idea is that any correct sequence of terminal and nonterminal symbols defined by the grammar is a legal module. The fragment language describes how such strings may be combined into larger strings, and is presented here using a graphical syntax, though the fragment language also has a textual syntax which is currently used by the Mjølner BETA System. A future version of the Mjølner BETA System will include support for a graphical syntax such as that used in this book.[1]

17.1.1 Forms

The BETA grammar in Appendix A has the following rule:

```
<ObjectDescriptor> ::= <PrefixOpt> <MainPart>
```

The following strings can be derived from the nonterminal `<ObjectDescriptor>`:

```
(1)     (# T: @Text do 'Hello'->T #)

(2)     (# P: <ObjectDescriptor>; R: ^P
        do (if <Evaluation> // true then &P[]->R[] if)
        #)
```

The first string consists only of terminal symbols. The second string has two unexpanded nonterminals, `<ObjectDescriptor>` and `<Evaluation>`. In Figure 17.1, other examples of strings derived from nonterminals of the BETA grammar are shown.

A string of terminal and nonterminal symbols derived from a nonterminal `A` is called an `A`-*form* , or sometimes just a *form* [2]. The derived strings in Figure 17.1 are all examples of forms. Forms are the basic elements used to define modules in the Mjølner BETA System. The fragment language has language constructs for combining forms into complete programs. Consider, for example, the forms 3 and 4 in Figure 17.1. By substituting the `DoPart` nonterminal of form 3 by form 4 we get the following form:

---

[1] In addition to the use of a graphical syntax, the fragment language described in this book is slightly more general than the actual implementation. For details, see the Mjølner BETA System manuals.

[2] In formal language theory this is called a *sentential form.*

	Nonterminal	Examples of derived forms
1.	<Attributes>	P: (# a,b: @integer #); R: ^P
2.	<AttributeDecl>	X: @integer
3.	<PatternDecl>	Foo: (# a,b,c: @integer enter(a,b) <DoPart> exit c #)
4.	<DoPart>	do a*b->c
5.	<Imp>	(if B//True then <Imp> if)
6.		(for <Index> repeat <IfImp> for)
7.	<IfImp>	(if B//True then <Imp> if)
8.	<ForImp>	(for <Index> repeat <IfImp> for)

Figure 17.1 Nonterminals and examples of corresponding derived forms.

```
Foo: (# a,b,c: @integer
     enter(a,b)
     do a*b->c
     exit c
     #)
```

The fragment language is a notation for describing how nonterminals in one form may be replaced by other forms.

17.1.2 Slots

A form may contain several nonterminals having the same syntactic category. This is the case in the following form:

```
Stack:
  (# Push: (# e: @integer enter e <DoPart> #);
     Pop: (# e: @integer <DoPart> exit e #)
  #)
```

which has two <DoPart> nonterminals. In the fragment language it is necessary to be able to refer separately to each nonterminal. Each nonterminal must therefore have a name which uniquely identifies it.

In the Mjølner BETA System, several tools manipulate forms, thus not all nonterminals are necessarily to be used by the fragment system. The nonterminals used by the fragment language are called *slots* since they define openings where other forms may be inserted. They are marked by the keyword `SLOT`. A nonterminal defining a slot has the syntax:

```
<<SLOT T:A>>
```

where `T` is the name of the slot and `A` is the syntactic category. Also note that slots are enclosed by `<<` and `>>` instead of `<` and `>`. This is done purely for technical reasons. A nonterminal must begin with a symbol (here `<<`), which is not in the vocabulary of the language. Since `<` is used as `less than` in BETA, it cannot be used to begin a nonterminal.

The above form may instead be described as follows:

```
Stack:
  (# Push: (# e: @integer enter e <<SLOT Push:DoPart>> #);
     Pop: (# e: @integer <<SLOT Pop:DoPart>> exit e #)
  #)
```

Slot names and BETA names belong to different languages, thus there is no possibility of confusing BETA names and slot names. In the above example there is a pattern called `Push` and a slot called `Push`. As we shall see later, it is conventional to use identical names in this manner.

17.1.3 Fragment-form

In the fragment language, each form must be given a name and its syntactic category specified. A *fragment-form* is a form associated with a name and a syntactic category having the following syntax. As noted earlier, the syntax of the fragment language is mainly graphical:

F:A
`ff`

`F` is the name of the fragment-form, `A` is the syntactic category, and `ff` is a form, i.e. `ff` is a string of terminal and nonterminal symbols derived from `A`.

The following is an example of a fragment-form:

Counter:PatternDecl

```
Counter:
  (# Up: (# n: @integer enter n <<SLOT Up:DoPart>> #);
     Down: (# n: @integer <<SLOT Down:DoPart>> exit n #)
  #)
```

17.1.4 Fragment-group

Often it is convenient to define a set of logically related fragment-forms together. For this purpose it is possible to define a group of fragments, called a *fragment-group*, which has the following syntax:

```
NAME 'F'
F1:A1
ff1
F2:A2
ff2
...
Fn:An
ffn
```

that defines a fragment-group with the name `F` consisting of n fragment-forms. The name of fragment-form i is `Fi`, its syntactic category is `Ai` and the actual fragment-form is `ffi`.

The following is an example of a fragment-group:

```
Up:DoPart
do n+7->n
Down:DoPart
do n-5->n
```

The term *fragment* refers to either a fragment-form or a fragment-group.

17.1.5 Fragment library

The fragment system handles the storing of fragment-groups in a library, called the *fragment library*. The fragment library is usually implemented on top of the computer's file system or database system. The fragment language has constructs for describing how to combine fragments into compound fragments and eventually complete programs. The fragment language refers to fragment-groups stored in the fragment library by means of a *fragment name* (or just *name*). The Mjølner BETA System assumes a hierarchical name structure in the style of UNIX directories or Macintosh folders[3], as shown in Figure 17.2.

[3]The reader is assumed to have some knowledge of such hierarchical file systems.

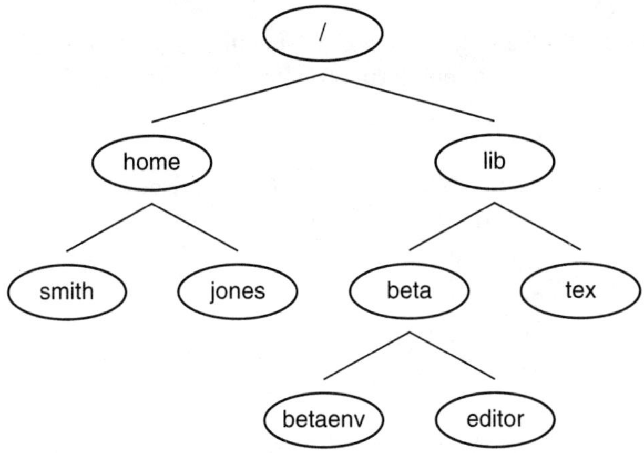

Figure 17.2 Hierarchical directory structure.

In the Mjølner BETA System, fragment-groups are represented as files in such a directory. The name of a fragment-group is given by means of a UNIX-path enclosed in quotes ('). The path:

```
'/home/smith/CounterGroup'
```

denotes a file `CounterGroup` which is supposed to contain a fragment. `CounterGroup` resides in the directory/folder `/home/smith`. In the following examples, the name of a fragment-group will often be given as shown below:

```
NAME '/home/smith/CounterGroup'
----------------------------------
Counter:PatternDecl
----------------------------------
Counter:
  (# Up: (# n: @integer enter n <<SLOT Up:DoPart>> #);
     Down: (# n: @integer <<SLOT Down:DoPart>> exit n #)
  #)
```

For fragment-groups consisting of only one fragment-form, one should not confuse the name of the file/folder containing the fragment-group with the name of the fragment-form. In the above example, `CounterGroup` is the fragment-group (and file/folder) name and `Counter` is the fragment-form name. The file/folder name and the fragment-form name may be identical.

17.1.6 Origin of a fragment-group

The *origin part* of a fragment-group specifies a fragment-group that is used when binding fragment-forms to slots. Consider the following example:

NAME '/home/smith/CounterBody'
origin '/home/smith/CounterGroup'

Up:DoPart
do n+7->n

Down:DoPart
do n-5->n

The origin of `CounterBody` is the fragment-group `/home/smith/CounterGroup`. The origin must have free slots corresponding to `Up` and `Down`. The origin construct specifies that the fragment-forms `Up` and `Down` are substituted for the corresponding slots in `CounterGroup`. The result of this substitution is a form, called the extent of the fragment, as defined below.

A fragment defines a unique form, called the *extent* of the fragment. The extent of the above fragment is a combination of `CounterBody` and `CounterGroup`. The combination is obtained by filling in the slots in the origin with the corresponding fragment-forms. In the above example this gives the following form:

```
Counter:
  (# Up: (# n: @integer enter n do n+7->n #);
     Down: (# n: @integer do n-5->n exit n #)
  #)
```

17.1.7 The basic environment

The Mjølner BETA System provides a basic environment that defines the most important standard patterns and objects. In addition, this environment initiates and terminates the execution of any BETA program. The basic BETA environment is the fragment `betaenv`[4] shown in Figure 17.3. As can be seen, this fragment defines a number of standard patterns. In addition, the fragment has two slots: `PROGRAM` and `LIB`.

A complete BETA program that makes use of `betaenv` may be defined by defining the `PROGRAM` slot. The following fragment-form is an example of a very simple BETA program:

[4] In the rest of this chapter, simple names without directory paths are used for specifying the names of fragment-groups.

```
NAME 'betaenv'
betaenv:ObjectDescriptor
{****** The basic BETA environment ******}
(# Put: (# ch: @char enter ch ... #);
   PutInt: (# n: @integer enter n do ... #);
   PutText: (# T: @Text enter T do ...#);
   NewLine: (# ... #);
   PutLine: (# T:@Text enter T do T->putText; newLine #);
   Text: ...;
   File: ...;
   integer: (# ... #);
   char: (# ... #);
   ... {Definition of other standard attributes}
   <<SLOT LIB: Attributes>>
do {Initialize for execution}
   <<SLOT PROGRAM:ObjectDescriptor>>;
   {Terminate execution}
#)
```

Figure 17.3 The basic BETA environment.

```
NAME 'mini1'
origin 'betaenv'
PROGRAM:ObjectDescriptor
(#
do 'Hello world!'->PutLine
#)
```

The extent of the fragment `mini1` is the following form:

```
{****** The basic BETA environment ******}
(# ...
   PutLine:...
   ...
do {Initialize for execution}
   (#
   do 'Hello world!'->PutLine
   #)
   {Terminate execution}
#)
```

As can be seen, the `PROGRAM` fragment has been substituted for the `PROGRAM` slot in `betaenv`. In the `PROGRAM` fragment it is therefore possible to use any name which is visible at the point of the `PROGRAM` slot in `betaenv`. `PutLine` is visible at the `PROGRAM` slot and is therefore visible in the `PROGRAM` fragment. It would also have been possible to make use of patterns like `integer`, `char`, `Text`, etc. In Section 17.6 we shall return to the question of visibility.

The `LIB` slot in `betaenv` is intended for making a set of general patterns to be used by other programs. The difference between such a library and a program is that the library is a list of patterns whereas the program is a single object-descriptor. The following example is an example of a library consisting of two patterns:

NAME 'mylib'
origin 'betaenv'

LIB:attributes
`Hello: (# do 'Hello'->PutText #);` `World: (# do 'World'->PutText #)`

By substituting the `LIB` slot in `betaenv` with the `LIB` fragment-form we obtain the following form:

```
{****** The basic BETA environment ******}
(# ...
   Hello: (# do 'Hello'->PutText #);
   World: (# do 'World'->PutText #)
do {Initialize for execution}
   <<SLOT PROGRAM:ObjectDescriptor>>;
   {Terminate execution}
#)
```

As can be seen, the library patterns are inserted at the point of the `LIB` slot. This means that in the `LIB` fragment-form it is possible to see all names visible at the point of the `LIB` slot in `betaenv`.

Note that the extent of `mylib` is not an executable program, since the `PROGRAM` slot has not been defined. In the next section we shall show how to make use of a library in a program.

17.1.8 Include

When making libraries like `mylib`, we need a mechanism for combining several fragments into one fragment. The **include** construct makes this possible. In the following example we have a program that makes use of the `mylib` library:

NAME 'mini2'
origin 'betaenv'
include 'mylib'

PROGRAM:ObjectDescriptor
(# do Hello; World; newLine #)

The effect of the **include** 'mylib' is that the patterns defined in `myLib` can be used in the `PROGRAM` fragment-form. Formally the fragment-forms of `mylib` become part of the fragment `mini2`. In the above example `mini2` may be understood as a fragment-group consisting of the fragment-forms in `mylib` and the `PROGRAM` fragment-form. This implies that the extent of `mini2` is obtained by substituting the `LIB` slot in `betaenv` by the `LIB` fragment-form in `mylib` and by substituting the `PROGRAM` slot in `betaenv` by the `PROGRAM` fragment-form in `mini2`. This gives the following form as a result:

```
{****** The basic BETA environment ******}
(# ...
   Hello: (# do 'Hello'->PutText #);
   World: (# do 'World'->PutText #)
do {Initialize for execution}
   (#
   do Hello; World; newLine
   #)
   {Terminate execution}
#)
```

Since the patterns in `mylib` are inserted at the point of the `LIB` slot, they are visible at the point of the `PROGRAM` slot. This is where the `PROGRAM` fragment-form in `mini2` is inserted, i.e. the patterns `Hello` and `World` are visible inside the `PROGRAM` fragment-form.

A fragment-form may have more than one include. This makes it possible to use several library fragments in the same fragment.

17.1.9 Body

When defining a fragment it is often desirable to be able to specify one or more fragments that must always be included when using the fragment.

This is often the case when a fragment is separated into an interface fragment and one or more implementation fragments. Here we introduce the construct for specifying this, but delay further explanation until Section 17.2. The **body** construct specifies a fragment that is always part of the extent. Consider the following fragments:

```
NAME 'counter'
origin 'betaenv'
body 'counterbody'
---
LIB:Attributes
---
Counter:
  (# Up: (# n: @integer enter n <<SLOT Up:DoPart>> #);
     Down: (# n: @integer <<SLOT Down:DoPart>> exit n #);
     Private: @ <<SLOT Private:ObjectDescriptor>>
  #)
```

The `counter` fragment has a body specification which specifies that a fragment called `counterbody` is always part of the extent of `counter`. The `counterbody` fragment could be described as follows:

```
NAME 'counterbody'
origin 'counter'
---
Up:DoPart
---
do n+7->n
---
Down:DoPart
---
do n-5->n
---
Private:ObjectDescriptor
---
(# V: @integer #)
```

The `counter` fragment could be used by the following fragment:

```
NAME 'mini3'
origin 'betaenv'
include 'counter'
---
PROGRAM:ObjectDescriptor
---
(# C: @Counter; N: @integer
do 3->C.up; C.down->N
#)
```

The extent of mini3 is obtained by combining the PROGRAM fragment-form in mini3, **origin** 'betaenv' and **include** 'counter'. In addition the **body** 'counterbody' in counter implies that the counterBody fragment is also included in the extent. The resulting form looks as follows:

```
{****** The basic BETA environment ******}
(# ...
   Counter:
     (# Up: (# n: @integer enter n do n+7->n #);
        Down: (# n: @integer do n-5->n exit n #);
        Private: @(# V: @integer #)
     #)
do {Initialize for execution}
   (# C: @Counter; N: @integer
   do 3->C.up; C.down->N
   #);
   {Terminate execution}
#)
```

As stated earlier, the patterns defined in LIB are visible in mini3 through the use of **include**. However, the counterbody is not visible from mini3. This means that an evaluation like:

```
C.private.V+1->C.private.V
```

is not possible within mini3. That is even if the extent of mini3 includes the counterbody fragment, it is not visible within mini3.

The *domain* of a fragment F is that part of the extent of F which is visible within F. The domain of F consists of the fragment-forms in F, plus the domain of the origin of F plus the domain of possible included fragments.

The domain of mini3 takes the following form:

```
{****** The basic BETA environment ******}
(# ...
   Counter:
     (# Up: (# n: @integer enter n <<SLOT Up:DoPart>> #);
        Down: (# n: @integer<<SLOT Down:DoPart>>exit n#);
        Private: @ <<SLOT Private:ObjectDescriptor>>
     #)
do {Initialize for execution}
   (# C: @Counter; N: @integer
   do 3->C.up; C.down->N
   #);
   {Terminate execution}
#)
```

The domain of `mini3` is constructed as follows:

- The domain of `mini3` consists of the `PROGRAM` fragment-form in `mini3`, the domain of `betaenv` (its origin), plus the domain of the included fragment `counter`.
- The domain of `betaenv` is the form in Figure 17.3.
- The domain of the `counter` fragment consists of the form defining the pattern `Counter`, plus the domain of `betaenv`. Note that the **body** part of `Counter` does not contribute to the domain.

In Section 17.6 the concepts of extent and domain are described further.

17.2 Separation of interface and implementation

Organizing a program as a collection of fragments (modules) is one way of dealing with the complexity of large programs. A large system, however, consists of a large number of fragments. A fragment may use a number of other fragments (via origin, include or body), and be itself used by a number of other fragments. The result may in fact be a fairly complicated structure. For this reason it is necessary to limit the interconnections between fragments. Furthermore, knowledge about the details of a fragment should be limited whenever possible.

A fundamental technique in the design of software systems is to distinguish between the *interface* and *implementation* of a module. The *interface* of a module describes the part of the module which is visible from modules that use it. This includes a description of how to use the module and is sometimes called the 'outside view' of the module. The *implementation* of a module is the part of the module which is necessary to realize it on a computer. This is sometimes called the 'inside' view of the module.

An important issue is the notion of *encapsulation* or *information hiding*. Encapsulation means that access to the implementation part of a module is not possible from outside the module, i.e. the implementation of a module is hidden. This means that the usage of a module cannot depend upon internal details of its implementation, and thus it is possible to change the implementation of a module without affecting its usage.

Encapsulation and separation of interface and implementation may also save compilation time. In the Mjølner BETA System, as in most other systems, fragments (modules) can be separately compiled. A change in an implementation module can then be made without recompilation of the interface module and modules using the interface module. This can yield significant savings in compilation time. On the other hand, a change in an interface module implies that all modules using it must be recompiled. This can be extremely time consuming, therefore we recommend carefully designing critical interfaces to reduce the need for future changes. It is, however, not possible to avoid such changes since the requirements for an interface usually change over time.

Programming takes place at different abstraction levels. The interface part of a module describes a view of objects and patterns meaningful at the abstraction level where the module is used. The implementation level describes how objects and patterns at the interface level are realized using other objects and patterns.

To sum up, encapsulation and separation of interface and implementation have the following advantages:

- The user of a module can only access its interface and thus cannot make use of implementation details.
- It is possible to change the implementation without affecting the usage of a module.
- A change in an implementation module can be made without recompilation of the interface module and modules using the interface module.

The fragment language supports encapsulation and separation of interface and implementation. One fragment defines the interface while others define the implementation.

Figure 17.4 shows the `textlib` fragment which defines the interface of a library text manipulating patterns. The library consists of two patterns, each having a slot as its do-part. This slot should be filled with a `<DoPart>` defining the implementation of the pattern. The `textlibbody` fragment in Figure 17.5 is the implementation part of the library.

The **body** 'textlibbody' part of `textlib` specifies that the fragment `textlibbody` is automatically included in any fragment using `textlib`. A fragment using `textlib` will not be able to access attributes described in `textlibbody`. In other words; the extent of `textlib` includes `textlib` and `textlibbody`, whereas the domain of `textlib` does not include `textlibbody`. Figure 17.6 shows a `program` fragment which makes use of `textlib`.

```
NAME 'textlib'
origin 'betaenv'
body 'textlibbody'
---
LIB:attributes
 SpreadText:
    {A blank is inserted between all chars in the text 'T'}
    (# T: @Text
    enter T
    <<SLOT SpreadText:DoPart>>
    exit T
    #);
 BreakIntoLines:
   {'T' refers to a Text which is to be split into a}
   {no. of lines. 'w' is the width of the lines.}
   (# T: ^Text; w: @integer
   enter(T[],w)
   <<SLOT BreakIntoLines: DoPart>>
   #)
```

Figure 17.4 Interface fragment of the simple text library.

```
NAME 'textlibbody'
origin 'textlib'
---
SpreadText: DoPart
do (# L: @integer
   do (for i: (T.length->L)-1 repeat
          (' ',L-i+1)->T.InsertCh
   for)#)
---
BreakIntoLines: DoPart
do T.scan
   (# sepInx,i,l: @integer;
   do i+1->i; l+1->l;
      (if (ch<=' ' )// true then i->sepInx if);
      (if l//w then
          (nl,sepInx)->T.InxPut;
          i-sepInx->l
   if)#);
   T.newline;
```

Figure 17.5 Implementation fragment of the simple text library.

```
NAME 'libuser2'
origin 'betaenv'
include 'textlib'
---
program:ObjectDescriptor
  (# T: @Text;
  do 'Here I am!'->SpreadText->PutLine;
     'Once upon a time in the west '->T;
     'a man came riding from east'->T.putText;
     (T[],10)->BreakIntoLines;
     T->putText;
  #)
```

Figure 17.6 The fragment `libuser2` includes `textlib`.

17.2.1 Abstract data types

One of the fundamental concepts in program development is the notion of *abstract data type*. In the context of BETA, an abstract data type is a class pattern whose instances are completely characterized by a set of (procedure) pattern attributes – sometimes referred to as its 'operations.' These operations constitute the outside view of the objects, whereas reference attributes and details of the pattern attributes belong to the inside view (the implementation).

The fragments in Figures 17.7 and 17.8 show an example of an abstract data type in BETA. The fragments define the interface and implementation of a stack of text references. A stack is completely characterized by its operations `Push`, `Pop`, `New` and `isEmpty`. The `stack` may be used as shown in Figure 17.9

Since the domain of `stack` does not include its implementation, the stack can only be used by means of its operations. It is good practice to define most class patterns as 'abstract data types,' i.e. restrict their interface to be pattern operations. In some languages (e.g. Smalltalk), class patterns are always abstract data types.

```
NAME 'stack'
origin 'betaenv'
body 'arraystack'
LIB: Attributes
Stack:
  (# Private: @ <<SLOT private: ObjectDescriptor>>;
     Push: (# e: ^Text enter e[] <<SLOT Push: DoPart>> #);
     Pop: (# e: ^Text <<SLOT Pop: DoPart>> exit e[] #);
     New: (# <<SLOT New: DoPart>> #);
     isEmpty:
       (# Result: @boolean
       <<SLOT isEmpty: DoPart>>
       exit Result
       #)
  #)
```

Figure 17.7 The interface part of the `Stack` pattern.

NAME `'arraystack'`
origin 'stack'
private: ObjectDescriptor
`(# A: [100] ^Text; Top : @integer #)`
Push: DoPart
`do private.top+1->private.top; e[]->private.A[private.top][]`
Pop: DoPart
`do private.A[private.top][]->e[]; private.top-1->private.top`
new: DoPart
`do 0->private.top`
isEmpty: DoPart
`do (0 = private.Top)->result`

Figure 17.8 The implementation part of `Stack`.

NAME 'libuser3'
origin 'betaenv'
include 'stack'

program:ObjectDescriptor

```
(# T: @Text; S: @Stack
do  'To be or not to be'->T; T.reset;
    Get:
      cycle
      (# T1: ^Text
      do &Text[]->T1[]; T.getText-> T1;
         (if T1.empty // True then leave Get if);
         T1[]->S.push
     #);
   Print:
     cycle
     (# T1: ^Text
     do (if S.isEmpty // true then leave Print if);
        S.pop->T1[];
        T1->putText; ' '->put
     #)
#)
```

Figure 17.9 A fragment using the stack interface.

17.3 Alternative implementations

It is possible to have several implementations of a given interface module. In general, this means that different fragments may define different bindings for slots in a given fragment.

Suppose that we want to define an alternate implementation of the `stack` from the previous section. In the alternate implementation stack objects are represented as a linked list. The list implementation is shown in Figure 17.10.

We have to remove the body specification of the `stack` fragment, since it forces the `arrayStack` to always be included as part of the extent of `stack`. Instead, the user of `stack` should have a body part specifying the appropriate implementation.

```
NAME 'listStack'
origin 'stack'
---
private: ObjectDescriptor
    (# head: ^elm; elm: (# T:^Text; next: ^elm #)
    #)
---
Push: DoPart
do (# R: ^private.elm
    do &private.elm[]->R[]; private.head[]->R.next[];
       e[]->R.T[]; R[]->private.head[];
    #)
---
Pop: DoPart
    do private.head.T[]->e[];
       private.head.next[]->private.head[];
---
new: DoPart
    do NONE->private.head[]
---
isEmpty: DoPart
    do (NONE=private.head[])->result ;
```

Figure 17.10 List implementation of stack.

To sum up:

- The `stack` must have no body:

```
NAME 'stack'
origin 'betaenv'
---
LIB: Attributes
---
Stack:
  (# ...
  #)
```

- A user of the stack must have a body selecting an implementation. The following fragment makes use of the list implementation:

```
NAME 'libuser4'
origin 'betaenv'
include 'stack'
body 'listStack'
---
program:ObjectDescriptor
---
(# T: @Text; S: @Stack
do ...
#)
```

- The following fragment makes use of the array implementation:

```
NAME 'libuser5'
origin 'betaenv'
include 'stack'
body 'arrayStack'
---
program:ObjectDescriptor
---
(# T: @Text; S: @Stack
do ...
#)
```

Sometimes it is not desirable to select the implementation of the stack at the point where it is used. Consider a fragment using the `stack` without specifying an implementation:

```
NAME 'libuser6'
origin 'betaenv'
include 'stack'
program:ObjectDescriptor
   (# T: @Text; S: @Stack
   do ...
   #)
```

The fragment `libuser6` has, however, not been completely specified since the free slots in `stack` have not been bound. The simplest way of doing this is to specify a fragment that only adds a body specification:

```
NAME 'libuser7'
origin 'libuser6'
body 'arrayStack'
```

The fragment `libuser7` is a complete program.

17.4 Program variants

Often, several variants of a given program are needed, usually if variants of a given program have to exist for several computers. The main part of the program is often the same for each computer. For maintenance purposes, it is highly desirable to have only one version of the common part. In the Mjølner BETA System program, variants are handled in the same way as alternative implementations of a module, i.e. different variants of a module bind some of the slots differently.

As an example, assume that two variants of a program are needed. Assume that they vary with respect to the implementation of the `stack` pattern. The fragment in Figure 17.11 is like the `libuser6` fragment above, except that it has been extended with a slot. This slot is supposed to print information about the variant. The fragment in Figure 17.12 is an example of a variant of the `libuser8` fragment. A similar variant may be defined using `stackList`.

```
NAME 'libuser8'
origin 'betaenv'
include 'stack'
-- program:ObjectDescriptor --
(# T: @Text; S: @Stack
do  'Program Hamlet. '-> PutText;
     <<SLOT hamlet:ObjectDescriptor>>;
    'To be or not to be'->T; T.reset;
     Get:
       cycle(# T1: ^Text
       do &Text[]->T1[]; T.getText-> T1;
          (if T1.empty // True then leave Get if);
          T1[]->S.push
       #);
    Print:
      cycle(# T1: ^Text
      do (if S.isEmpty // true then leave Print if);
         S.pop->T1[]; T1->putText; ' '->put
      #)
#)
```

Figure 17.11 The `libuser8` fragment.

```
NAME 'libuser9'
origin 'libuser8'
body 'listStack'
-- hamlet:ObjectDescriptor --
(#do 'Variant using list implementation of stack'
      ->putLine;
#)
```

Figure 17.12 The `libuser9` fragment.

17.5 Using several libraries

The examples of libraries until now have only shown how to use one library from a program. The syntactic category of a slot like `SLOT LIB:attributes` describes a list of declarations. It is thus possible to bind an arbitrary number of `LIB` fragments to such a slot. Figure 17.13 shows a fragment that includes two libraries.

17.6 Visibility and binding rules

We now summarize the rules for binding slots, and give a precise definition of the extent and domain of a fragment. A general skeleton of a fragment is shown in Figure 17.14. The origin `G` is optional, and there may be zero or more includes. The case $m = 0$ means that there are no includes. Similarly, $k = 0$ corresponds to a fragment with no bodies.

The *origin-chain* of `F` is a list of fragments:

```
G, G1, G2, ... Gn
```

where `G` is the origin of `F`, `G1` is the origin of `G`, etc. The fragment `Gn` has no origin. Usually, `Gn` will be the basic environment `betaenv`. The origin-chain must be finite without duplicates.

The fragment-forms in `F` are bound by searching for free slots in the origin chain, starting with `G`.

```
NAME 'libuser10'
origin 'betaenv'
include 'mylib'
include 'textlib'
program:ObjectDescriptor
  (# T: @Text;
  do Hello; World; newline;
     'Here I am!'->SpreadText->PutLine;
     'Once upon a time in the west '->T;
     'a man came riding from east'->T.putText;
     (T[],10)->BreakIntoLines;
     T->putText;
  #)
```

Figure 17.13 Example of a fragment including two other fragments.

NAME 'F'
origin 'G'
include 'A1'
include 'A2'
...
include 'Am'
body 'B1'
body 'B2'
...
body 'Bk'
F1: S1
`ff1`
F2: S2
`ff2`
...
Fn: Sn
`ffn`

Figure 17.14 A general fragment.

The *fragment-dependency graph* of `F` has a node for each fragment referred to via origin, include and body. The dependency graph is constructed as follows:

(1) A directed edge is made **from** `F` **to** its origin.

(2) A directed edge is made **from** `F` **to** each fragment it includes.

(3) Construct the dependency graph for each body fragment `F`.

(4) Steps 1-3 are repeated for each fragment referred by origin, include and body.

The dependency graph must be acyclic, i.e. there should be no loops. This means that a fragment cannot include itself directly or indirectly via other fragments. The dependency graph for fragment `libuser9` of Figure 17.12 is shown in Figure 17.15

The extent of `F` is the extent of its origin, the extent of all fragments included, plus the extent of all bodies, and finally `F` itself. This may be described using the following equation, where we rely on the reader's intuition for the definition of the operator $\oplus$:

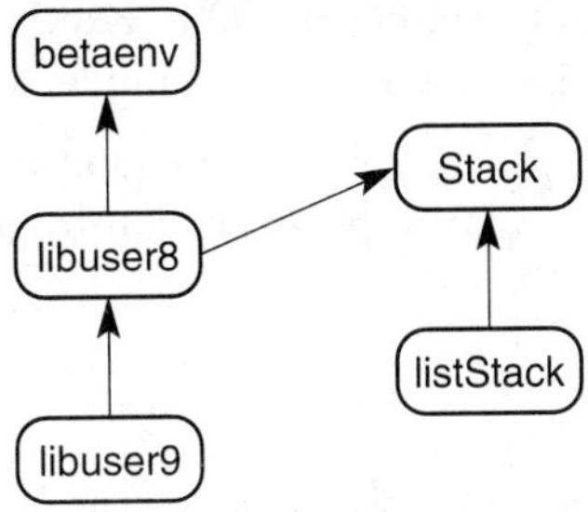

Figure 17.15 Dependency graph for `libuser9`.

$$\begin{aligned}\mathbf{Extent}(F) &= \mathbf{Extent}(G) \oplus \\ &\quad \mathbf{Extent}(A1) \oplus \mathbf{Extent}(A2) \ldots \oplus \mathbf{Extent}(Am) \oplus \\ &\quad \mathbf{Extent}(B1) \oplus \mathbf{Extent}(B2) \ldots \oplus \mathbf{Extent}(Bk) \oplus \\ &\quad \texttt{ff1} \oplus \texttt{ff2} \oplus \ldots \oplus \texttt{ffn}\end{aligned}$$

Note the recursive nature of extent. Anything in the extent of the origin is part of the extent of `F`, and similarly for include and body. The recursion is finite since the dependency graph is acyclic. Eventually, there will be a fragment without an origin and fragments without include and body parts.

The domain of `F` has a similar recursive definition. The domain of `F` includes the domain of the origin, the domain of all included fragments and the fragment itself. The body fragments are not included in the domain. The following equation describes the domain:

$$\begin{aligned}\mathbf{Domain}(F) &= \mathbf{Domain}(G) \oplus \\ &\quad \mathbf{Domain}(A1) \oplus \mathbf{Domain}(A2) \ldots \oplus \mathbf{Domain}(Am) \\ &\quad \oplus \texttt{ff1} \oplus \texttt{ff2} \oplus \ldots \oplus \texttt{ffn}\end{aligned}$$

17.7 Exercises

(1) Define an interface fragment and an implementation fragment for the `Register` pattern in Chapter 9.

(2) Develop an alternative implementation for the `Register` pattern where the elements are stored in a linked list.

(3) Redo the soda- and vending machine Exercise 2 in Chapter 7 and split the program into interface- and implementation fragments.

(4) Redo the bank system Exercise 3 in Chapter 7 by splitting the program into interface- and implementation fragments.

17.8 Notes

The grammar-based principle used to define the Mjølner BETA Fragment System was originally proposed by (Kristensen *et al.*, 1983a).

The handling of modularization differs from language to language. Some languages, like the original version of Pascal, have no mechanisms for supporting modularization. Other languages like Modula 2 and Ada have modularization constructs as part of the language. In these languages the interface of the data type has been textually separated from the implementation. In C and C++ a module corresponds to a file.

In (DeRemer and Krohn, 1976) the term 'programming in the large' was introduced to characterize the construction of large and complex systems. The main point made by DeRemer and Krohn is that structuring a large collection of modules to form a system (programming in the large) is essentially a different activity from that of constructing the individual modules (programming in the small). They propose the use of different languages for the two activities: a *module interconnection language* should be used for describing the modular structure, and a conventional programming language should be used for describing the contents of modules. They also propose a module interconnection language called MIL 75. The BETA Fragment System is an example of such a module interconnection language.

Chapter 18

Conceptual Framework

In Chapter 2 a short introduction to the conceptual framework underlying BETA was given. This chapter will present a more detailed description of the framework. We will introduce concepts such as information processes and systems and discuss abstraction, concepts, classification and composition. The framework provides a means to be used when modeling phenomena and concepts from the real world, it is thus a fundamental basis for object-oriented analysis and design. It is, however, also important for implementation, since it provides a means for structuring and understanding the objects and patterns generated by a program execution. The approach presented in this book is that analysis, design and implementation are programming or modeling activities, but at different abstraction levels.

Object-orientation is also being applied to databases. This book is not about databases, but the framework and BETA language presented here are also relevant for object-oriented databases. Data modeling is the same activity for databases and programming. There are, of course, additional aspects of databases which are not covered by this book. In (Atkinson *et al.*, 1990) the following is mentioned: persistence of objects; secondary storage management; recovery and query facilities.

In the rest of this chapter a number of definitions of various concepts are given. The definitions are given in English, and it is in most cases not possible to give a precise definition. The level of preciseness is intended to be like that of a dictionary. Most of the concepts being defined are examples of so-called 'prototypical' concepts (see below). The examples following the definitions are therefore of great importance for understanding the concepts. Despite the difficulties in making precise definitions, the experience is that the concepts introduced are useful, but that some practical experience is necessary before a satisfactory understanding of the concepts can be obtained. This experience may be obtained by using BETA in practical system development projects.

18.1 Physical modeling

The conceptual framework presented here reflects a certain perspective on programming. It is deliberately presented as one of many possibilities: in Chapter 2 other perspectives such as procedural programming, functional programming and constraint programming were briefly mentioned. We define perspective as follows:

Definition 18.1 *A* perspective *is the means a person uses to structure her/his thinking and understanding in relation to situations within some domain.*

The means determine the nature of properties which may be considered important for a given situation, and thereby also the nature of properties that are ignored. The means also provide concepts and other methods of organization to be used in the interpretation of the selected and considered properties.

For functional and constraint programming, the means include mathematics. For procedural programming the means include the concept of a programmable calculator. In this chapter (some of) the means of the object-oriented perspective are presented.

In Chapter 2, the object-oriented perspective on programming was defined as follows:

Definition 18.2 *A program execution is regarded as a physical model simulating the behavior of either a real or imaginary part of the world.*

The key word is 'physical.' The term 'physical model' is used to distinguish these models from, for instance, mathematical models. Part of reality may often be described using mathematical equations: Newton's Laws are an example of this. A physical model is a model constructed from some physical material like Lego bricks. Elements of the physical model represent phenomena from the application domain. Objects are the computerized material used to construct computerized physical models. Objects may be viewed as a kind of electronic Lego bricks.

A collection of things which may be used to generate a set of phenomena may be called a *phenomena generator*. If the phenomena generated are processes, the collection may be called a *process generator*. The set of processes that might be generated may be called the *process set* of the process generator.

A collection of Lego pieces is a phenomena generator. The phenomena generated will usually be regarded as static, and a building set for toy railroads is a better example of a process generator. With this very general description, almost anything could be regarded as a phenomena generator.

In practice we will of course use it in a much more restricted context – that of informatics and of modeling and design.

A given phenomena/process generator puts some restrictions on which aspects of reality can be modeled. In addition, it defines the possibilities for obtaining a physical similarity between reality and the model. Most 'Lego houses' would probably have some commonly accepted physical likeness to houses people live in. A toy model of a railway shunting yard may be used for serious analysis of aspects of the real yard's operation, and the physical similarity is obvious. The building set may, however, also be used to model cars moving on a road, but with a questionable realism, since for example, a car represented by a toy locomotive will not be able to pass another car, represented by another locomotive, except at predetermined locations on the 'road' and using rules that do not correspond to passing on real roads.

An analog computer, consisting of capacitors, resistance and other electric components, may of course be used to model the electric behavior of a certain class of circuitry – the process set of the analog computer. But it may (and has) also be used successfully to model the management of water reservoirs in a hydroelectric power supply system. In this case there is no physical similarity between the reality and the model.

The definition of object-oriented programming implies that all program executions are models of some other existing systems. For new systems this also holds, even though the existing system in that case is a system existing in the mind(s) of the programmer(s). The distinction between a *real* or an *imaginary* part of the world needs further elaboration.

Let us consider modeling parts of the real world. Examples of this are simulation programs – a program simulating a railway system is clearly a model of part of the real world. The trains, stations, passengers, etc., involved in the simulation may all be represented as objects in the program execution. The first object-oriented language, Simula, was in fact invented with the purpose of simulation.

Consider next a library. A library consists of books, card files and files for the registration of loans. Each of the files consists of a number of cards describing books or loans. A computer system handling these files may be considered as a physical model of the library (which is a real part of the world). The cards in the files may naturally be represented by objects in the program execution, etc. This is an example of how to make a physical model of a manually operated administrative system.

The creation of computer systems of course includes a great deal of invention. These inventions may be imagined as new phenomena and concepts with a well defined role in the problem domain. They will then subsequently be realized as objects and patterns in the program execution. Often it is also a matter of taste as to whether or not an object is a representation of some real world phenomenon or a new kind of phenomenon. Is a patient record a representation of a patient or a new kind of object?

There are also examples of computerized models where initially the system was conceived of as a model of some existing part of the world. However, as time goes on, the EDP-system completely replaces the original manual system and becomes part of reality itself. An example of this is a computer system for organizing securities like stocks and bonds. When constructing such a system it is natural to represent the securities as objects and all the trading with securities are then replicated in the EDP-system. In some countries, like Denmark, the objects become the securities themselves, i.e. the 'real stocks and bonds' are the objects and not the paper representations. Eventually, people will forget about paper-based securities and only think of object-based securities.

Referent and model systems

The real or imaginary part of the world being modeled will in the following be called the *referent system*, and the program execution constituting the physical model will be called the *model system*.[1] Figure 18.1 illustrates the programming process as a modeling process between a referent and a model system.

The programming process involves identification of relevant concepts and phenomena in the referent system and representation of these concepts and phenomena in the model system. This process consists of three sub-processes: abstraction in the referent system; abstraction in the model system; and modeling. Please note that intentionally we do not impose any ordering among the sub-processes. Abstraction in the referent system is the process where we are perceiving and structuring knowledge about phenomena and concepts in the referent system with particular emphasis on the problem domain in question. We say that we are creating *problem-specific concepts* in the referent system. Abstraction in the model system is the process where we build structures that should support the model we are intending to create in the computer. We say that we create *realized concepts* in the model system. Finally, *modeling* is the process where we connect the problem specific concepts in the referent system with the realized concepts in the model system. In the model system, objects and properties of these objects represent phenomena and their properties in the referent system.

The programming process involves identification of concepts and phenomena in the referent system and their subsequent representation in

[1] Later in this chapter a definition of the term *system* will be given.

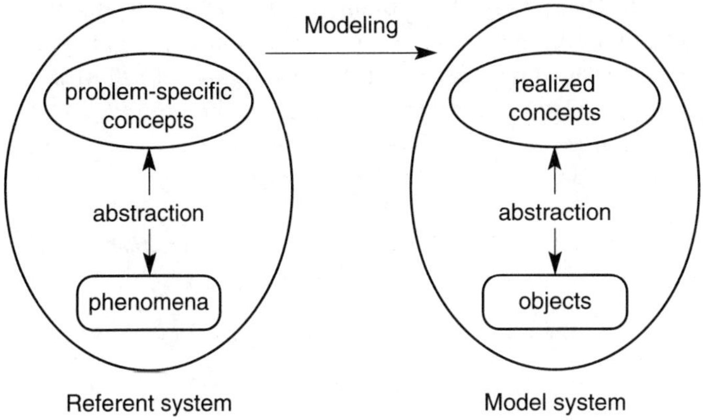

Figure 18.1 Modeling.

terms of objects and patterns. Ultimately this is a question about how to identify the patterns and objects of our program executions. It is not all aspects of the real (or imaginary) world that can be modeled as a program execution. We therefore have to identity the kind of phenomena that we want to model as program executions. The physical models we are interested in are those parts of reality we want to regard as *information processes*. In the next section we will introduce the notion of information process, which will give us some guidelines about identifying objects.

Patterns are means for representing concepts of the referent system. To 'find the patterns' it is therefore necessary to discuss subjects like the notion of concepts and their relations to phenomena, and important aspects of the abstraction process. Concepts and abstraction will be dealt with further in Section 18.3.

18.2 Information processes

It is not all aspects of reality that can be modeled as program executions. In this section we will look at the kind of phenomena we can represent as computerized models. Perhaps the most important phenomena studied in informatics are information processes. Program executions are information processes, and information handling in offices, planning in corporations, etc., are other examples of such processes. The above definition of informatics does not imply that all phenomena to which we may associate information aspects 'belong' to informatics. Informatics represents one perspective for looking at phenomena. Data processing in a post office may be regarded as an information process, as an economic process or as a social process, and thus 'belong' to informatics, economics or sociology, depending upon the perspective chosen.

An information process is a special kind of process, and we define it in the following way:

Definition 18.3 *An* information process *is a process where the qualities considered are:*

- *Its* substance, *the physical material that it transforms.*
- Measurable properties *of its substance, the results of measurement represented by values.*
- Transformations *of its substance and thus its measurable properties.*

The notion of an information process gives certain guidelines for identifying concepts and phenomena in the referent systems.

Substance This is the physical material that is transformed by an information process. Phenomena like 'Socrates', 'Mount Everest', a medical record, and a memory cell in a computer are all examples of phenomena which have substance. Substance is characterized by a certain volume and a unique location in time and space. A major aspect of substance is *identity*. Two pieces of substance have the same identity only if they are the same substance. They may have identical properties: 'Socrates' and 'your teacher' may have the same weight, age and eye color, but they are not the same person.

Measurable properties of substance Substance has no inherent properties besides having a certain volume and a unique location in time and space. All other properties associated with substance have to be obtained by *measurements*. A given property of some substance may be observed by performing a measurement resulting in a measure result (measurement). A measurement may be a simple counting of the number of petals on a flower or it may be performed using advanced equipment, such as measuring radiation from a computer screen. In general, a sequence of actions is involved in performing the measurement.

Weight, blood pressure and eye color of a person are examples of measurable properties. The state of a memory cell of a computer is a measurable property.

The results of measurements are usually described by values to capture them for the purpose of comparing them. This is so common that one often does not distinguish between measurements and the values describing them. The value '82.5 kg' may describe the weight of some person. The value '82.5 kg' is actually an abstraction classifying a set of measurements on a weight. We may think of '82.5 kg' as a concept and the measurements of the weight as part of its extension. Because of this confusion values are often considered the phenomena instead of the actual measurements.

Abstractions such as values, functions and types have been developed to describe measurable properties of substance.

Transformations on substance An information process is characterized by transformations which change its substance and thereby its measurable properties. Transformations are partially ordered sequences of events. An event changes the state of the information process, and events are ordered in time. The ordering is partial. The events are the only means for changing the measurable properties of the substance.

The following phenomena are examples of events: pushing a specific button at a specific point in time; 'the birth of Hans Christian Andersen', and 'the transition between spring and summer 1984.' Phenomena may also be sequences of events like 'Hannibal's march across the Alps', 'Columbus' America-expedition' and 'eating.'

The notion of information processes gives certain guidelines for the selection of phenomena. We have to consider tangible things where the main aspect is substance, we have to consider measurable properties of substance, and finally, we have to consider the transformations on the substance.

Information systems

The definition of an information process is very general, and in this section we will put a *system perspective* on information processes. The term *system* is often encountered within informatics, and it has been frequently used in this book. We define a system in the following way:

Definition 18.4 *A* system *is a part of the world that a person (or group of persons)* chooses *to regard as a whole consisting of* components, *each component characterized by* properties *and by actions related to these properties and those of other components.*

According to this definition, no part of the world 'is a system' as an inherent property. It is a system if we choose a system perspective.

In a system perspective, substance of information processes is organized/perceived in terms of components. The (measurable properties) of substance are the measurable properties of components. The transformations on the substance are perceived as actions performed by components. In the definition of system, terms like 'properties' and 'actions' are used. There are many different kinds of properties that may be associated with components, and there are many ways of organizing actions within a system. Program executions are information processes, and may be regarded as systems in the above sense. In this book we are mainly interested in program executions, and the notion of BETA program executions presented here is one specific way of understanding and describing systems.

We are now able to give a more precise definition of program execution:

Definition 18.5 *A* program execution *is an information process regarded as a system developing through transformations of its state.*

- *The substance is organized as* objects, *which are computerized material.*
- *A measurable property of the substance is a measurable property of one or more objects.*
- *Transformations of state are regarded as partially ordered sequences of actions associated with objects.*
- *Concepts are represented by* patterns *which are attributes of objects.*

The components of a program execution are *objects*. The properties of components (objects) are attributes. A BETA program execution can be more precisely defined as follows:

Definition 18.6 *A* BETA program execution *consists of a collection of objects. An object is characterized by a set of* attributes *and an* action-part. *An attribute may be: A* reference *to an object, a* part-object *or a* pattern.

A BETA program execution has three kinds of objects: item, component *and* system. *Items may have their action-part executed by other objects, components may execute their action-part alternately with other components, and systems may execute their action-part concurrently with other systems.*

18.3 Concepts and abstraction

Abstraction is probably the most powerful tool available to the human intellect for understanding complex phenomena. In the real world we are confronted with a huge number of different phenomena such as physical objects, situations, events and processes. All phenomena are different; there are no two identical persons, two identical cars, or two identical flowers. It is, however, impossible to deal with all single phenomena directly without tools for grouping similar phenomena. Abstraction arises from a recognition of similarities between phenomena and concepts and the decision to concentrate on these similarities and ignore the differences for the time being. The similarities are considered as fundamental and the differences as trivial. An abstraction covers a group of phenomena characterized by certain properties. A word or picture is usually introduced to symbolize the abstraction. An abstraction is also referred to as a *concept.*

18.3.1 Phenomena and concepts

Until now we have been rather vague about the terms phenomenon and concept. The following definitions give more precise definitions of these terms:

Definition 18.7 *A* phenomenon *is a thing that has definite, individual existence in reality or in the mind; anything real in itself*

Definition 18.8 *A* concept *is a generalized idea of a collection of phenomena, based on knowledge of common properties of instances in the collection*

The following individuals are all examples of phenomena: 'Winston Churchill', 'John F. Kennedy' and 'Charles de Gaulle.' They are all covered by the general concept 'Person', but also by the more specialized concept 'Statesman.' 'Bounty', 'Jutlandia' and 'Peder Pårs'[2] are examples of phenomena covered by the concept 'Ship.' 'Mount Everest', 'Mont Blanc' are examples of phenomena covered by the concept 'Mountain.'

The 'Statesman' concept is an example of a *role* played by persons. Other examples of roles are 'Employee', 'Owner', 'taxpayer' and 'Tenant.'

The above-mentioned phenomena are examples of phenomena that have substance.

Phenomena can also be events that happen. The following phenomena are examples of events: pushing a specific button at a specific point in time, and 'the birth of Hans Christian Andersen.' Phenomena may also be sequences of events like 'Hannibal's march across the Alps.' 'Columbus' America-expedition' and 'making a specific pizza.' For such phenomena we may develop concepts where the intension describes the sequences of events taking place.

[2] Jutlandia and Peder Pårs are well-known Danish ships.

We may also have phenomena that record events. An example of such a phenomenon is a 'Flight record' which may register certain data of a specific flight, like SK911 from Copenhagen to LA on December 12, 1989, etc. Another example is a 'System crash' which may be registered in a log book.

Measurable properties of some material are also examples of phenomena. Examples of these include the 'weight of a person', the 'blood pressure of a person' and 'the temperature in New York on December 24, 1984.'

Definition 18.9 *A* concept *is traditionally characterized by the following terms:*

- *The* extension *of a concept refers to the collection of phenomena that the concept somehow covers.*
- *The* intension *of a concept is a collection of properties that in some way characterize the phenomena in the extension of the concept.*
- *The* designation *of a concept is the collection of names (or pictures) by which the concept is known.*

The extension of the concept 'Person' includes the phenomena 'Winston Churchill', 'John F. Kennedy' and 'Charles de Gaulle.' The intension of 'Person' includes the following properties: 'able to think', 'walks upright' and 'uses tools.' In addition to 'Person' the designation includes 'Human Being' and '*Homo sapiens.*'

A phenomenon is a thing that has definite, individual existence in **reality** or in the **mind**. The above examples of phenomena exist in reality. Examples of phenomena existing in the mind include 'Sherlock Holmes', 'Donald Duck' and 'The Loch Ness Monster' (although some people think it exists in reality!). The extension of concepts like 'Unicorn', 'Pixy' and 'Nordic God' are examples of phenomena existing in the mind. The terms *concrete phenomena* and *abstract phenomena* are often used to distinguish between phenomena existing in reality or in the mind.

One philosophical issue here is whether or not it is useful to distinguish between phenomena and concepts. Concepts exist in the mind and may consequently be viewed as abstract phenomena. One consequence of this is that it is possible to imagine a concept where the extension consists of concepts. This situation is usually better described by means of generalization, as introduced below. In general, we think that it is useful to distinguish between concepts and abstract phenomena. A concept like 'Boat' covers a collection of phenomena, whereas an abstract phenomenon like 'Sherlock Holmes' is one individual phenomenon existing in the mind of people. However, at this point it may be appropriate to point out that most issues in this chapter are of a philosophical nature and therefore highly subjective.

In the above definition of concepts, the properties constituting the intension are those that 'in some way' characterize the phenomena in the extension. There are different views of concepts that give different interpretations to 'in some way.' In the next sections we look at two extremes in this respect.

18.3.2 Aristotelian view

The first of the two views has its origin in the classical Aristotelian logic. Here concepts are organized in a logical hierarchical concept structure and the extension of a concept contains phenomena that all satisfy some precisely defined requirements. This is expressed in the following characterization of the intension:

Definition 18.10 *The* intension *of a concept is a collection of properties that may be divided into two groups: the* defining properties *that all phenomena in the extension must have and the* characteristic properties *that the phenomena may or may not have. The nature of the properties is such that it is objectively determinable whether or not a phenomenon has a certain property.*

The defining properties determine a sharp border between members and non-members of a concept. Since it is objectively determinable whether or not a phenomenon has a certain property, it is also objectively determinable whether or not a phenomenon belongs to a given concept. In other words, the extension of a concept is uniquely defined by the intension.

The Aristotelian view of concepts has turned out to be useful for modeling systematic and 'scientific' concepts as found within well established fields like mathematics, physics, zoology and botany.

For the properties in the intension it is important that it is objectively determinable whether or not a phenomenon has a certain property. This results in a concept structure in which the concepts are characterized by sharp concept borders. In addition, the phenomena in the extension of an Aristotelian concept are relatively homogeneous. This is in line with the 'scientific' nature of the Aristotelian view of concepts.

The properties of an Aristotelian concept may be described by means of predicates, i.e. using mathematics. Within sciences like physics and biology, phenomena are often characterized using measurable properties, as described in Section 18.2. No matter how the properties are described, it is important that it is objectively decidable whether or not a given phenomenon has a certain property.

18.3.3 Prototypical view

As already mentioned, the Aristotelian view of concepts is useful for modeling systematic and 'scientific' concepts, and it has been used for many years with success especially within natural sciences, although not always without problems.

There are a large number of everyday concepts that cannot conveniently be described as Aristotelian concepts. Examples of such concepts are, 'rock music', 'intelligence' and 'food.' Also, some more technical concepts such as 'object-oriented programming' and 'structured programming' are difficult to describe as Aristotelian concepts. It is commonly not possible to find a collection of objectively decidable properties that define these concepts, but it is possible to find a collection of properties that may characterize these concepts. However, often it is not possible to objectively determine whether or not a given phenomenon has a certain property. This has led to the development of the so-called *prototypical view* of concepts (or *fuzzy view* or *prototype theory*). In the prototypical view the intension is defined in the following way:

Definition 18.11 *The* intension *of a concept consists of examples of properties that phenomena may have, together with a collection of typical phenomena covered by the concept, called* prototypes.

The prototypical view differs from the Aristotelian view in a number of ways:

(1) It may not be objectively decidable whether or not a phenomenon has a property of the intension.

(2) The intension is given by examples of properties. All phenomena will have some of the properties, but rarely all. A phenomenon having some of the properties may not belong to the extension of the concept.

(3) The prototypes are typical phenomena belonging to the extension of the concept.

The major consequence of this is that the extension of a prototypical concept is not uniquely determined by the intension. It requires a human judgement to decide whether or not a given phenomenon belongs to the concept. The phenomena in the extension will have varied typicality and the borders between concepts are blurred.

The prototypical view of concepts is more suited than the Aristotelian view to describe most everyday concepts. This is also often true for problem-specific concepts of the referent system. Below we discuss the consequences of this for the system development process.

18.3.4 Other views of concepts

The Aristotelian and prototypical view of concepts represent two extremes, and it is possible to imagine a number of intermediate views.

One difference between Aristotelian and prototypical views of concepts is whether or not it is objectively decidable if a given phenomena has a certain property or not.

Conceptual clustering Conceptual clustering is a variation of the Aristotelian view. The intension may have properties which may not be objectively decided, thus it is based on a human judgement whether or not a phenomenon is covered by the concept.

Prototypical concepts with objective properties It is of course possible to imagine prototypical concepts where all the properties are objectively decidable.

Defining *versus* characteristic properties The intension of an Aristotelian concept is divided into defining and characteristic properties. In theory, each of these two sets of properties may be empty. It is easy to imagine Aristotelian concepts without characteristic properties. It is more problematic to imagine Aristotelian concepts without defining properties. According to the definition of an Aristotelian concept, any phenomenon possessing the defining properties belongs to the extension of the concept. Consequently, a concept without defining properties has all phenomena in its extension. This is of course useless.

It is, however, still interesting to consider a variant of Aristotelian concepts that allows the defining properties to be empty. In this case the defining properties are supposed to be possessed by all phenomena in the extension, but not vice versa. It is then a matter of human judgement to decide if a given phenomenon belongs to the concept.

If properties are allowed to be non-objective, we are close to the prototypical view of concepts.

18.3.5 Representing concepts in BETA

A programming language like BETA is mainly useful for representing Aristotelian concepts: a pattern may be used for representing an Aristotelian concept. The instances of the pattern represent the extension of the concept, the object-descriptor represents the intension and the name of the pattern represents its designation. The intension of a concept is represented by means of an object-descriptor, i.e. an object-descriptor determines the kind of properties that can be represented. For an object-descriptor we have attributes and actions. The attributes may be part-objects, references to other objects and patterns.

18.4 The abstraction process

In both the referent and the model systems, concept structures are created. This implies that we have to discuss the process of producing and using knowledge, i.e. issues related to the theory of knowledge also called epistemology. The *process of knowledge* may be split into three levels:

(1) *The level of empirical concreteness.* At this level we conceive reality or individual phenomena as they are. We do not realize similarities between different phenomena, nor do we obtain any systematic understanding of the individual phenomena. We notice what happens, but neither understand why it happens nor the relations between the phenomena. In the programming process this corresponds to a level where we are trying to understand the single objects that constitute the system. We have little understanding of the relations between the objects, e.g. how to group them into classes.

(2) *The level of abstraction.* To understand the complications of the referent system, we have to analyze the phenomena and develop concepts for grasping the relevant properties of the phenomena that we consider. In the programming process this corresponds to designing the classes and their attributes and to organizing the classes into a class/sub-class hierarchy. At this level we obtain a simple and systematic understanding of the phenomena in the referent system.

(3) *The level of thought concreteness.* The understanding corresponding to the abstract level is further developed to obtain an understanding of the totality of the referent system. By having organized the phenomena of the referent system by means of concepts, we may be able to understand relations between phenomena that we did not understand at the level of empirical concreteness. We may also be able to explain why things happen and to predict what will happen.

The above is an identification of three levels appearing in the process of creating and producing knowledge. In this process the perspective provides us with various means for organizing and understanding our knowledge. The following are three fundamental means of organization for apprehending the real world:

(1) *Identification of phenomena and their properties.* In perceiving the real world people identify phenomena and their properties. The result of this is a number of *singular phenomena* characterized by a

selected set of properties. The phenomena are singular since they have not been classified in terms of concepts.

Selection of the relevant properties of phenomena is highly domain specific. In this book the domain is information processes, as explained in Section 18.2. Within information processes there is still a great deal of variety depending on the kind of information system to be constructed.

(2) *Classification.* Classification is the means by which we form and distinguish between different classes of phenomena. That is we form concepts. Having identified phenomena and their properties and concepts, we group similar phenomena and concepts. A classification is often called a *taxonomy.* It is very common to construct taxonomies to compare various subjects. When classification is applied repeatedly, *classification hierarchies* may be obtained.

(3) *Composition.* A phenomenon may be understood as a composition of other phenomena, i.e. there is a distinction between whole phenomena and their component phenomena. A car consists of body, four wheels, motor, etc. A process of making a pizza may be understood as a composition of several sub-processes, including: making the dough, making the tomato sauce, preparing the topping, etc. Repeated application of composition leads to *composition hierarchies.*

In general, the process of creating new concepts cannot just be explained as consisting of the above sub-functions. In practice, the definition of concepts will undergo drastic changes. The understanding obtained during the development process will usually influence previous steps. It is, however, useful to be aware of whether a problem is approached top-down or bottom-up. In the same way it is useful to be aware of the above-mentioned sub-functions of abstraction.

In the next section we take a closer look at classification and composition.

18.5 Classification and composition

In reality we have to deal with a huge number of concepts and phenomena, and it would not be possible to deal with that amount of complexity without tools for *hierarchical organization* of concepts and phenomena. Classification and composition are means to organize complexity in terms of hierarchies. The two terms are often used in two different, but complementary, ways. In some situations they are used as a description of sub-functions going on in the *process* of producing knowledge. In this process we constantly apply classification and composition to organize our knowledge. In other situations the two terms are used for describing (static) *relations* between phenomena and concepts identified during the process of identifying knowledge.

18.5.1 Classification

For classification we distinguish between the classification of phenomena and of concepts. In the following we define the terms 'clustering' and 'generalization.' By *classification* we then mean either clustering or generalization:

Clustering Is a means to focus on similarities between a number of phenomena and to ignore their differences, i.e. clustering is a classification of phenomena.

Definition 18.12 *To* cluster *is to form a concept that covers a collection of similar phenomena.* To exemplify *is to identify a phenomenon in the extension of a concept. Exemplification is the inverse of clustering.*

Clustering/exemplification corresponds to the *instance-of* relationship.

Definition 18.13 *The* instance-of *relationship holds between a concept and a phenomenon in the extension of the concept.*

Generalization Is a means to focus on similarities between a number of concepts and to ignore their differences, i.e. generalization is classification of concepts.

Definition 18.14 *To* generalize *is to form a concept that covers a number of more special concepts based on similarities of the special concepts. The intension of the general concept is a collection of properties that are all part of the intension of the more special concepts. The extension of the general concept contains the union of the extensions of the more special concepts.*

To specialize *is to form a more special concept from a general one. Specialization is the inverse of generalization.*

The terms *generalization of* and *specialization of* are the names for the corresponding relations.

Definition 18.15 *A* generalization *is a relationship between a general concept and a number of more special concepts. A specialization is the inverse of a generalization.*

The term generalization is often used about the general concept and the term specialization is often used about one of the special concepts.

The concept 'Animal' is a generalization of the more special concepts 'Mammal', 'Fish', 'Bird' and 'Reptile', and all of these may in turn be considered specializations of 'Animal.' The concept 'Mammal' may be thought of as a generalization of the concepts 'Predator' and 'Rodent', which may be considered specializations of 'Mammal.'

The concept 'Reservation' may be considered a generalization of 'Flight Reservation', 'Train Reservation', 'Boat Reservation' and 'Hotel Reservation.'

The concept 'Movement' may be considered a generalization of the concepts 'Travel', 'Jump' and 'Run.'

Classification hierarchies

Classification is often used to define hierarchies of concepts and phenomena. An example of a classification hierarchy for animals is shown in Figure 2.2. This hierarchy is also an example of a generalization/specialization hierarchy since it only includes concepts.

The hierarchy in Figure 2.2 has an important property: it is *tree structured.* Each concept has at most one immediate generalization, implying that the extensions of two concepts with the same immediate generalization are disjoint. The concepts 'Predator' and 'Rodent' have the same generalization 'Mammal', and the extensions of 'Predator' and 'Rodent' are disjoint. The tree structured classification hierarchies are an important mechanism for organizing knowledge. They are applied in many disciplines such as biology and chemistry. The phenomena of interest are classified according to selected properties.

There are also examples of classification hierarchies that are not tree structured. An example of such a hierarchy is given in Figure 18.2,[3] which shows a classification of geometric figures. This hierarchy is not tree structured since, for example, the concept 'Square' has two immediate generalizations 'Rectangle' and 'Rhombus.'

It is often a desirable property of a classification hierarchy that it is tree structured since this gives a simpler and more systematic organization than using non-tree structured classifications. In practice, however, one often ends up with a classification hierarchy which is not tree structured. This may be the case if one is classifying the same phenomena according to independent properties. A non-tree structured hierarchy can always be made tree structured, which, however, often gives rise to clumsy hierarchies. Instead of one classification hierarchy one may instead make two or more classifications of the same phenomena. This will then result in two or more independent tree structured classification hierarchies.

---

[3]Borrowed from (Abelson and Sussmann, 1985).

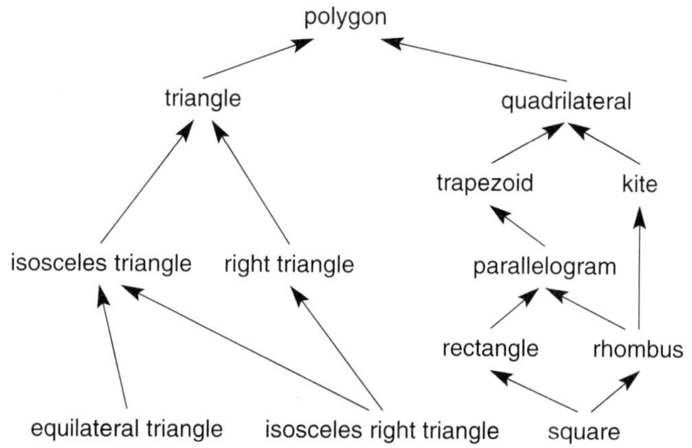

Figure 18.2 Classification of geometric objects.

Consider an example where several roles of people are of interest. It may then be of interest to classify people according to their profession, their nationality and their religion. This may result in three alternative tree structured classifications of the same phenomena.

Support for classification in BETA

Classification is supported in BETA by means of objects and patterns. Objects may be used to represent phenomena and their properties. Patterns may be used to represent concepts. Clearly, there is support for the instance-of relationship.

Sub-patterns and virtual patterns supports generalization/specialization. In Chapters 6–9 numerous examples of modeling of generalization/specialization hierarchies are shown.

It is obvious that the sub-pattern mechanism only supports tree structured classification hierarchies. In addition, BETA does not support the possibility of representing more than one classification hierarchy of the same objects. In BETA it may therefore be necessary to represent such classification hierarchies by another mechanism.

Some programming languages like Clos, C++ and Eiffel make use of *multiple inheritance*. In the cases where this is used to represent alternative classifications, like the role example above, it may lead to complicated structures. See Section 6.8 for a further discussion of multiple inheritance.

18.5.2 Composition

Composition is a means to organize phenomena and concepts in terms of components of other phenomena and concepts. There are a number of different ways of composing phenomena into compound phenomena.

A car may be viewed as consisting of a body, four wheels, etc. These components are physical parts of the car. A tree may be viewed as consisting of branches, a trunk, roots and leaves.

A 'Hotel Reservation' may be viewed as a composition of a 'Person', a 'Hotel', a 'Room' and a 'Date.' It is, however, not meaningful to view, for instance, the person as a physical part of the hotel reservation. The corresponding component is better viewed as a *reference* to a person.

We define composition in the following way:

Definition 18.16 *To* compose *is to form a compound phenomenon/concept by means of a number of component phenomena/concepts. Properties in the intension of the compound phenomenon/concept are described using the component phenomena/concepts. The extension of the compound phenomenon/concept consists of phenomena which have components belonging to the extension of the component phenomena/concepts.*

To decompose *is to identify a component phenomenon/concept of a phenomenon/concept. Decomposition is the inverse of composition.*

Composition gives rise to the *component-of* relation:

Definition 18.17 *The* component-of *relation is a relationship between a phenomenon/concept and one of its component phenomena/concepts.*

There are a number of different means for making compositions. They may all be defined as special cases of composition and component-of. In the following we introduce four of these means: whole-part composition; reference composition; localization; and concept composition. They will only be introduced as relations, and no name for the corresponding subfunction of composition will be given, although this could be done. The four cases of composition are not independent in the sense that the same components may be part of two or more of the relations. The reader may find the distinction between some of the verbal definitions below quite subtle. However, hopefully the illustration of the relations in BETA will make the distinction clear.

Whole-part composition

One important form of composition is the structuring of phenomena into wholes and parts. A 'Person' may naturally be viewed as consisting of parts like 'Head', 'Body', 'Arms' and 'Legs.' In turn, the 'Legs' consist of 'Lower leg', 'Foot', etc.

Definition 18.18 *The* part-of *relation is a relation between a phenomenon and one of its part phenomena.*

A 'Car' may be considered as consisting of parts like 'SteeringWheel', 'Motor', 'Body' and 'Wheel', i.e. 'Wheel' is a part-of a 'Car', a 'Motor' is a part-of a 'Car', etc.

The following example shows how whole-part composition is supported in BETA. The example describes a pattern representing the concept of a 'Car':

```
Car:
   (# aSteeringWheel: @SteeringWheel;
      aMotor: @Motor;
      aBody: @Body;
      wheels: [4] @Wheel
   #)
```

The part-of relation gives rise to a *part hierarchy.*

For more examples of modeling whole-part hierachies in BETA, see Chapter 10.

Reference composition

A reference is a component of a phenomenon that denotes another phenomenon. The 'Person' component of a 'Reservation' is actually a reference to a 'Person.' Similarly, for the 'Hotel' and 'Room' components. Composition of references gives rise to the *has-ref-to* relation:

Definition 18.19 *The* has-ref-to *relation is a relationship between a phenomenon and one of its components, being a reference to another phenomenon.*

The following examples shows how reference composition is supported in BETA. The example describes the concept of a 'Hotel Reservation':

```
HotelReservation:
   (# aPerson: ^Person;
      aHotel: ^Hotel;
      aRoom: ^Room;
      aDate: @Date
    #)
```

The components 'aPerson', 'aHotel' and 'aRoom' are reference components of a 'Hotel Reservation.'

The component 'aDate' is represented as a part-object. It is, however, not intuitively useful to model the date of a hotel reservation as a part object. The date is a measurable property of a hotel reservation. Modeling of measurable properties is further discussed in Section 18.7

For more examples of modeling reference composition in BETA, see Section 10.1.1.

Localization

Localization is a means for describing/organizing that the existence of phenomena/concepts are restricted to the context of a given phenomenon, i.e. the local component phenomena/concepts are dependent upon the composite phenomenon. The properties of a given phenomenon may be singularly defined phenomena or concepts which only have a meaning as components of the compound phenomenon/concept.

Definition 18.20 *The* is-local-to *relation is a relationship between a compound phenomenon and a locally defined dependent component phenomenon/concept.*

In Chapter 8 a number of examples of localization are given. Block structure is the BETA mechanism for supporting localization.

Concept composition

Concept composition is a means to define a compound phenomenon/concept by means of a number of independent component concepts. Concept composition is thus a relationship between a phenomenon/concept and a number of concepts. Independence means that the component concepts have a meaning independent of the compound phenomenon/concept being defined.

Definition 18.21 *A* concept composition *is a relationship between a compound phenomenon/concept and a number of independent component concepts.*

A certain relationship between the concepts 'Person', 'Hotel', 'Room' and 'Date' may be considered as the concept composition 'Reservation.' The concepts 'Person', 'Hotel', 'Room' and 'Date' are independent, since they have a meaning without the concept of 'Reservation.' Note that a concept like 'Reservation' may be viewed as both a reference composition and a concept composition. In general, a concept or phenomena may be viewed as one or more of the four forms of composition.

The concept 'Travel' may be viewed as a concept composition of concepts like 'Source', 'Destination', 'Duration' and 'Subtravels.'

The concept 'Car' may be thought of as a concept composition of the concepts: 'Horsepower', 'Body', 'Wheel', 'Motor', etc.

18.6 Relations

Relations are a common form of abstraction used for organizing knowledge:

Definition 18.22 *A* relation *is a union or connection of phenomena and/or concepts*

Some of the above abstraction mechanisms may all be viewed as special kinds of relations. For classification and composition we have already introduced a number of corresponding relations, including instance-of, part-of, has-ref-to, etc. These relations are examples of *structural relations* implied by the abstraction principles. In a given problem domain there may be a large number of *special relations* that we may be interested in modeling.

Reference composition is actually a means for representing simple binary relations between phenomena. An example of such a relation is 'Employee has-a Boss', which is a binary relationship between an employee and his or her boss. Other examples are 'Vehicle is-owned-by Person', 'Part is-manufactured-by Supplier', 'Hotel room is-reserved-by Person' and 'Company has President.' In Section 10.1.1 a number of examples of how to represent relations in BETA are shown, including the relationship between a book and its author, and between a vehicle and its owner. In addition, the difference between *one-way* and *two-way* relations was discussed.

Another important aspect of relations metioned in Section 10.1.1 is the functionality of the relation. Consider a relation 'A R B' meaning that instances of 'A' are in the relation 'R' to instances of 'B.' Relationships involving instances of two classes can be classified into the following forms, depending on the number of instances involved in each instance of the relationship:

One-to-one: In each instance of the relationship, at most one instance of 'A' can be in relation to at most one 'B.'

One-to-many: In each instance of the relationship, at most one instance of 'A' can be in relation to many instances of 'B.'

Many-to-many: In each instance of the relationship, many instances of 'A' can be in relation to many instances of 'B.'

For each of the forms the phrase 'at most one' could be 'exactly one.' This is, for example, the case with a vehicle that always has an owner. Similarly, the phrase 'many' can mean either ' zero or more' or 'one or more' or a fixed number.

Section 10.1.1 also mentioned that it may be useful to represent relationships as instances of patterns. This may be the case for relations that are not binary or if additional attributes are needed to characterize the relation. 'The Beatles', 'The Mills Brothers', and 'Simon and Garfunkel' are examples of phenomena that belong to the extensions of concepts such as 'Quartet', 'Trio' and 'Duo.' As an example of a relation that includes attributes other than just dynamic references, the 'owner/owns' relation for vehicles was given.

The use of relations for modeling phenomena and concepts have been used extensively in the area of databases for many years. The most widely used model is the *extended entity-relationship model*, where information is represented by means of three primitive concepts:

(1) *Entities*, which represent the phenomena being modeled.

(2) *Attributes*, which represent the properties of those phenomena.

(3) *Relationships*, which represent the associations among phenomena.

The extended EER model fits well with object-oriented modeling in the sense that an EER model can be developed as part of an object-oriented model. The EER entities correspond to objects, and the EER attributes correspond to measurable properties. The relationships may be represented as simple references or as patterns, as shown above.

18.7 Representative elements of a description

BETA may be used as a tool for analysis, modeling and design. The BETA language provides support for representing certain parts of reality. There are, however, various parts of reality that cannot be described directly in BETA. It will therefore be necessary to represent such aspects by means of some other BETA elements.

Let us first discuss aspects that can be directly represented in BETA. These include:

- Concepts can be represented by patterns.
- Material can be represented by objects.
- Classification hierarchies can be represented by sub-pattern hierarchies and objects.

- Composition hierarchies corresponding to whole-part composition, reference composition, localization and concept composition can be represented.
- Relations can be represented by reference composition or by relational objects.

The `balance` property of an `Account` is an example of a property that cannot be represented directly in BETA. In Chapter 3, the `balance` property is represented as an `integer` part-object. `Balance` is an example of a measurable property, and the substance of the `integer` part-object does not correspond to a phenomenon in the referent system.

Consider next the *speed* of a vehicle. This is an another example of a property that does not have substance. It is, however, an observable and measurable property, by for example the car's speedometer or the police radar, and the measuring devices do have substance. The measurement maps an observation of the speed on a value space with km/hr (miles/hr) as the unit. There are a number of alternatives for representing a measurable property in BETA. The speed attribute may be represented by an object as in:

```
Vehicle:
  (# Body: @(# ... #);
     owner: ^Person;
     speed: @real
  #)
```

There is, however, a great difference between the description of the `speed` property and the other attributes of `Vehicle`. The `real` object representing speed does not correspond to a phenomenon in the referent system. It is important to be aware of which elements of a BETA description correspond to phenomena/concepts in the referent system and which do not. For this reason we introduce the following definition:

Definition 18.23 *A* representative element *of a BETA description is a BETA element corresponding to a phenomenon or concept in the referent system. BETA elements which are not representative are called* non-representative.

In the above description of `Vehicle`, `Body` and `owner` may be viewed as representative whereas `speed` is not.

Speed is an example of a measurable property, and to measure a property a measurement must be performed. The speed property could thus be represented by a pattern representing a classification of all measurements of the speed. This gives us the the following version of `Vehicle`:

NAME 'vehicle'
origin 'betaenv'
body 'vehiclebody'

LIB:Attributes

```
Vehicle:
  (# Body @(# ... #)
     owner: ^Person;
     Speed: (# V: @real do <<SLOT Speed:DoPart>> exit V #)
     private: @<<SLOT private:ObjectDescriptor>>
  #)
```

NAME 'vehiclebody'
origin 'vehicle'

Speed:DoPart

```
do private.speed -> V
```

private:ObjectDescriptor

```
(# speed: @real #)
```

Figure 18.3 Separation of the `Vehicle` description into representative and non-representative parts.

```
Vehicle:
  (# Body: @(# ... #);
     owner: ^Person;
     Speed: (# V: @real do ... exit V #)
  #)
```

The `Speed` pattern is now intended to perform a measurement producing the 'speed' of the vehicle. How can we complete the description of `Speed`?

One possibility is to have a private `Real` object representing the `Speed`. This may leave us close to the first alternative of representing `Speed` directly as a `Real` object. We may, however, separate the actual representation of the speed from the `Vehicle` pattern using the fragment system, as described in Chapter 17. Figure 18.3 shows how a description of `Vehicle` can be separated into representative and non-representative parts.

18.8 Graphical notation

The syntax of the BETA language used in this book has been textual. In Chapter 17 a diagrammatic notation for the fragment language has been used. It may also be possible to use a diagrammatic or graphical notation for the BETA language, especially useful in analysis and design, since a diagrammatic notation may provide a better overview of key objects and patterns and their relations. In this book certain diagrams have been used to illustrate language concepts.

It is possible to define an alternative graphical syntax for the BETA language, and one proposal for this was given by (Bertelsen *et al.*, 1986). This proposal gave a graphical syntax for all language constructs in BETA. It is not obvious that it is useful to have a graphical notation for all language elements, since perhaps not all details are best presented graphically. The Mjølner BETA System includes an editor that provides a diagrammatic notation for the overall structure of a BETA description. The syntax of these diagrams is similar to the diagrams used in this book.

One advantage of a graphical notation is that it can illustrate certain semantic relations more directly than the textual representation. One example of this is classification hierarchies, as shown in Figure 6.1. The classification structure is defined as sub-patterns, where the names of super-patterns refer to the corresponding super-patterns. Using a graphical notation, it is possible to show the relationship between a pattern and its sub-patterns more directly by using, for example, lines.

A graphical notation can also be used to show composition hierarchies, specified relations, active *versus* passive objects and communication connections between objects.

Graphical notations have been used for many years to support analysis and design. This is especially the case for methods based on structured analysis/structured design. Recently, a number of graphical design notations for supporting object-oriented analysis and design have appeared.

CASE tools

It may be impractical to use a graphical notation without the support of a computer-based tool. A number of so-called *CASE tools* have been developed to support the various different development methods. In general such tools support construction and manipulation of a graphical notation for analysis and/or design. In addition, such tools may support the generation of code skeletons in some programming language, which may then be filled in to produce a final program. There may be a number of problems with such tools depending on the differences between the graphical notation and the programming language. The following problems have been recognized:

(1) There may be language mechanisms in the graphical language which are not supported by the programming language. This may make it difficult to recognize the original design in the code skeletons.

(2) Ideally, a CASE tool should make it possible to make a full specification that can be used to generate a complete executable program. With current specification languages this is not practical, since it would be just as complex as writing the program directly. Most CASE tools thus generate a code skeleton which must be completed to get a full implementation. The distance between the (graphical) specification language used by the CASE tool and the programming language is referred to as the *CASE gap*.

(3) In the process of developing the code skeletons into complete programs, it may happen that it is necessary to reorganize the code. This means that the CASE diagrams will have to be updated, otherwise there will be inconsistencies between the diagrams and the code. The problem of going back from the code to the CASE diagrams is called *reverse engineering*.

The above problems with CASE tools are due to the fact that the CASE language and the programming language differ. By using an object-oriented approach it is possible to design a CASE language and a programming language based on the same abstract language. The graphical notation being developed for BETA is just an alternative syntax for the same underlying abstract language. The graphical notation and the textual notation are two alternative representations of the same language. It is therefore possible to develop a CASE tool/editor[4] that makes it possible to alternate between using the graphical notation and the textual notation. It is easy to generate the textual notation from the graphical notation, and vice versa.

The problems with CASE tools are typical for CASE tools based on structured analysis/structured design. The reason is that there is a major shift in language between analysis, design and implementation. For CASE tools based on an object-oriented approach the problem is in general less obvious. It is, however, often the case that there are differences between the CASE language and the programming language. The BETA approach is that the same underlying (abstract) language should be used for analysis, design and implementation. This will make it easier to alternate between analysis, design and implementation.

[4]Such a CASE tool/editor is currently being developed for the Mjølner BETA System.

18.9 Elements of a method

In this section we summarize some of the important tasks involved in an object-oriented approach. Note that this is not intended to be a fully-fledged method, since there are more elements of a method than presented here. According to (Andersen *et al.*, 1986), a method is characterized by application area, perspective(s) (e.g. language), and guidelines, i.e. techniques, tools and principles of organization.

The approach presented in this chapter consists of creating a physical model (called the model system) of part of reality (called the referent system). The system development process, which is the process of creating a model system, has traditionally been organized into analysis, design and implementation. The analysis phase is primarily concerned with understanding the problem domain; the design phase is concerned with construction of the physical model; implementation is concerned with realizing this model on a computer.

The conceptual framework presented in the previous sections may be applied to all three phases. Each phase represents three different domains: the domain of the referent system is the phenomena and concepts of the application domain; the domain of the model system is the phenomena and concepts of the model, i.e. the representative objects and patterns; the domain of the implementation are the objects and patterns used to implement the model. Thus, one main difference between the three phases is the domain; another is the degree of formality, as we shall see below.

The separation of the system development process into analysis, design and implementation is not a sequential organization in the sense that phase one is analysis, phase two is design and phase three is implementation. Often these phases are completely intermixed, and it may be difficult to distinguish between them. Many developers are not even aware of whether they are doing one or the other. In practice it is very difficult to do analysis without doing some design, and similarly doing design without doing some implementation. The system development process is evolutionary with respect to analysis, design and implementation. One implication of this could be that it is perhaps not useful to distinguish between analysis, design and implementation. Below we argue that this is in fact useful.

18.9.1 General approach

The BETA language and associated conceptual framework is to various degrees useful for analysis, design and implementation. In this section we summarize the overall approach to all these phases. In later sections we discuss how the approach differs for analysis, design and implementation.

In the following the domain can be the referent system, the model system or the computer system. Within a given domain, the following steps should be taken. Again the steps are not supposed to be sequential, merely a check list:

(1) Select (relevant) phenomena and concepts from the domain and select the (relevant) properties of these phenomena and concepts. This includes:

    (a) Select the material (objects) of the domain.

    The section of relevant properties of the material includes selection of:

    (b) Measurable properties.

    (c) Possible physical parts of the material, i.e. whole-part composition.

    (d) Possible reference attributes, i.e. reference composition.

    (e) Possible local concepts: procedure patterns, class patterns, etc., i.e. localization.

    (f) Possible non-local concepts used for describing properties, i.e. concept composition.

    (g) Classification of objects as either active or passive.

    For active objects describe the action-sequences they perform. This includes their participation into concurrent action sequences with other objects, and their involvement in alternating action sequences.

(2) Select concepts. Describe concepts as prototypical, Aristotelian, etc. Describe the intension of the concepts.

(3) Select relations between phenomena and concepts.

    It must be decided whether a relation is one-to-one, one-to-many or many-to-many, and whether a relation should be represented by a pattern or just by means of reference attributes.

(4) Determine classification hierarchies, including clustering and generalization/specialization. It must be considered which of the classification hierarchies are single/tree structured and which are multiple, and whether there should be several alternative classifications of the same phenomena/concepts.

(5) Determine composition hierarchies.

    The composition hierarchies such as whole-part composition, reference composition, localization and concept composition should be determined.

18.9.2 Analysis

The analysis phase is primarily concerned with understanding the problem domain, i.e. the referent system. The domain referred to in the general approach is thus the referent system. We are therefore concerned with the selection of relevant phenomena and concepts from the referent system.

In this phase it is important that the developer is not restricted to the (formal) mechanism of a programming language like BETA. This also applies to any other formal language proposed for analysis including the many proposals for a graphical notation. If the developer is restricted to the use of a formal notation this may impose too narrow a view on the referent system. The developer should make use of any means available when doing analysis, including informal descriptions, graphics and the conceptual framework presented in this chapter.

Prototypical concepts may be useful for understanding the problem domain. Problem-specific concepts are often prototypical. BETA (and other programming languages) is primarily suited for representing Aristotelian concepts. It is possible to use a pseudo formal notation for describing prototypical concepts. Such a description will often include an English description.

The realized concepts in the model have to be Aristotelian. Part of the modeling function is thus concerned with giving prototypical concepts an Aristotelian interpretation. This will often make the resulting computer system appear inflexible to the user. It is important that the developer is not forced to use Aristotelian concepts at too early a stage in the development process. In addition, it is useful to be aware of concepts that are best described as prototypical, but have been transformed into an Aristotelian concept. Of course, the developer should make use of Aristotelian concepts whenever possible.

A major characteristic of analysis is that it may be necessary to relax on the formal notation provided by the language. Examples include the use of prototypical concepts, and describing alternative classifications and multiple inheritance. The developer should have the ability to extend the language to at least informally describe the desired aspects of the referent system.

18.9.3 Design

The design phase is concerned with the construction of a physical model that can be refined into an executable program. The domain referred to in the general approach is thus the objects and patterns of the model.

The (possibly informal) descriptions of phenomena and concepts identified during analysis have to be transformed into formal descriptions in terms of objects and patterns, including giving Aristotelian definitions of prototypical concepts.

As can be seen, the programming process is faced with the problem that not only do we restrict the realism of our model by only considering a part of the world, but equally important, the modeling process *has* to take into account the restrictions imposed by modeling a possible prototypical concept structure in the referent system into an Aristotelian concept structure in the model system. In general, the expressiveness is limited by the language used to describe the model. Other examples of this include the support for classification hierarchies: it may be necessary to transform multiple classification hierarchies into single hierarchies, or into the particular interpretation of multiple inheritance in the programming language, just as it may be awkward to represent several classifications.

A large part of design may be to invent new things and concepts. Remember that the model system is a physical model simulating the behavior of either a real or imaginary part of the world. The imaginary part has to be invented during design: the new phenomena and concepts must have a meaning in the referent system.

The formal notation can be a programming language or a graphical design language. If BETA is used a mixture of graphical and textual syntax can be used. In the design phase it is important to remember that the whole description/specification must be representative with respect to the reference system. A design description in BETA will thus be a fairly abstract program.

Design may also involve the design of a user interface. It is outside the scope of this book to discuss the design of user interfaces. The general approach of an object-oriented user interface is that representative elements of the model should have a representation on the screen. The user should have a feeling of manipulating the physical model directly. Of course, only selected parts of the model may be represented at any given time, but the user should be able to navigate in the model.

During design it may be useful to construct scenarios and/or prototypes of the system. The latter will involve implementation.

At some point during design it may be necessary to make a requirement specification, and in such a specification it should be possible to use part of the design. Selected objects and their attributes, class patterns, procedure patterns, etc., classification hierarchies and composition hierarchies should be relatively easy to present for the users. The form of the presentation may be a mixture of diagrams, program text and English descriptions, depending on the background of the user.

18.9.4 Implementation

Here the domain of the general approach is the computer system. Phenomena and concepts are the objects and patterns necessary to implement the design. In the implementation phase the design description is refined into an implementation that can be executed. It is very important to make a clear separation of representable and non-representable parts of the description.

18.10 Exercises

(1) Develop a set of concepts that capture what you consider to be the essential properties of a restaurant.

(a) Develop a generalization hierarchy with concepts that are more general than *Restaurant* and concepts that are more special than *Restaurant*.

(b) Develop a composition hierarchy. Identify possible parts, references and concepts of a restaurant. Identify possible concepts/phenomena where a restaurant may be a component.

(c) Identify one or more phenomena in the extensions of the concepts.

(d) Describe the intension of the developed concepts. Describe defining and characteristic properties of the concepts.

(e) Are the developed concepts Aristotelian or prototypical?

(f) Identify substance, measurable properties and transformations.

(g) Try to model the process of serving a customer in a restaurant. This may include concepts like 'customer', 'table', 'waiter.' It may include actions like 'get a table', 'get a menu', 'order food' and 'pay the bill.' For each object in your model, identify which of its attributes are measurable properties, part objects, references to separate objects and local concepts.

(h) Include modeling of the restaurant's food preparation process as well.

(i) For which type of applications are the concepts useful? For customers using restaurants, for the owner of a restaurant, for the city administration, etc.?

18.11 Notes

Some authors use the term *paradigm* instead of perspective as used in this book, i.e. terms like the object-oriented paradigm and functional paradigm are used instead of object-oriented perspective and functional perspective. (Nygaard and Sørgaard, 1987) argue that according to Kuhn, paradigms are defined to deal with major shifts in understanding within science, which is not the case with for example the difference between functional programming and object-oriented programming. Object-oriented programming and functional programming may often both be used in the same program.

Various authors use different words for classification and composition. Some of the terms like classification and composition and their more special variants – clustering, generalization/specialization, whole-part composition, reference composition, localization, concept composition – are widely accepted, whereas others are not. The term classification is generally accepted although some authors use classification for what has been called clustering here. The term generalization/specialization is widely accepted, with the same meaning as here. It is more problematic with terms for composition: the term *aggregation* is often used instead of composition. However, there is no commonly agreed definition of aggregation. Most authors define aggregation to be whole-part composition. Others define it to be localization or concept composition. In (Smith and Smith, 1977a) aggregation seems to be defined similarly to concept composition.

Relations have been an important aspect of databases, analysis and design for many years. The entity-relationship model was introduced in (Chen, 1976). Relations have not played a central role within object-oriented programming, but are included in most books on object-oriented databases and object-oriented analysis and design (see (Hughes, 1991; Coad and Yourdon, 1990; Coad and Yourdon, 1991; Booch, 1991; Rumbaugh *et al.*, 1991; Wirfs-Brock *et al.*, 1991)).

The conceptual framework presented here has been influenced by similar developments within artificial intelligence and databases (Smith and Smith, 1977a; Smith and Smith, 1977b). The development of a conceptual framework has been an important part of the development of BETA. It does not seem to have played a role in the development of other object-oriented languages. It is, however, of major importance in the area of object-oriented analysis, modeling and design, as presented, in for example, (Booch, 1991; Coad and Yourdon, 1990; Coad and Yourdon, 1991; Shlaer and Mellor, 1988; Rumbaugh *et al.*, 1991; Wirfs-Brock *et al.*, 1991). The BETA approach is, however, that analysis, design and programming should not be considered as different issues: it is all programming at different abstraction levels. The conceptual framework presented here is heavily influenced by (Knudsen and Thomsen, 1985). The use of characteristic properties for Aristotelian concepts is discussed in (Faber and Krukow, 1990). The process of knowledge is from (Mathiassen, 1981), but originates from Karl Marx.

Object-oriented CASE for BETA is discussed in (Sandvad, 1990).

Appendix A

Grammar for BETA

This appendix describes a grammar for the implemented subset of BETA. The grammar formalism used in the Mjølner BETA System is a variant of context-free grammars. A *structured context-free grammar* is a context-free grammar (CFG) where the rules (productions) satisfy a certain structure. Each nonterminal must be defined by exactly one of the following rules:

1. An *alternation rule* has the following form:

   ```
   <A0> ::| <A1>  |  <A2>  | ... | <An>
   ```

   where <A0>, <A1>, ..., <An> are nonterminal symbols. The rule specifies that <A0> derives one of <A1>, <A2>, ..., or <An>.

2. A *constructor rule* has the following form:

   ```
   <A0> ::= w0  <t1:A1>  w1  ... <tn:An> wn
   ```

   where <A0>, <t1:A1>, ..., <tn:An> are nonterminal symbols and w0, w1, ..., wn are possibly empty strings of terminal symbols. This rule describes that <A0> derives the string:

   ```
   w0 <A1> w1 ... <An> wn
   ```

   A nonterminal on the right side of the rule has the form <t:A> where t is a tag-name and A is the syntactic category. Tag-names are used to distinguish between nonterminals belonging to the same syntactic category, consequently all tag-names in a rule must be different. If no tag-name is provided then the name of the syntactic category is used as a tag-name.

3. A *list rule* has one of the following forms:

```
<A> ::+ <B> w
<A> ::* <B> w
```

where <B> is a nonterminal and w is a possibly empty string of terminal symbols. The nonterminal <A> generates a list of <B>s separated by ws:

```
<B> w <B> w ... w <B>
```

The +-rule specifies that at least one element is generated; the *-rule specifies that the list may be empty.

4. An *optional rule* has the following form:

```
<A> ::? <B>
```

where <B> is a nonterminal. The nonterminal <A> may generate the empty string or <B>.

There are four predefined nonterminal symbols named <NameDecl>, <NameAppl>, <String> and <Const>. These nonterminals are called *lexem-symbols*, and they derive identifiers, character-strings and integer constants. A lexem-symbol may also have a tag-name like <Title:NameAppl>.

The start symbol of the grammar is <BetaForm>, which may derive either an <ObjectDescriptor>, an <Attributes> or a <DoPart>. These nonterminals are those that can be used to define fragment-forms/slots, cf. Chapter 17.

The grammar

```
<BetaForm> ::| <DescriptorForm>
            | <AttributesForm>
<DescriptorForm> ::= <ObjectDescriptor>
<AttributesForm> ::= <Attributes>
<ObjectDescriptor> ::= <SuperPattenrOpt> <MainPart>
<MainPart> ::= (# <Attributes> <ActionPart> #)
<Attributes> ::+ <AttributeDeclOpt> ;
<SuperPattern> ::? <SuperPattern>
<SuperPattern> ::= <AttributeDenotation>
<AttributeDeclOpt> ::? <AttributeDecl>
```

```
<AttributeDecl> ::| <PatternDecl>
                  | <SimpleDecl>
                  | <RepetitionDecl>
                  | <VirtualDecl>
                  | <BindingDecl>
                  | <FinalBindingDecl>
                  | <VariablePatternDecl>
<PatternDecl> ::= <Names> : <ObjectDescriptor>
<SimpleDecl> ::= <Names> : <referenceSpecification>
<RepetitionDecl>::= <Names> : [ <index> ] <referenceSpecification>
<VirtualDecl> ::= <Names> :< <ObjectSpecification>
<BindingDecl> ::= <Names> :: < <ObjectSpecification>
<FinalBindingDecl> ::= <Names> :: <ObjectSpecification>
<VariablePatternDecl> ::= <Names> : ## <AttributeDenotation>
<referenceSpecification> ::| <StaticItem>
                           | <DynamicItem>
                           | <StaticComponent>
                           | <DynamicComponent>
<StaticItem> ::= @ <ObjectSpecification>
<DynamicItem> ::= ^ <AttributeDenotation>
<StaticComponent> ::= @ | <ObjectSpecification>
<DynamicComponent> ::= ^ | <AttributeDenotation>
<ObjectSpecification> ::| <ObjectDescriptor>
                        | <AttributeDenotation>
<Index> ::| <SimpleIndex>
          | <NamedIndex>
<NamedIndex> ::= <NameDcl> : <Evaluation>
<ActionPart> ::= <EnterPartOpt> <DoPartOpt> <ExitPartOpt>
<EnterPartOpt> ::? <EnterPart>
<DoPartOpt> ::? <DoPart>
<ExitPartOpt> ::? <ExitPart>
<EnterPart> ::= enter <Evaluation>
<DoPart> ::= do <Imperatives>
<ExitPart> ::= exit <Evaluation>
<Imperatives> ::+ <ImpOpt> ;
<ImpOpt> ::? <Imp>
<Imp> ::| <LabelledImp>
        | <LabelledCompoundImp>
        | <ForImp>
        | <IfImp>
        | <LeaveImp>
        | <RestartImp>
        | <InnerImp>
        | <SuspendImp>
        | <Evaluation>
```

```
<LabelledImp> ::= <NameDcl> : <Imp>
<LabelledCompoundImp> ::= ( <NameDcl> <Imperatives> <NameDcl> )
<ForImp> ::= (for <Index> repeat <Imperatives> for)
<IfImp> ::= (if <Evaluation> <Alternatives> <ElsePartOpt> if)
<Alternatives> ::+ <Alternative>
<Alternative> ::= <Selections> then <Imperatives>
<Selections>::+ <Selection>
<Selection> ::| <CaseSelection>
<CaseSelection> ::= // <evaluation>
<ElsePartOpt> ::? <ElsePart>
<ElsePart> ::= else <Imperatives>
<LeaveImp> ::= leave <NameApl>
<RestartImp> ::= restart <NameApl>
<InnerImp> ::= inner <NameAplOpt>
<NameAplOpt> ::? <NameApl>
<SuspendImp>  ::= suspend
<Evaluations> ::+ <Evaluation> ,
<Evaluation> ::| <Expression>
               | <AssignmentEvaluation>
<AssignmentEvaluation> ::= <Evaluation> -> <Transaction>
<Transaction> ::| <ObjectEvaluation>
                | <ComputedObjectEvaluation>
                | <ObjectReference>
                | <EvalList>
                | <StructureReference>
<ObjectEvaluation> ::| <InsertedItem>
                     | <reference>
<Reference> ::| <ObjectDenotation>
              | <DynamicObjectGeneration>
<DynamicObjectGeneration> ::| <DynamicItemGeneration>
                            | <DynamicComponentGeneration>
<InsertedItem> ::= <ObjectDescriptor>
<ObjectDenotation> ::= <AttributeDenotation>
<ComputedObjectEvaluation> ::= <ObjectEvaluation> !
<ObjectReference> ::= <Reference> []
<StructureReference> ::= <AttributeDenotation> ##
<EvalList> ::= ( <Evaluations> )
<DynamicItemGeneration> ::= & <ObjectSpecification>
<DynamicComponentGeneration> ::= & | <ObjectSpecification>
<AttributeDenotation>::| <NameApl>
                       | <Remote>
                       | <ComputedRemote>
                       | <Indexed>
                       | <ThisObject>
<Remote> ::= <AttributeDenotation> . <NameApl>
<ComputedRemote> ::= ( <Evaluations> ) . <NameApl>
```

```
<Indexed> ::= <AttributeDenotation> [ <Evaluation> ]
<ThisObject> ::= this ( <NameApl> )
<Expression> ::| <RelationalExp> | <SimpleExp>
<RelationalExp>::| <EqExp> | <LtExp> | <LeExp>
                 | <GtExp> | <GeExp> | <NeExp>
<SimpleExp> ::| <AddExp> | <SignedTerm> | <Term>
<AddExp>  ::| <PlusExp> | <MinusExp> | <OrExp>
<SignedTerm> ::| <unaryPlusExp> | <unaryMinusexp>
<Term> ::| <MulExp> | <Factor>
<MulExp> ::| <TimesExp> | <DivExp> | <ModExp> | <AndExp>
<EqExp> ::= <Operand1:SimpleExp> = <Operand2:SimpleExp>
<LtExp> ::= <Operand1:SimpleExp> < <Operand2:SimpleExp>
<LeExp> ::= <Operand1:SimpleExp> <= <Operand2:SimpleExp>
<GtExp> ::= <Operand1:SimpleExp> > <Operand2:SimpleExp>
<GeExp> ::= <Operand1:SimpleExp> >= <Operand2:SimpleExp>
<NeExp> ::= <Operand1:SimpleExp> <> <Operand2:SimpleExp>
<PlusExp> ::= <SimpleExp> + <Term>
<MinusExp> ::= <SimpleExp> - <Term>
<OrExp> ::= <SimpleExp> or <Term>
<unaryPlusExp> ::= + <Term>
<unaryMinusExp> ::= - <Term>
<TimesExp> ::= <Term> * <Factor>
<DivExp> ::= <Term> div <Factor>
<ModExp> ::= <Term> mod <Factor>
<AndExp> ::= <Term> and <Factor>
<Factor> ::| <TextConst>
           | <IntegerConst>
           | <NotExp>
           | <NoneExp>
           | <RepetitionSlice>
           | <Transaction>
<RepetitionSlice> ::= <AttributeDenotation>
                 [ <Evaluation> : <Evaluation> ]
<notExp> ::= not <factor>
<noneExp> ::= none
<Names> ::+ <NameDcl> ,
<NameDcl> ::= <NameDecl>
<NameApl> ::= <NameAppl>
<SimpleEntry> ::? <TextConst>
<TextConst> ::= <String>
<IntegerConst> ::= <Const>
<SimpleIndex> ::= <Evaluation>
```

Appendix B

The Mjølner BETA System

The Mjølner BETA System is a programming environment for object-oriented programming, which includes an implementation of BETA.

The BETA implementation has native code generation, garbage collection, separate compilation, configuration control, interface to C, and assembly, source-level debugger and persistent objects. There is a large library of class patterns and application frameworks:

- Class patterns for text, file, set, multiset, set with subsets, hashtable, list, stack, queue, priority queue, deque, etc.
- Powerful and easy to use application frameworks on top of the X Window System, Athena Widgets and Motif.
- Powerful and easy to use application frameworks on top of the Macintosh Toolbox.
- Powerful metaprogramming system for manipulating programs as data.
- Interface to operating system and external languages.
- Powerful graphical system based on the Stencil & Paint imaging model.

A pre-release is available of the Hyper Structure Editor for programs and text documents supporting integrated syntax directed and textual editing, incremental parsing, abstract presentation and browsing, integration of documentation and comments, hypertext facilities, and adaptive pretty printing.

A demo version is available of the Mjølner BETA CASE Tool, with support for design diagrams and simultaneous editing of design diagrams and program text. This eliminates the CASE gap by using one single abstract language (BETA) for design as well as for implementation.

The Mjølner BETA System is available on the following platforms: Macintosh, 8 MB RAM, at least a 68020 CPU, MPW; Sun-3, Sun-4 (SPARC), 16 MB RAM, SunOS 4.0, Solaris; HP 9000/300, 400, 700; 16

MB RAM, HP/UX 8. Mjølner Informatics ApS offers to port the MBS to other platforms. Ask for more information.

A general overview of the Mjølner BETA System may be found in (Knudsen *et al.*, 1989). (Knudsen *et al.*, 1990) give an example of using the object-oriented BETA interface on top of the Macintosh Toolbox.

Further information about the Mjølner BETA System is available from:

Mjølner Informatics ApS,	Phone:	+45 86 20 20 00
Science Park Aarhus,	Fax:	+45 86 20 12 22
Gustav Wiedsvej 10,	E-mail:	`mjolner@mjolner.dk`
DK-8000 Aarhus C, DENMARK.		

The following sections describe the main components of the Mjølner BETA System.

B.1 Implementation of BETA

The Mjølner BETA System includes an implementation of the BETA programming language. The implementation has the following characteristics:

- Native code generation. The compiler generates assembly code.
- Garbage collection. Automatic storage management and garbage collection is used. The techniques used for garbage collection are generation-based scavenging and mark-sweep.
- Separate compilation. Programs may be divided into smaller fragments (modules) for separate compilation. The compiler makes an automatic dependency analysis on the fragments structure. When a fragment has been changed, the system keeps track of the dependent fragments that must be recompiled.
- Interface to C and assembly languages. There is a general interface to C and assembly languages, including the call of C procedures, call-back and parameter transfer of simple types, text and C structures. For Macintosh there is also a Pascal interface.
- Source-level debugger. A source-level debugger for the BETA language is available on the UNIX platform, containing facilities for specifying break-points, single stepping, inspection of object states, inspecting the run-time organization, etc. The debugger uses a graphical interface running under the X Window System.
- Persistent objects. Support for saving any kind of objects generated by a BETA program execution on secondary storage and restoring them

in another BETA program execution. The persistent store is fully type safe. An object-oriented database for BETA objects is currently under development.

- Distributed objects. Support for distribution of objects to support a client-server model is being developed.
- Implementation language. The entire Mjølner BETA System is written in BETA, except for a few run-time routines.

B.2 The Mjølner BETA fragment system

The fragment system is used for splitting BETA programs into smaller pieces (fragments). The fragment system is responsible for the dependencies between different fragment files, defining a given library or program. Due to the generality of the fragment system, a BETA program can be divided into smaller pieces in many different ways:

Modularization Programs can be split into modules of logically related elements called fragments. A fragment is not restricted to a specific BETA element such as a pattern. A fragment may, for example, contain one or more patterns, a set of attributes of a pattern, or the imperative bodies of one or more procedure patterns.

Separation of interface and implementation A fragment can be split into interface fragments and implementation fragments. It is thus possible to hide the implementation details of a fragment from the client fragments using the fragment.

Alternative implementations and variant control It is possible to have alternative implementations of a fragment. Such alternative fragments may be machine dependent and used for organizing different variants of the same fragment.

Configuration control The system automatically combines the necessary fragments needed for a complete program, including the selection of machine dependent fragments. The system handles the organization of code for different machines.

Units for separate compilation A fragment may be separately compiled. The compilation compiler makes an automatic dependency analysis on the fragment structure. When fragments have been changed, the system keeps track of dependent fragments that must be recompiled.

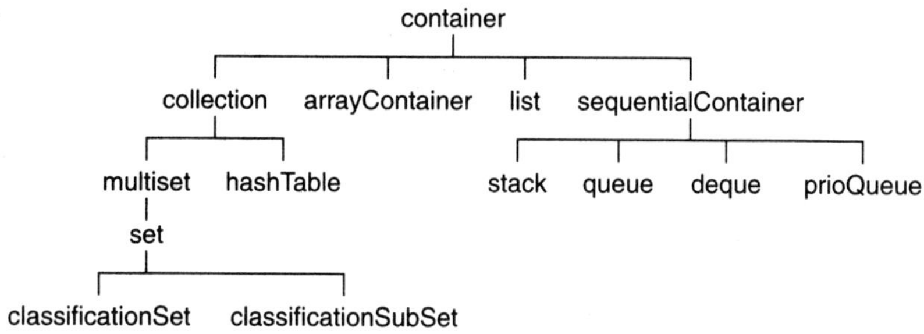

Figure B.1 Classification hierarchy for container patterns.

Grammar-based The fragment system is grammar-based in the sense that a fragment is a legal sequence of terminal and nonterminal symbols of the grammar. The fragment system may thus be used to implement a fragment structure for any language, based on its context-free syntax.

Metaprogramming The fragment system is part of the metaprogramming system Yggdrasil, and enables the management and manipulation of coherent BETA programs located in different files.

B.3 Basic libraries

Container patterns

The standard container data structures are organized in the classification hierarchy shown in Figure B.1:

Container patterns are generic patterns in the sense that the element type of the elements kept in the container can vary between different container instances. `MultiSet` is an unstructured collection of element references, where duplicates are allowed. `Set` is like `multiSet`, except that duplicates are not allowed. `ClassificationSet` (and the accompanying `classificationSubset`) is used for dynamic classification of objects. `HashTable` implements a standard hash table data structure. `ArrayContainer` is an abstraction of an element repetition, augmented with sorting operations. `Stack` implements a stack data structure, `Queue` implements a queue data structure, `Deque` implements a double-ended queue data structure, `PrioQueue` implements a priority queue data structure, and `List` implements a list data structure. Lists may be recursive (i.e. lists may have sublists).

Basic patterns

The basic patterns are the object-oriented variants of the standard simple datatypes, such as `char`, `boolean`, `integer` and `real`. For example, these patterns make it possible to treat integers as ordinary objects. The basic patterns also include the `Object` pattern, which is the implicit super-pattern for all those patterns that have no explicit super-pattern.

Stream patterns

A `Stream` is a generalization of internal and external text objects. An internal text object (`Text`) is a sequence (repetition) of chars. An external text object (`File`) corresponds to a traditional text file. `Stream`, `Text` and `File` are organized in the following hierarchy:

```
Stream: (# ... #);
  Text: Stream(# ... #);
  File: Stream(# ... #);
    UnixFile: File(# ... #);
    MacFile: File(# ... #);
```

As part of the interface to the operating system, the basic libraries include patterns for accessing the directory structures of hierarchical file systems:

```
Directory: (# ... #);
  UnixDirectory: Directory(# ... #);
  MacDirectory: Directory(# ... #);
```

Process patterns

The process interface facilitates execution of sub-processes, communication between several independent processes, client/server architectures, and it is even possible to establish communication between UNIX and Macintosh processes.

Concurrency patterns

The basic libraries define various patterns for dealing with concurrency, synchronization and communication. These patterns are `system`, `semaphore`, `fork`, `monitor`, `port`, `restrictedPort`, `objectPort`, `qualifiedPort`, `conc` and `alt`.

External language interface patterns

To enable interfacing into external languages (such as C), the basic libraries define the `external`, `cStruct` and `externalRecord` patterns.

B.4 Yggdrasil — The Mjølner BETA metaprogramming system

Yggdrasil — The Mjølner BETA metaprogramming system A metaprogram is a program that manipulates other programs. Yggdrasil[1] is a metaprogramming system that supports the creation of metaprograms, and is grammar-based: a metaprogramming environment may be generated from the grammar of any language.

Metaprograms manipulate programs through a common representation called abstract syntax trees (AST). An AST is modeled as an instance of a pattern; there is a pattern corresponding to each syntactic category (nonterminal) of the grammar. The grammar hierarchy is modeled by a corresponding pattern hierarchy, derived automatically from the grammar.

Grammar-based interface

The grammar for a specific language results in a grammar-based interface – a metaprogramming environment with a set of patterns for the language. A metaprogram using the grammar-based interface will thus be language-specific. Examples of tools that benefit from using the grammar-based interface are semantic checkers, program analyzers, interpreters, browsers and graphical presentation tools.

Three levels of support

The AST may be manipulated at different levels of specialization:

- **Tree level** Here the AST is viewed as a tree. Examples of tools accessing the AST using the tree level are table-driven parsers and syntax-directed editors.
- **Context-free level** This is the grammar-based interface generated automatically from the grammar. Graphical presentation tools and browsers are examples of tools using the context-free level.

[1]Yggdrasil is the tree of the world, the ash tree of which the crown covers the whole world. The tree gets power from the gods, from the evil giants and from the kingdom of death. Everything in the world happens under the mighty crown of Yggdrasil.

- **Semantic level** At this level semantic attributes may be added to the AST. The compiler is an example of a tool using the semantic level to access the AST.

Users may develop their own metaprogramming tools. Yggdrasil supports the generation of metaprogramming environments from a grammar, and users can then use this environment to develop their own metaprogramming tools – tools that manipulate other programs.

Fragment system

The fragment system is a part of Yggdrasil, and enables the management and manipulation of coherent ASTs located in different files. The functionality of the fragment system allows splitting of an AST into a number of sub-ASTs (sub-trees) by allowing some inferior nodes in the original AST to be replaced by special nodes. The AST, originally positioned at the position of that node, is called a fragment, and may be located in a totally different file.

B.5 Valhalla — The Mjølner BETA debugger

The Mjølner BETA Debugger Valhalla[2] is a symbolic source level debugger with an easy-to-use graphical user interface.

Using the Mjølner BETA Debugger you may

- Trace the execution of a BETA program by setting break-points and stepping at the level of single BETA source lines, stepping over procedure-calls, and even single step at the level of machine code instructions.
- Simultaneously examine the state of any number of objects.
- Examine the execution stack and view code and objects on the stack.
- Examine the program heaps and view objects on the heaps.
- Relative to any object, find and display the object that is the value of an expression.
- Simultaneously view any number of windows containing source code.
- Execute the program until a run-time error occurs and then examine the program state.

[2]Valhalla is Odin's hall, where all the dead warriors come when they have fallen as heroes in battle. Odin is the highest of all gods in Asgaard.

The Mjølner BETA Debugger is currently available on the UNIX systems supported by the Mjølner BETA System. It runs under the X Window System.

B.6 XtEnv — Object-oriented interface to X Toolkit Widgets

The Mjølner BETA object-oriented interface to the X Toolkit Intrinsics (Xt) is called XtEnv. This pattern contains the basic patterns common for many user-interface toolkits built upon the X Window System, but it does not contain any higher level user interface elements. It is typically used together with a widget set containing such user interface elements built on top of it. Examples of such widget sets are the Athena Widgets, OPEN LOOK and Motif. The Mjølner BETA system currently includes object-oriented interfaces to the Athena Widgets (AwEnv) and to Motif (MotifEnv):

XtEnv `XtEnv` includes patterns corresponding to the widgets of the X Toolkit Intrinsics, i.e. `Core, Composite, Constraint` and the various `Shell` sub-classes. It also includes an interface to Xt resources, displays, translations, actions, timers and work procedures. An application is created by specializing the `XtEnv pattern`, creating various widgets and initializing them. When the `XtEnv` pattern starts executing it does some initialization itself. Then it calls the BETA construct `INNER`, thus allowing the specialization to initialize itself. When the control returns to `XtEnv`, a global event handler is started, which distributes events to the various widgets. In `Xt`, the widgets form a hierarchy, used for distributing events and when specifying resources. The block structure of the BETA program is used to determine the hierarchy automatically. This is a major enhancement compared to the C interface of `Xt`.

AwEnv `AwEnv` is a specialization of `XtEnv`, which adds the patterns corresponding to the Athena Widgets. This includes the simple widgets `Label`, `Scrollbar`, `Grip, Stripchart, Command, Toggle` and `List`. It also includes the text editor called AsciiText, menus and submenus. Finally, it includes the layout widgets called `Form, Dialog` and `Box`.

MotifEnv `MotifEnv` is a specialization of `XtEnv` which adds the patterns corresponding to the Motif widgets and gadgets. This includes the primitive widgets `Label, Cascadebutton, Drawnbutton, Pushbutton, Togglebutton, Arrowbutton`, `List`, `Scrollbar`, `Separator` and `Text`; the Motif-specific shells like `DialogShell` and `MenuShell`; and the Manager widgets `BulletinBoard`, `RowColumn`, `ScrolledWindow`, `DrawingArea`, `VPaned`, `Frame`, `Scale`, `SelectionBox`, `MessageBox`, `Form`, `FileSelectionBox` and `CommandBox`. Patterns also exist for the corresponding gadgets (windowless widgets), and finally an interface to the Motif-specific resources like Motif Strings is included.

B.7 MacEnv — Object-oriented interface to the Macintosh Toolbox

`MacEnv` is a family of libraries abstracting the Macintosh Toolbox into an object-oriented framework. Every object in the Macintosh user interface, like windows and menus, has a corresponding BETA pattern definition in MacEnv. To create, say, a new window, you just create an instance of the `Window` pattern and tell it to display itself. All the other Macintosh user interface objects can be created and displayed in the same way. User-defined objects like dialog boxes are easily created by specializing the `Dialog` pattern, and using the various `Control` patterns defined in `MacEnv`. `MacEnv` includes a series of predefined patterns for making text editors, scrolling windows with pictures, object-oriented graphics with QuickDraw, easy interface to the Macintosh resources, files, clipboard, sound and QuickTime.

The object-oriented abstractions in `MacEnv` are more general, flexible and easier to use than, for example, MacApp of Apple Computer, Inc., due to the strengths and power of the BETA programming language.

Highlights of the object-oriented abstractions in MacEnv:

User interface objects All interface objects (menus, windows, graphical objects) are sub-patterns of the InterfaceObject pattern. The InterfaceObject defines two common properties of all interface objects: event handling and access to Macintosh resources.

Event handling One of the strengths of `MacEnv` is the ease with which the event handling is conducted. `MacEnv` takes care of all the details of the Macintosh event dispatching and handling, and converts all Macintosh event occurrences into invocations of special virtual patterns (event patterns) within the appropriate user interface object. The application programmer only has to further bind these event patterns of the individual user interface objects to specify the actions to be taken in response to user interaction.

Windows Macintosh windows are easily created and manipulated using the BETA pattern Window. The Window includes definitions of all standard actions, such as dragging, resizing and scrolling (using the Scroller pattern). A window can have sub-windows called **canvases**. A canvas is a sub-window inside a window, defining its own coordinate system and event handler. Floating windows can also be easily created using `MacEnv`.

Menus The Menu pattern interfaces to the Macintosh menu. Menus defined using resources can be easily created. Actions are bound to the items by virtual procedures. The standard menus **`Apple`**, **`File`** and **`Edit`** are predefined in `MacEnv`, and will always appear in a `MacEnv` application.

Object-oriented `MacEnv` This defines an object-oriented abstraction on top of the Macintosh QuickDraw graphics library. For each graphical entity (rectangle, region, line, text, etc.) a corresponding BETA user interface pattern is defined. Direct user interaction with these graphical entities, including interactive creation, is fully defined in the corresponding BETA pattern.

B.8 Bifrost — Interactive object-oriented graphics system

Bifrost[3] is based on the Stencil & Paint imaging model. Bifrost models computer graphics images by abstracting the geometric and color properties of graphical objects. The important new concept introduced in Bifrost is that there is one basic drawing primitive, the graphical object, uniting interaction, graphics modeling and graphics context. Bifrost includes extensive support for various kinds of interaction: interactive creation, reshaping, translation, scaling and rotation of graphical objects. The object-oriented approach makes extensibility and tailorability a simple task, and facilitates object-oriented drawing applications. One of the main goals of the development of Bifrost was to make the graphics system independent of underlying graphics and hardware systems. Important concepts of Bifrost:

Canvas Representation of the drawing surface, and is the connection between the display device and Bifrost. The canvas contains a picture, and all graphics shown in the canvas must be in the canvas picture.

[3] Bifrost is the luminous bridge, the rainbow, that leads from Midgaard to Asgaard. Midgaard is the place where the human beings live. Asgaard is the habitat of the gods in the middle of the world.

Picture Is a collection of graphical objects, and realizes the concept of graphics modeling. The graphical object is the smallest possible entity that can be drawn, and is complete in the sense that it contains all necessary information about how the graphical object appears on the canvas, and is therefore independent of any other graphical objects in the picture.

Graphical object shape The graphical object concept is a composition of two concepts: shape and paint. The shape describes the outline of the object, and the paint describes the color or raster to be pushed through the shape of the object, thus making it appear in the canvas. The shape of a graphical object is described by segments – a segment is either a straight line segment or a spline segment (used to describe curves). The shape is analogous to the stencil in the Stencil & Paint imaging model.

Paint The paint of Bifrost represents what is pushed through the shape of the graphical object. The Paint can be simple solid colors using a predefined name of the color or relative to some color space, e.g. RGB, HSV, CMY. Tiles and rasters (e.g. scanned images) can also be used as paint.

The basic imaging model of Bifrost is thus very simple: define a shape that represents the outline of the object you want to draw, select a paint as the color for the object, construct a graphical object with the shape and paint just defined, and draw the object in a canvas, i.e. insert the graphical object into the canvas picture. If the object must have several different colors the object must be split into more graphical objects and assembled in a picture. The picture is a graphical object itself, and can thus be drawn on a canvas. Bifrost is currently available on UNIX models only.

B.9 Sif — Mjølner BETA hyper structure editor

Sif[4] is a hyper structure editor with the following features:

Syntax-directed editing Syntax directed editing makes it possible to construct and edit programs or other documents without introducing syntax errors. Syntax-directed editing is especially useful for application-oriented languages intended for end-users, casual users and beginners who may have difficulty in remembering the concrete syntax. Also a program

[4] The wife of Thor is Sif with the golden hair.

constructed by syntax-directed editing need not be parsed, thereby saving time in the development phase. One characteristic of syntax-directed editing is choosing templates from a menu, containing only the legal choices at any time.

Abstract presentation and browsing The editor is able to present a program at any level of detail. At the top-level of a program the user may get an overview of classes and procedures. It is then possible to browse through modules and procedures to see more and more details. This mechanism is completely general since the user may decide the level of granularity. The three dots ... , called contractions, indicate details that are suppressed. By clicking on contractions the next level of detail is shown.

Adaptive pretty-printing The editor includes an adaptive pretty-printing algorithm which prints the program or document such that it always fits within the size of the window or paper.

Text editing and incremental parsing The programmer may freely alternate between syntax directed editing and textual editing. Any program part may be textually edited using keyboard, mouse and menus in the usual style known from the Macintosh or the X Window System, respectively. Any program part that has been textually edited is immediately parsed.

Fragment manipulation and browsing The editor provides an interface to the fragment system. It is possible to browse in the fragment structure and to create and combine fragments.

Grammar basis The editor is generic and may be adapted to specific languages. An editor for a given language is generated from a context-free grammar for that language. Grammars exist for a number of programming languages, including BETA, Simula, Modula-2, Pascal, Standard ML and Object-Oriented SDL. Grammars have also been made for the query language SQL and for various document types in the style of SGML and ODA.

Integration of program and documentation The user may add a comment at any place in a program. The user decides whether or not to display a comment, and whether to display a comment as part of the program or in another window; in the latter case a comment is indicated by means of (*). Using abstract presentation it is possible to obtain a pretty-print of a program which includes just the classes and procedure headings and corresponding comments. This makes it possible to extract a functional specification from the program.

This facility, together with abstract presentation, has turned out to be one of the most useful features of the editor. Programmers are motivated for integrating code and documentation since it is easy to extract part of the program and the comments as functional specifications and other kinds of documentation.

Hypertext facilities The editor includes hypertext facilities. The facility for handling comments is an example of a hyperlink between a program and a text document. Another type of hyperlink is a link from the use of a name to the declaration of the name (this is only implemented for BETA). Examples of such semantic links are putInt and putText that are used in Employee and defined in Stream. Another kind of link are those between program and documentation. Anchors (i.e. link end-points) are indicated by means of the special symbol (ˆ).

Availability At the time of writing, Sif is only available as a pre-release. It will become part of the commercial Mjølner BETA System.

B.10 Freja — Mjølner BETA CASE tool

Freja,[5] the Mjølner BETA CASE tool, provides:

- graphical structure editing of design diagrams
- textual structure editing of programs
- automatic program generation from design diagrams
- reverse engineering from programs to design diagrams
- simultaneous editing of design diagrams and programs.

No CASE gap One single abstract language is used throughout analysis, design and implementation. Different concrete syntaxes are used to present the different models:

- graphical syntax for design
- textual syntax for programs.

[5]Freja is the goddess of love; she lives in Folkvang and is the most beautiful of all women in Asgaard. She owns the golden Brisingemen jewelry.

This gives a significant advantage compared to other object-oriented CASE tools that support object-oriented notations for analysis and design that are isolated from the language used for implementation. Isolated notations for analysis and design introduce a new CASE gap because there are still consistency problems between design and implementation. The single language approach puts strong requirements on the language used. It must be executable, and it must be powerful enough to model the application domain. BETA meets these requirements.

Implementation

- common representation for design diagrams and programs
- graphical abstract presentations of the common representation in the graphical structure editor Freja
- textual abstract and detailed presentations of the common representation in the Sif textual structure editor
- the common representation is abstract syntax trees
- experimental version exists on UNIX workstations
- Freja is implemented on top of Design/OA.

Availability At the time of writing, the Mjølner BETA CASE tool is available on UNIX systems as an experimental version. It will become part of the commercial Mjølner BETA System. The CASE Tool requires Design/OA.

Bibliography

(Abelson and Sussmann, 1985) G. Abelson, G.J. Sussmann with J. Sussmann. *The Structure and Interpretation of Computer Programs.* Cambridge MA: MIT Press, 1985.

(Agesen *et al.*, 1990) O. Agesen, S. Frølund, M.H. Olsen. *Persistent and Shared Objects in BETA.* Technical Report IR-89, Computer Science Department, Aarhus University, 1990.

(Andersen *et al.*, 1986) N. E. Andersen, F. Kensing, M. Lassen J. Lundin, L. Mathiassen, A. Munck-Madsen, P. Sørgaard. *Professional System Development.* Teknisk Forlag, 1986 (in Danish).

(Atkinson *et al.*, 1990) M. Atkinson, F. Bancilhou, D.DeWitt, K. Dittrich, D. Maier, S. Zdonick. Object-Oriented Database System Manifesto. In *Deductive and Object-Oriented Databases* (W. Kim, J.M. Nicolas, eds.). Amsterdam: North-Holland, 1990.

(Bertelsen *et al.*, 1986) S. Bertelsen, S. Hvidbjerg, P. Sørensen. Graphical Programming Environments – Applied to BETA. *Masters thesis,* Computer Science Department, Aarhus University, 1986.

(Blake and Cook, 1987) E. Blake, S. Cook. On Including Part Hierarchies in Object-Oriented Languages, with an Implementation in Smalltalk. In *Proc. Euro. Conf. Object-Oriented Programming,* Paris, France, July, 1987 (*Lecture Notes in Computer Science, Vol 276*, Berlin: Springer-Verlag).

(Bobrow and Stefik, 1983) D.G. Bobrow, M. Stefik. *The LOOPS Manual.* Palo Alto CA: Xerox Corporation, 1983.

(Booch, 1986) G. Booch. Object-Oriented Development. *IEEE Trans. Software Engineering,* **12**(2), 1986.

(Booch, 1991) G. Booch. *Object-Oriented Design with Applications.* New York NY: Benjamin/Cummings, 1991.

(Borning and Ingalls, 1981) A.H. Borning, D.H. Ingalls. *A Type Declaration and Inference System for Smalltalk.* University of Washington, 1981.

(Brinch-Hansen, 1975) P. Brinch-Hansen. The Programming Language Concurrent PASCAL. *IEEE Trans. Software Engineering,* **1**(2), 149-207, 1975.

(Cannon, 1982) H. Cannon. *Flavors, A Non-Hierarchical Approach to Object-Oriented Programming.* Draft 1982 .

(Chambers, 1992) C. Chambers. Object-Oriented Multi-Methods in Cecil. In *Proc. Euro. Conf. Object-Oriented Programming,* Utrecht, Netherlands, June/July, 1992 (*Lecture Notes in Computer Science, Vol 615*, Berlin: Springer-Verlag).

(Chen, 1976) P.P.S Chen. The Entity Relationship Model: Towards a Unified View of Data. *ACM Trans. Database Systems,* **1**(1), 1976.

(Coad and Yourdon, 1990) P. Coad, E. Yourdon. *Object-Oriented Analysis.* Englewood Cliffs NY: Prentice-Hall/Yourdon Press, 1990.

(Coad and Yourdon, 1991) P. Coad, E. Yourdon. *Object-Oriented Design.* Englewood Cliffs NY: Prentice-Hall/Yourdon Press, 1991.

(Conway, 1963) M.E. Conway. Design of a Separable Transition – Diagram Compiler. *Comm. ACM,* **6**(7), 396-408, 1963.

(Cook, 1988) S. Cook. Impressions of ECOOP'88. *J. of Object-Oriented Programming,* **1**(4), 1988.

(Cox, 1984) B.R. Cox. Message/Object, An Evolutionary Change. *IEEE SOFTWARE,* Jan. 1984.

(Dahl and Hoare, 1972) Dahl O.-J., C.A.R Hoare. Hierarchical Program Structures. In *Structured Programming* (O-J. Dahl, E.W. Dijkstra, C.A.R.Hoare), Academic Press, 1972.

(Dahl *et al.*, 1968) O.J. Dahl, B. Myrhaug, K. Nygaard. *SIMULA 67 Common Base Language.* Norwegian Computing Center, Oslo, 1968.

(Dahle *et al.*, 1986) H.P. Dahle, M. Løfgren, O.L. Madsen, B. Magnusson. *The Mjølner Project – A Highly Efficient Programming Environment* for Industrial Use. Mjølner report no. 1, Oslo, Malmø, Aarhus, Lund 1986.

(DeRemer and Krohn, 1976) F.L. DeRemer, H. Krohn. Programming-in-the-Large versus Programming-in-the-Small. *IEEE Transactions on Software Engineering,* **2**(2), 80-86, 1976.

(Dijkstra, 1968) E. W. Dijkstra. Co-operating Sequential Processes. In *Programming Languages* (F. Genuys, ed.), New York NY: Academic Press, 1968.

(ECOOP 1987–1992) ECOOP, European Conference on Object-Oriented Programming. Conference Proceedings 1987-92. *Lecture Notes in Computer Science,* Berlin: Springer-Verlag, 1987–1992.

(Eiffel, 1989) "Interactive Software Engineering Inc.. Eiffel: The Language, Version 2.2. *Santa Barbara, CA, USA, 1989.*

(Faber and Krukow, 1990) L. Faber, L. Krukow. This Town is Big Enough for Most of It – Modelling in OOP. *Masters thesis,* Computer Science Department, Aarhus University, 1990.

(Goldberg and Robson, 1989) A. Goldberg, D. Robson. *Smalltalk-80, The Language and its Implementation.* Reading MA: Addison-Wesley, 1989.

(Goodenough, 1975) J.B. Goodenough. Exception Handling: Issues and a Proposed Notion. *Comm. ACM,* **18**(12), 436-49, 1975.

(Griswold *et al.*, 1981) R.E Griswold, D.R Hanson, J.T. Korb. Generators in Icon. *ACM Trans. on Programming Languages and Systems,* **3**(2), 144-61, 1981.

(Grune, 1977) D. Grune. A view of Coroutines. *ACM Sigplan Notices,*75-81, July 1977.

(Hanson, 1981) Hanson D.R.. Is Block Structure Necessary?. *Software Practice and Experience,* **11**, 853-66, 1981.

(Henry, 1987) R. Henry. BSI Modula-2 Working Group: Coroutines and Processes. *The Modus Quarterly,* **8**, 1987.

(Hoare, 1972) C. A. R. Hoare. Proof of Correctness of Data Representation. *Acta Informatica,* **4**, 271-281, 1972.

(Hoare, 1978) C.A.R Hoare. Communicating Sequential Processes. *Comm. ACM,* **21**(8), 666-677, 1978.

(Hoare, 1981) C.A.R Hoare. The Emperor's old Clothes. *Comm. ACM,* **24**(2), 75-83, 1981.

(Holbæk-Hanssen *et al.*, 1975) E. Holbæk-Hanssen, P. Håndlykken, K. Nygaard. *System Description and the Delta Language.* Norwegian Computing Center, Publ. no 523, 1975.

(Holbæk-Hanssen *et al.*, 1981) P. Håndlykken, K. Nygaard. The DELTA System Description Language: Motivation, Main Concepts and Experience from use. In *Software Engineering Environments* (H. Hunke, ed.). Amsterdam: North-Holland, 1981.

(Horowitz, 1983) E. Horowitz. *Fundamentals of Programming Languages.* Berlin: Springer-Verlag 1983.

(Hughes, 1991) J.G. Hughes. *Object-Oriented Databases.* Englewood Cliffs NJ: Prentice-Hall, 1991.

(Jackson, 1983) M. Jackson. *System Development.* Englewood Cliffs NJ: Prentice-Hall, 1983.

(Jensen and Wirth, 1975) K. Jensen, N. Wirth. *Pascal User Manual and Report.* Berlin: Springer-Verlag, 1975.

(Kahn and MacQueen, 1977) G. Kahn, D. MacQueen. Coroutines and Networks of Parallel Processes. *Information Processing 77,* B. Gilchrist (ed.), 993-998. Amsterdam: North-Holland, 1977.

(Keene, 1989) S.E. Keene. *Object-Oriented Programming in* COMMON LISP – *A Programmer's Guide to CLOS.* Reading MA: Addison-Wesley 1989.

(Kernighan and Ritchie, 1978) B.W. Kernighan, D.M Ritchie. *The C Programming Language* 2nd edn. Englewood Cliffs NJ: Prentice-Hall, 1988.

(Kim *et al.*, 1987) W. Kim, J. Banerjee, H.-T. Chou, J.F. Garza, D.Woelk. Composite Object Support in an Object-Oriented Database System. In *Proc. Object-Oriented Programming, Languages, Systems and Applications,* Orlando, FL, 1987, (*ACM Sigplan Notices*, **22**(12)).

(Knudsen, 1984) J. L. Knudsen. Exception Handling – A Static Approach. *Software Practice and Experience,* 429-49, May 1984.

(Knudsen, 1987) J. L. Knudsen. Better-Exception Handling in Block-Structured Systems. *IEEE Software,* 40-49, May 1987.

(Knudsen and Thomsen, 1985) J. Lindskov Knudsen and K. Stougård Thomsen. *A Conceptual Framework for Programming Languages.* DAIMI PB-192, Aarhus University, April 1985.

(Knudsen *et al.*, 1989) J.L. Knudsen, O.L. Madsen, C. Nørgaard, L.B. Petersen, E. Sandvad. *An Overview of the Mjølner BETA System.* Computer Science Department, Aarhus University, Draft, Dec. 1989.

(Knudsen *et al.*, 1990) J.L. Knudsen, O.L. Madsen, C. Nørgaard, L.B. Petersen, E. Sandvad. Teaching Object-Oriented Programming Using BETA. In *Proc. Apple European University Consortium Annual Conf.*, Salamanca, 1990.

(Knudsen *et al.*, 1992) J.L. Knudsen, M. Løfgren, O.L. Madsen, B. Magnusson (eds.). *Object-Oriented Environments – The Mjølner Approach.* Englewood Cliffs NJ: Prentice-Hall, 1993.

(Kristensen *et al.*, 1976) B.B. Kristensen, O.L. Madsen, B. Møller-Pedersen, K. Nygaard. *BETA Project Working Notes 1-8.* Norwegian Computing Center, Oslo and Computer Science Department, Aarhus University, Aarhus, 1976–1982 .

(Kristensen *et al.*, 1983a) B.B. Kristensen, O.L Madsen, B. Møller-Pedersen, K. Nygaard. Syntax Directed Program Modularization. In *Interactive Computing Systems* (P. Degano, E. Sandewall, eds.). Amsterdam: North-Holland, 1983.

(Kristensen *et al.*, 1983b) B.B. Kristensen, O.L. Madsen, B. Møller-Pedersen, K. Nygaard. Abstraction Mechanisms in the BETA Programming Language. In *Proc. 10th ACM Symp. Principles of Programming Languages,* Austin TX, January 24-26 1983.

(Kristensen *et al.*, 1985) B.B. Kristensen, O.L. Madsen, B. Møller Pedersen, K. Nygaard. Multisequential Execution in the BETA Programming Language. *Sigplan Notices,* **4**(20), 1985.

(Kristensen *et al.*, 1987a) B.B. Kristensen, O.L. Madsen, B. Møller-Pedersen, K. Nygaard. The BETA Programming Language. In *Research Directions in Object Oriented Programming* (B.D. Shriver, P .Wegner, eds.). Cambridge: MIT Press, 1987.

(Kristensen *et al.*, 1987b) B.B. Kristensen, O.L. Madsen, B. Møller-Pedersen, K. Nygaard. Classification of Actions or Inheritance also for Methods. In *Proc. Euro. Conf. Object-Oriented Programming,* Paris, France, June, 1987 (*Lecture Notes in Computer Science Vol. 276,* Berlin: Springer-Verlag).

(Kristensen *et al.*, 1988) B.B. Kristensen, O.L. Madsen, B. Møller-Pedersen, K. Nygaard. Coroutine Sequencing in BETA. *Hawaii*

International Conference on System Sciences, **21**, January 5-8, 1988.

(Krogdahl and Olsen, 1986) S. Krogdahl, K.A. Olsen. Modular and Object-Oriented Programming. *DataTid* No. 9, Sept. 1986 (in Norwegian).

(Lampson *et al.*, 1977) Lampson B.W. *et al.*. Report on the Programming Language Euclid. *SIGPLAN Notices,* **12**(2), 1977.

(Leler, 1987) W. Leler. *Constraint Programming – Their Specification and Generation.* Reading MA: Addison-Wesley, 1987.

(Lindstrom and Soffa, 1981) G. Lindstrom, M. L. Soffa. Referencing and Retention in Block-Structured Coroutines. *ACM Trans. on Programming Languages and Systems,* **3**(3), 263-292, 1981.

(Liskov and Zilles, 1974) B. Liskov, S. Zilles. Programming with Abstract Data Types. *ACM Sigplan Notices,* **9**(4), 50-59, 1974.

(Liskov *et al.*, 1977) B. Liskov, A. Snyder, R. Atkinson, C. Schaffert. Abstraction Mechanisms in CLU. *Comm. ACM,* **20**(8), 564-576, 1977.

(Madsen, 1987) O.L. Madsen. Block Structure and Object Oriented Languages. In: *Research Directions in Object Oriented Programming* (B.D. Shriver, P. Wegner, eds.). Cambridge MA: MIT Press, 1987.

(Madsen and Møller-Pedersen, 1988b) O.L. Madsen, B. Møller-Pedersen. What Object-Oriented Programming may be — and what it does not have to be. In *Proc. Euro. Conf. Object-Oriented Programming*, Oslo, Norway, August, 1988 (*Lecture Notes in Computer Science Vol 322,* Berlin: Springer-Verlag).

(Madsen and Møller-Pedersen, 1989a) O.L. Madsen, B. Møller-Pedersen. Basic Principles of the BETA Programming Language. In *Object-Oriented Programming Systems* (G. Blair, D. Hutchinson, D. Shephard, eds.). London: Pitman Publishing, 1989.

(Madsen and Møller-Pedersen, 1989b) O.L. Madsen, B. Møller-Pedersen. Virtual Classes — A Powerful Mechanism in Object-Oriented Programming. In *Proc. Object-Oriented Programming, Languages, Systems and Applications,* New Orleans, LS, 1989, (*ACM Sigplan Notices*, **24**(10)).

(Madsen and Møller-Pedersen, 1992) O.L. Madsen B. Møller-Pedersen. Part Objects and their Location. *Technology of Object-Oriented Languages and Systems* — TOOLS 7, Dortmund. Englewood Cliffs NJ: Prentice-Hall 1992.

(Madsen *et al.*, 1983) O.L. Madsen, B. Møller-Pedersen, K. Nygaard. From SIMULA 67 to BETA. In *Proc. 11th SIMULA 67 User's Conf.*, Paris 1983. Norwegian Computing Center, 1983.

(Madsen *et al.*, 1990) O.L. Madsen, B. Magnusson, B. Møller-Pedersen. Strong Typing of Object-Oriented Languages Revisited. In *Proc. Object-Oriented Programming, Languages, Systems and Applications,* Ottawa, Canada, 1990, (*ACM Sigplan Notices*, **25**(10)).

(Marlin, 1980) C.D. Marlin. Coroutines – A Programming Methodology, a Language Design and an Implementation. *Lecture Notes in Computer Science, Vol 95.* Berlin: Springer-Verlag, 1980.

(Mathiassen, 1981) L. Mathiassen. Systems Development and Systems Development Methods (in Danish). *Ph.D. thesis.* Institute of Informatics, Oslo University, 1981.

(Meyer, 1987a) B. Meyer. Genericity versus Inheritance. In *Proc. Object-Oriented Programming, Languages, Systems and Applications*, Portland, OR, 1986, (*ACM Sigplan Notices*, **21**(11)).

(Meyer, 1987b) B. Meyer. Reusability: The Case for Object-Oriented Design. *IEEE Software,* **2**(4), March 1987.

(Meyer, 1988) B. Meyer. *Object-Oriented Software Construction.* Englewood Cliffs NJ: Prentice-Hall, 1988.

(Møller-Pedersen *et al.*, 1987) B. Møller-Pedersen, D. Belsnes, H.P. Dahle. Rationale and Tutorial on OSDL: An Object-Oriented Extension of SDL. *Computer Networks & ISDN Systems,* **13**, 97-117, 1987.

(Naur, 1962) P. Naur (ed.). Revised Report on The Algorithmic Language ALGOL 60. *Regnecentralen.* Copenhagen, 1962.

(Nygaard, 1986) K. Nygaard. Basic Concepts in Object Oriented Programming. *ACM Sigplan Notices,* **21**(10), 1986.

(Nygaard and Dahl, 1981) K. Nygaard, O.-J. Dahl. Simula 67. In *History of Programming Languages* (R.W. Wexelblat, ed.). Reading MA: Addison-Wesley, 1981.

(Nygaard and Sørgaard, 1987) K. Nygaard, P. Sørgaard. The Perspective Concept in Informatics. In *Computers and Democracy – A Scandinavian Challenge* (G. Bjerkness, P. Ehn, M. Kyng, eds.). Aldershot: Gower, 1987.

(OOPSLA 1986–1992) OOPSLA, Object-Oriented Programming Systems, Languages and Applications. Conference Proceedings, 1986–1992. *ACM Sigplan Notices.*

(Raj and Levy, 1989) R.K. Raj, H.M. Levy. A compositional Model for Software Reuse. In *Proc. Euro. Conf. Object-Oriented Programming*, Nottingham, England, July, 1989 (*BCS Workshop Series*, Cambridge: CUP).

(Rees and Clinger, 1986) J. Rees and W. Clinger (ed.). *Revised Report on the Algorithmic Language Scheme.* MIT, TR no. 174, August 1986.

(Rumbaugh *et al.*, 1991) J. Rumgaugh, M. Blaha, W. Premerlani, F. Eddy, W. Lorensen. *Object-Oriented Modeling and Design.* Englewood Cliffs NJ: Prentice-Hall, 1991.

(Sakkinen, 1989) M. Sakkinen. Disciplined Inheritance. In *Proc. Euro. Conf. Object-Oriented Programming*, Nottingham, England, July, 1989 (*BCS Workshop Series,* Cambridge: CUP).

(Sandvad, 1990) E. Sandvad. *Object-Oriented Development – Integrating Analysis, Design and Implementation.* Computer Science Department, DAIMI PB-302, April 1990.

(Shlaer and Mellor, 1988) S. Shlaer and S.J. Mellor. *Object-Oriented Systems Analysis – Modeling the World in Data.* Englewood Cliffs NJ: Prentice-Hall/Yourdon Press, 1988.

(Shriver and Wegner, 1987) B. Shriver, P. Wegner (eds.). *Research Directions in Object-Oriented Languages.* Cambridge: MA: MIT Press, 1987.

(Smith, 1984) B. Smith. Personal Communication. *Stanford 1984.*

(Smith and Smith, 1977a) J.M. Smith and D.C.P. Smith. Data Base Abstractions: Aggregation. *Comm. ACM,* **20**(6), 396-404, 1977.

(Smith and Smith, 1977b) J.M. Smith and D.C.P. Smith. Data Base Abstractions: Aggregation and Generalization. *ACM Transactions on Database Systems,* **2**(2), 105-133, 1977.

(Stefik and Bobrow, 1984) M. Stefik, D.G. Bobrow. Object-Oriented Programming: Themes and Variations. *AI Magazine,* **6**(4), 40-62, 1984.

(Stroustrup, 1991) B. Stroustrup. *The C++ Programming Language* 2nd edn. Reading MA: Addison-Wesley, 1986.

(Swedish Standard, 1987) Swedish Standard. Data Processing – Programming Languages – SIMULA. *Swedish Standard SS 63 61 14,* ISBN 91-7162-234-9, 1987.

(Sørgaard, 1988) P. Sørgaard. Object-Oriented Programming and Computerised Shared Material. In *Proc. Euro. Conf. Object-Oriented Programming,* Oslo, Norway, August, 1988 (*Lecture Notes in Computer Science, Vol 322,* Berlin: Springer-Verlag).

(Tennent, 1977) R.D. Tennent. Language Design Methods based on Semantic Principles. *Acta Informatica,* **8**(2), 97-112, 1977.

(Tennent, 1982) R.D. Tennent. Two Examples of Block Structuring. *Software-Practice and Experience,* **12**, 385-392, 1982.

(Thomsen, 1987) K.S. Thomsen. Inheritance on Processes, Exemplified on Distributed Termination Detection. *International Journal of Parallel Programming,* **16**(1), 17-52, 1987.

(Ungar and Smith, 1987) D. Ungar, R.B. Smith. SELF: The Power of Simplicity. In *Proc. Object-Oriented Programming, Languages, Systems and Applications,* Orlando, FL, 1987, (*ACM Sigplan Notices,* **22**(12)).

(US Department of Defense, 1980) *Ada Reference Manual* . Proposed Standard Document. United States Department of Defense, July 1980.

(Vaucher, 1975) J. Vaucher. Prefixed Procedures: A Structuring Concept for Operations. *Infor,* **13**(3), 1975.

(Wang and Dahl, 1971) A. Wang, O.-J. Dahl. Coroutine Sequencing in a Block Structured Environment. *BIT,* **11**, 425-449, 1971.

(Wang, 1982) A. Wang. *Coroutine Sequencing in Simula, Parts I-III.* Norwegian Computing Center, 1982.

(Wegner, 1983) P. Wegner. On the Unification of Data and Program Abstraction in Ada. In *Proc. 10th ACM Symp. on Principles of Programming Languages,* Austin, TX, 24-26 January 1983.

(Wegner, 1987) P. Wegner. *Dimensions of Object-Based Language Design.* Tech. Report No. CS-87-14, Brown University, 1987.

(Wikstrøm, 1987) A. Wikstrøm. *Functional Programming Using Standard ML.* Englewood Cliffs NJ: Prentice-Hall, 1987.

(Wirfs-Brock *et al.*, 1991) R. Wirfs-Brock, B. Wilkerson, L. Wiener. *Designing Object-Oriented Software.* Englewood Cliffs NJ: Prentice-Hall, 1990.

(Wirth, 1982) N. Wirth. *Programming in Modula-2.* Berlin: Springer-Verlag, 1982.

(Wulf and Shaw, 1973) W.A. Wulf, M. Shaw. Global Variables Considered Harmful. *Sigplan Notices,* **8**, 28-34, 1973.

Index